Music in Developmental Therapy
A Curriculum Guide

MUSIC IN DEVELOPMENTAL THERAPY

A Curriculum Guide

Edited by **Jennie Purvis, M.M., M.Ed., RMT** and **Shelley Samet, M.Ed., RMT**

Coordinator of Training/Music Therapy
Chatham-Effingham Psychoeducational
    Center
Savannah, Georgia

Coordinator of Music Therapy
North Metro Children's Center
Atlanta, Georgia

with contributions by **Clementine Gigliotti, M.Ed., RMT, Beleta Griffith, M.Ed., RMT,**
and **Sarah McGinley, M.Ed., RMT**

University Park Press
Baltimore • London • Tokyo

UNIVERSITY PARK PRESS
International Publishers in Science and Medicine
Chamber of Commerce Building
Baltimore, Maryland 21202

Typeset by The Composing Room of Michigan, Inc.
Manufactured in the United States of America by Collins Lithographing
and Printing Co.

Library of Congress Cataloging in Publication Data

Main entry under title:

Music in developmental therapy.

Bibliography: p.
Includes indexes.
1. Music therapy. I. Purvis, Jennie. II. Samet,
Shelley.
ML3920.M8965   615'.837   76-15197
ISBN 0-8391-0895-8

Contents

(continued)

Foreword

According to the 1970 Report of the Joint Commission on Mental Health of Children there are an estimated 10 million children in the United States who are in need of mental health services. This is an awesome number, and the teachers or therapists of these children have a formidable task. The task is challenging because of the complexities involved in providing programs that have individual significance in the rehabilitation of every child. Communication must be established as a basis for trust if there is to be subsequent growth; and of all the ways to communicate, perhaps music is the most universal. In one form or another, music reaches everyone. A child may be extremely disoriented or driven by impulses he cannot control. Another may be impoverished by emotional deprivation, sometimes retreating from his confusing, unhappy world or lashing back in retaliation. Whatever form the disturbance takes, and whatever the age of the child, there is a way to reach each child through music in order to begin the gradual movements toward healthier responses.

This book testifies to the conviction that music is a powerful tool for reaching therapeutic goals. Music can provide a nonverbal means of expressing feelings. It can be used as a springboard for oral communication with children who cannot or will not communicate. Because music is its own intensely real experience it provides a nonthreatening medium for responding through which children can meet with pleasure and success. This invariably leads to increased self-confidence and a willingness to venture into other nonthreatening group experiences. Teachers and therapists have found that music helps set the tone or mood for experiences in the classroom. Sometimes there is a need for arousing, stimulating music activities; at other times, a need for activities that require a more relaxed, subdued response. Music can also be used to teach basic academic tasks involving concepts, colors, visual and auditory discrimination, numeration, sets, and left-right orientation in ways that are highly motivating and enjoyable.

There is no doubt that music is a natural mode of expression for most children. Through chanting, singing, moving rhythmically, or combining sounds from instruments, spontaneous, creative elements in nearly every child can be tapped. It is because of this potential that a natural alliance exists between music and Developmental Therapy.

Developmental Therapy emphasizes that there are healthy, normal, creative aspects to every child regardless of the type or severity of his handicap. It also emphasizes the universal nature of certain developmental milestones which almost all children master during the maturational process. Music provides an effective way of facilitating mastery of these milestones through experiences which can be pleasurable and positive and can encourage the active participation of each child. Furthermore, music activities can be planned to meet almost all of the developmental milestones included as Developmental Therapy objectives. These music activities can be sequenced to meet the individual needs of children at each stage of Developmental Therapy. Finally, music activities are especially well suited to the group setting, which is emphasized for socialization and communication in Developmental Therapy.

The activities described in this book are based on activities actually implemented in Developmental Therapy classes for seriously disturbed youngsters at the Rutland Center in Athens, Georgia. As the demonstration site for the Rutland Center-Developmental Therapy Model for treating emotionally disturbed children, this program has incorporated music therapy into its treatment classes since 1971. Children between the ages of 2 and 14 years of all developmental stages and all types of disturbance have been served. The most successful and widely used music activities which were implemented during 1973–1974 were compiled and re-evaluated with 125 enrolled children. It is important to note that while these music activities were designed specifically for use in the Developmental Therapy model, the activities can be used for children with other handicapping conditions as well as with nonhandicapped youngsters. Because the activities are planned for objectives based upon universal milestones of development, they can be adapted into other therapeutic intervention models.

Let me share one brief vignette that I was privileged to observe. During a group rhythm activity with drums, one severely withdrawn schizophrenic boy randomly moved his stick across the top of his drum. Intermittently he lifted his stick and let it fall in a lifeless, detached manner. But each time he did this the therapist responded directly to him with a strong single beat from her drum. After several such responses the boy suddenly dropped the stick with an incredulous look that was followed by an enormous grin. The therapist responded warmly, redirected him to his drum and together they exchanged beats. In a most vivid breakthrough this boy had recognized that the reciprocal beat was coming from her, in *response* to *him!* A first step in the process of social interaction had begun.

This exciting vehicle for therapy need not be limited to music therapists. There are many music activities that can be used by people who have had little or no training in the fundamentals of music or in the use of music in therapy. With this in mind, the music activities in this book were developed for anyone who works with emotionally disturbed children: special educators, therapists, and parents as well as music therapists.

What is most important is that all disturbed children can be reached, their inner worlds can be touched, and they can be started back toward constructive, healthy responses better able to participate in the experiences of childhood. The authors have given us clear directions for ways to do this, using music to assure that this will happen.

Mary M. Wood
Division for Exceptional Children,
University of Georgia and
Director of Training
Rutland Center

Acknowledgments

The editors wish to express their sincere appreciation to the following individuals for their contributions to this endeavor:

To **Dr. Mary M. Wood,** who provided the inspiration and impetus for the writing of this book. Her enthusiasm and belief in the therapeutic value of music served as a constant source of encouragement throughout the development of this curriculum guide. We are deeply indebted to her for freely sharing her wisdom and guidance with us in helping to make this book a reality.

To **Dr. William W. Swan,** whose sincerity, infinite patience, and never-ending support aided us in meeting unforeseen problems throughout each phase of the development of the manuscript. We are grateful to him for giving us the benefit of his clear, logical thinking and his practical suggestions.

To **Ms. Diane Weller,** whose ideas, talent, and leadership guided us in the practical aspects of implementing the music therapy program at the Rutland Center.

To **the Rutland Center staff,** whose whole-hearted cooperation provided us with the opportunities for implementing the music activities in this book.

To **the following music therapy students,** who used the material in this curriculum guide and who made many valuable and constructive suggestions:

Margaret Bailey	Myra Jordan	Nell Sins
Marcia Cansdale	Robbie Krizan	Sara Williams
Twyla Drace	Jack Pray	Sandy Williamson
Suzanne Hosch	Maxine Robbins	Laura Steinberg

To **John and Johnsie Purvis,** who spent many hours hand copying the original musical selections.

To **Daisy Fleming, Sandra Libby, Nora Mitchell, and Eileen Patrick,** who cheerfully and patiently typed the numerous drafts of the manuscript.

To **Mrs. Mignon Lawton,** director, and the staff at the Chatham-Effingham Psychoeducational Center, Savannah, Georgia, and to **Dr. Arthur Bilyeu,** director, and the staff at the North Metro Children's Center, Atlanta, Georgia, whose belief in the value of music for emotionally disturbed children is demonstrated by their support and encouragement of the music therapy programs at their respective facilities.

To **our family and friends,** whose interest and understanding have always been a source of steadfast support.

chapter 1

INSTRUCTIONS FOR USE OF CURRICULUM GUIDE

This curriculum guide presents a developmental approach to music therapy for emotionally disturbed children based on the systematic use of music in the Developmental Therapy model (Wood, 1972; 1975). Developmental Therapy is defined as "a psychoeducational approach to therapeutic intervention with young children who have serious emotional and behavioral disorders" (Wood, 1975, p. 3). In this context, music therapy refers to the application of music and music-related activities within the framework of the Developmental Therapy curriculum.

In the Developmental Therapy model, a set of curriculum objectives provides a structure for the treatment process. These objectives are arranged in a hierarchy over five sequential stages of therapy within four curriculum areas: behavior, communication, socialization, and academics. Therefore, in each curriculum area and for each stage of therapy there is a series of Developmental Therapy objectives which serves as a guide for planning and implementing sequential learning experiences.

Music in Developmental Therapy offers specific music therapy learning experiences which may be used to aid children in the mastery of these Developmental Therapy objectives. A variety of music activities has been developed for Developmental Therapy objectives in each curriculum area for the first four stages of therapy. Stage Five music activities are excluded from this text since children at this stage no longer need to attend treatment classes and are not directly involved in the music therapy program.

In the implementation of these music therapy learning experiences it is essential to keep in mind the tenets of the Developmental Therapy model. It is strongly suggested, therefore, that *Developmental Music Therapy* [1] (1974) and *Developmental*

Therapy (Wood, 1975) be used in conjunction with this curriculum guide.

In the effort to adhere to the Developmental Therapy model it is prudent to devote primary attention to several aspects of that model. First, children are grouped in Developmental Therapy treatment classes, not by chronological age, but, according to their stage of development in the areas of behavior, communication, socialization, and academics. Consequently, when implementing a specific music therapy learning experience, careful consideration should be given to the stage of therapy for which the music activity was intended. Children participating in any particular music activity should be functioning at approximately the same stage of therapy.

Second, the Developmental Therapy model places an emphasis on children's strengths rather than on their deficits. A positive approach is the essence of an effective treatment program. Music therapy learning experiences must be planned and implemented so as to meet children's needs at the stage at which they are functioning and to allow them to experience frequent success as they progress through sequential music activities.

Third, the success of the learning experiences outlined in this curriculum guide is dependent upon the therapist's ability to effectively and therapeutically interact with the children with whom he is working. Procedures, techniques, and materials must be modified and adapted to meet the unique needs of individual children and different groups of children.

All of the music therapy learning experiences recorded in this curriculum guide have been successfully implemented in Developmental Therapy treatment classes. The classes with which they have been used are composed of small groups of four to six children who are functioning at approximately the same stage of Developmental Therapy. Music is one of the regularly scheduled activities for each class, with music ther-

---

[1] *Developmental Music Therapy* [Monograph] was developed pursuant to a grant from the Office of Education, United States Department of Health, Education and Welfare (OEG-0-73-5585).

apists conducting music sessions two to five times per week for each group of children. The music therapists plan and implement music activities which focus on specific Developmental Therapy objectives designated as target objectives for the children in the class.

Detailed descriptions of the music activities are recorded by the music therapists using the Music Therapy Learning Experience forms (Figure 1). The music activities contained in this curriculum guide are notated on these forms. An explanation of the notation format (Figure 1) is given below:

(1) The Developmental Therapy objective which is the primary focus for the music activity is identified by a letter and a number. The letter (B, C, S, A) designates the curriculum area, i.e., Behavior, Communication, Socialization, Academics, and the number refers to the specific objective number in the set of Developmental Therapy objectives (Wood, 1975).

(2) The Developmental Therapy objective which is the primary focus for the music activity is stated in written form.

(3) The identification number for the music therapy learning experience is found in the upper corner. This number identifies the curriculum area, objective number, and sequence number within the series of learning experiences planned for a specific objective. An identification number of C-8.2, for example, refers to a music therapy learning experience which has as a focus Developmental Therapy objective number 8 in the area of Communication. The 2 indicates that it is the second music activity in a series of learning experiences planned for that objective.

(4) The curriculum area in which the primary objective is found is stated as Behavior, Communication, Socialization, or Academics.

(5) The stage of therapy in which the primary objective falls is noted by circling I, II, III, or IV to indicate Stages One, Two, Three, or Four.

(6) The kinds of participation called for in the music experience are indicated by circling one or more of the listed categories. These categories include listening, playing (instruments), singing, moving, creating, and verbalizing.

(7) Under the columns headed "Music Activity," the music therapy learning experience is explained in detail. This begins with an "Introduction" which describes the desired arrangement of the children, music materials, and classroom. The "Implementation" section consists of the sequence of steps used in implementing the activity. The third section provides instruction in techniques relevant to the designated stage of therapy and suggestions for modifying the music activity.

(8) The "Resource" column lists the materials used in the activity, e.g., records, instruments, audiovisual aids, etc.

(9) The "Cross Reference Objectives" section lists by number those Developmental Therapy objectives in each curriculum area, other than the primary objective, which are focused upon in the music therapy learning experience. This section is necessary since any one music activity almost always involves more than one Developmental Therapy objective. In addition to encompassing those objectives within the stage of the primary objective, the cross reference objectives can include the two final objectives of the stage which immediately precedes the stage in question and the first two objectives of the next sequential stage. For example, if the Developmental Therapy objective for which the music activity is planned is a Stage Two objective, then the possibilities for the cross reference objectives include all of the Stage Two objectives, the last two objectives in each curriculum area for Stage One, and the first two objectives in each curriculum area for Stage Three. This procedure is followed

Figure 1. Music Therapy Learning Experience ③

Developmental Therapy Objective ① / ②

Type of Activity ⑥	Area ④
Listening	Stage ⑤
Playing	I
Singing	I
Moving	II
Creating	III
Verbalizing	IV

MUSIC ACTIVITY ⑦

   I.   **Introduction**

   II. **Implementation**

III.   **Techniques and Modifications**

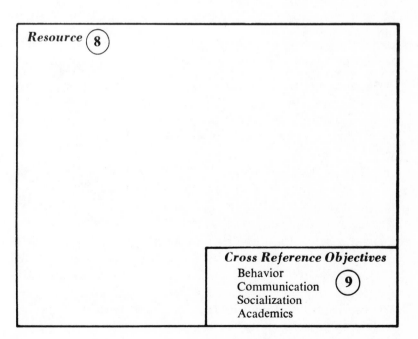

Resource ⑧

Cross Reference Objectives
Behavior
Communication ⑨
Socialization
Academics

to designate activities for children at one stage of therapy who may be working on several objectives at a lower or higher stage in some of the curriculum areas. In this way the music therapist can allow for differences among individual group members and between various groups.

The music therapy learning experiences are contained in Chapter 3. They are grouped into the four curriculum areas—Behavior, Communication, Socialization, and Academics—and are in sequential order within each area. The "Key to Music Therapy Learning Experiences" (Chapter 2) should be used as a guide for locating desired music activities. This chapter contains the Developmental Therapy objectives (Wood, 1975) for Stages One through Four. The objectives are grouped into the four curriculum areas and are sequenced within each of the areas, progressing from Stage One to Stage Four. Under each objective are listed the music therapy learning experiences which apply in some way to that particular objective. Using the identification numbers of these learning experiences, the reader can locate the suggested music activities in Chapter 3.

Chapter 4 ("Original Resource Materials") contains songs and stories referred to in the music therapy learning experiences which are not available in other publications. The number in the upper corner of each song or story is the number that is referred to in the resource section of the music therapy learning experience form.

The "Index of Resource Materials" lists all of the records, songs, and stories used in the curriculum guide. With each reference is given the identification numbers of the music therapy learning experiences in which the resource material is used.

The "Index to Music Therapy Learning Experiences" categorizes the music activities by the type of participation called for in the learning experiences, i.e., listening, playing (instruments), singing, moving, creating, verbalizing. Using this index, one can easily locate music therapy learning experiences which call for a specific type of musical involvement, e.g., Stage One activities involving playing instruments, Stage Three singing activities, etc.

It should be remembered that music therapy sessions can encompass one or more music therapy learning experiences and these can vary widely in the type of activity, materials used, etc. Careful sequencing from session to session as well as within one session is recommended to assure that the children have the necessary prerequisite musical and nonmusical skills and behaviors needed for successful participation in the activities.

In closing, the reader is cautioned against rigid adherence to the music activities in this curriculum guide. Instead, it is hoped that the music therapy learning experiences can serve as a guide and an impetus for planning activities which will be effective in meeting the needs of children at all stages of therapy.

chapter 2

Key to Music Therapy Learning Experiences

Developmental Therapy Curriculum Objectives

Behavior Objectives

[Objectives from *Developmental Therapy*, M. M. Wood (Ed.), University Park Press, Baltimore, Maryland, 1975, pp. 263–290.]

STAGE I:
Responding to the Environment with Pleasure

STAGE I BEHAVIOR GOAL: *TO TRUST OWN BODY AND SKILLS*

■ 1. to respond to sensory stimulus by attending to source of stimulus by body response or by looking directly at object or person [in situations using tactile, kinesthetic, visual, auditory, gustatory, and olfactory modalities]. (Same as Academic objective A-1.)
Music Therapy Learning Experiences:
    B-1.1; B-2.1; B-3.1; C-1.1; C-3.1; C-3.2; C-4.1; C-5.1; C-7.1; S-2.1; S-7.1; A-6.1; A-7.1; A-7.2

■ 2. to respond to stimulus by sustained attending to source of stimulus [continued looking at object or person after initial stimulus-response has occurred]. (Same as Academic objective A-2.)
Music Therapy Learning Experiences:
    B-1.1; B-2.1; B-3.1; C-1.1; C-3.1; C-3.2; C-4.1; C-5.1; C-7.1; S-1.1; S-2.1; S-4.1; S-4.2; S-7.1; A-5.1; A-6.1; A-7.1; A-7.2; A-10.1

■ 3. to respond with motor behavior to single environmental stimulus: object, person, sound. (Same as Academic objective A-3.)
Music Therapy Learning Experiences:
    B-1.1; B-3.1; C-1.1; C-7.1; S-1.1

■ 4. to respond with motor and body responses to complex environmental and verbal stimuli [through imitation "Do this"; through completion of verbal direction; minimal participation in the routine; given physical intervention and verbal cues]. (Same as Academic objective A-4.)
Music Therapy Learning Experiences:
    B-1.1; B-2.1; B-3.1; B-4.1; B-4.2; B-4.3; B-5.1; C-2.1; C-3.1; C-4.1; C-5.1; C-6.1; C-7.1; S-2.1; S-3.1; S-3.2; S-4.1; S-4.2; S-4.3; S-7.1; S-11.1; A-5.1; A-6.1; A-7.1; A-7.2; A-10.1; A-11.1; A-12.1; A-13.1; A-13.2; A-13.3; A-14.1; A-15.1; A-15.2; A-16.1; A-16.2; A-17.1; A-17.2

■ 5. to actively assist in learning self-help skills [toileting, washing hands, dressing, putting arms in coat when held (should be based upon chronological age expectations in combination with developmental expectations; mastery not essential)].
Music Therapy Learning Experiences:
    B-5.1; A-16.2

■ 6. to respond independently to play material. [Verbal cues may be used; age-appropriate play is not necessary.]
Music Therapy Learning Experiences:
    B-6.1; S-5.1

■ 7. to respond with recall to the routine spontaneously. [Child moves to next planned activity without physical stimulus; verbal cues or touch may be used.]
Music Therapy Learning Experiences:
    B-6.1; B-7.1; B-12.1; B-12.2; S-5.1

STAGE II:
Responding to the Environment with Success

STAGE II BEHAVIOR GOAL: *TO SUCCESSFULLY PARTICIPATE IN ROUTINES AND ACTIVITIES*

- 8. to use play materials appropriately, simulating normal play experience.
  Music Therapy Learning Experiences:
  B-6.1; B-8.1; C-1.1; S-5.1; A-18.1
- 9. to wait without physical intervention by teachers. [Verbal support or touch may be used.] (Same as Socialization objective S-14.)
  Music Therapy Learning Experiences:
  B-9.1; B-9.2; B-9.3; B-9.4; B-11.3; B-11.4; B-12.1; C-4.1; C-5.1; C-8.1; C-10.2; C-10.3; C-11.1; C-12.1; C-13.1; S-4.3; S-15.1; S-16.1; S-18.2; S-18.3; S-18.4; S-18.5; S-18.6; S-18.7; A-7.1; A-7.2; A-15.2; A-16.1; A-19.1; A-21.1; A-21.2; A-22.1; A-23.2; A-23.3; A-30.1
- 10. to participate in activities such as Work time, Story time, Talking time, Juice and Cookie time without physical intervention by teacher. [Verbal support or touch may be used.]
  Music Therapy Learning Experiences:
  B-10.1; A-31.1
- 11. to participate in activities such as Play time, Mat time, Games, Music, Art time without physical intervention by teacher. [Verbal support or touch may be used.]
  Music Therapy Learning Experience:
  B-8.1; B-9.1; B-9.2; B-9.3; B-9.4; B-10.1; B-11.1; B-11.2; B-11.3; B-11.4; B-19.1; B-19.2; C-8.1; C-8.2; C-9.1; C-10.1; C-10.3; C-11.1; C-11.2; C-12.1; C-13.1; C-16.1; S-13.1; S-13.2; S-15.1; S-16.1; S-17.1; S-18.1; S-18.2; S-18.3; S-18.4; S-18.5; S-18.6; S-18.7; S-19.2; S-19.3; S-20.4; S-20.5; A-18.1; A-19.2; A-20.1; A-21.1; A-21.2; A-22.1; A-23.1; A-23.3; A-24.1; A-26.1; A-27.1; A-28.1; A-28.2; A-29.2; A-30.1; A-31.1; A-32.1; A-33.1; A-34.2; A-35.1; A-35.2; A-39.1; A-39.3; A-44.3; A-44.4; A-44.5; A-48.1
- 12. to spontaneously participate in routines without physical intervention. [Verbal support or touch may be used, but child indicates some personal initiative to comply with routine.]
  Music Therapy Learning Experience:
  B-10.1; B-11.4; B-12.1; B-12.2; B-13.1; B-14.2; C-8.2; C-9.1; C-11.1; C-11.2; C-12.1; C-13.1; S-15.1; S-17.1; S-18.1; S-18.5; S-19.2; S-22.1; S-23.1; A-19.1; A-20.1; A-21.2; A-27.1; A-28.2; A-30.1; A-34.2; A-44.4; A-47.1

STAGE III:
Learning Skills for Successful Group Participation

STAGE III BEHAVIOR GOAL: *TO APPLY INDIVIDUAL SKILLS IN GROUP PROCESSES*

■ 13. to verbally recall group rules and procedure. (Same as Communication objective C-15.)
Music Therapy Learning Experience:
B-11.3; B-11.4; B-13.1; B-14.1; B-14.2; B-15.1; B-16.1; C-19.1; S-18.6; S-19.1; S-19.3; S-20.4; A-33.2; A-35.1; A-44.4

■ 14. to contribute to making group expectations of conduct and procedure. (Same as Communication objective C-17.)
Music Therapy Learning Experience:
B-11.4; B-14.1; B-14.2; B-15.1; B-16.1; C-19.1; S-20.2; S-20.4; A-38.1

■ 15. to verbalize consequences if group's expectations are not reached. (Same as Communication objective C-18.)
Music Therapy Learning Experience:
B-14.1; B-14.2; B-15.1; B-16.1; C-19.1; S-20.4

■ 16. to give simple reasons for group's expectations. [Verbal cues from teacher may be used.] (Same as Communication objective C-21.)
Music Therapy Learning Experience:
B-14.1; B-14.2; B-15.1; B-16.1; C-19.1

■ 17. to tell other, more appropriate ways to behave in a given situation; individual focus. [May not be able to implement alternatives.]
Music Therapy Learning Experience:
Specific music therapy learning experiences were not planned for this Developmental Therapy Objective. There should be frequent opportunities to work on this objective during regular Stage Three music activities.

■ 18. to refrain from inappropriate behavior or breaking group rules when others in the group are losing control [given verbal support by teacher].
Music Therapy Learning Experience:
Specific music therapy learning experiences were not planned for this Developmental Therapy Objective. There should be frequent opportunities to work on this objective during regular Stage Three music activities.

■ 19. to maintain self-control and comply with group procedures [given classroom structure and verbal support by teacher].
Music Therapy Learning Experiences:
B-13.1; B-14.2; B-15.1; B-19.1; B-19.2; B-19.3; B-19.4; B-19.5; B-19.6; B-20.1; B-20.2; B-20.3; B-20.4; C-14.1; C-19.1; C-20.1; C-20.2; C-25.2; S-19.1; S-19.3; S-19.4; S-20.1; S-20.3; S-20.4; S-20.5; S-20.6; S-22.1; S-22.2; S-22.3; S-24.1; S-25.1; S-30.1; A-32.1; A-33.1; A-33.2; A-33.3; A-34.2; A-35.1; A-38.1; A-39.3; A-40.1; A-44.2; A-44.4; A-44.5; A-45.1; A-47.1; A-48.1; A-52.1

STAGE IV:
Investing in Group Processes

STAGE IV BEHAVIOR GOAL: *TO CONTRIBUTE INDIVIDUAL EFFORT TO GROUP SUCCESS*

■ 20. to respond appropriately to choices for leadership in the group [either not being selected or being selected leader]. (Same as Socialization objective S-26.)

Music Therapy Learning Experiences:

B-13.1; B-14.2; B-20.1; B-20.2; B-20.3; B-20.4; S-19.1; S-22.1; S-22.2 S-22.3; S-25.1; A-33.2; A-33.3; A-35.1; A-36.1; A-39.1; A-39.3; A-45.1; A-52.1

■ 21. to spontaneously participate in activities previously avoided [without teacher structure]. (Same as Socialization objective S-27.)

Music Therapy Learning Experiences:

Specific music therapy learning experiences were not planned for this Developmental Therapy Objective. There should be frequent opportunities to work on this objective during regular Stage Four music activities.

■ 22. to implement appropriate alternative behavior toward others [minimal interpersonal interaction needed].

Music Therapy Learning Experiences:

Specific music therapy learning experiences were not planned for this Developmental Therapy Objective. There should be frequent opportunities to work on this objective during regular Stage Four music activities.

■ 23. to verbally express cause and effect relationship between feelings and behavior, between group members, and between individuals [group problem solving]. (Same as Communication objective C-29.)

Music Therapy Learning Experiences:

Specific music therapy learning experiences were not planned for this Developmental Therapy Objective. There should be frequent opportunities to work on this objective during regular Stage Four music activities.

■ 24. to respond to provocation with verbal and body control [with verbal support from teacher].

Music Therapy Learning Experiences:

Specific music therapy learning experiences were not planned for this Developmental Therapy Objective. There should be frequent oppor-

tunities to work on this objective during regular Stage Four music activities.

■ 25. to respond to suggestions of a new, real-life experience, or change with appropriate verbal and body control [can come either from teacher or another child].

Music Therapy Learning Experiences:

B-25.1; S-25.1

Communication Objectives

STAGE I:
Responding to the Environment with Pleasure

STAGE I COMMUNICATION GOAL: *TO USE WORDS TO GAIN NEEDS*

- 1. to attend to person speaking. [Child looks directly at adult when adult initiates verbal stimulus; eye contact not necessary.]
Music Therapy Learning Experiences:
  B-1.1; B-2.1; B-3.1; B-4.2; B-4.3; B-5.1; B-7.1; C-1.1; C-2.1; C-3.1; C-3.2; C-4.1; C-5.1; C-7.1; S-1.1; S-2.1; S-4.1; S-4.2; S-6.1; S-7.1; A-5.1; A-6.1; A-7.1; A-7.2; A-13.3; A-15.1; A-16.1; A-16.2; A-17.2
- 2. to respond to verbal stimulus with a motor behavior. [Following a command, child points to answer or makes a choice.]
Music Therapy Learning Experiences:
  B-1.1; B-2.1; B-3.1; B-4.2; B-4.3; B-5.1; C-1.1; C-2.1; C-3.1; C-4.1; C-5.1; S-1.1; S-2.1; S-4.1; S-4.2; S-6.1; S-7.1; S-11.1; A-5.1; A-6.1; A-7.1; A-7.2; A-11.1; A-13.2; A-13.3; A-15.1; A-15.2; A-16.1; A-16.2; A-17.2
- 3. to respond to verbal stimulus and single object with a recognizable approximation of the appropriate verbal response. [Child gives approximation, by word or gesture, to indicate use or correct answer to question, "What is this?"; object present; function or name acceptable.] (Same as Academic objective A-8.)
Music Therapy Learning Experiences:
  B-4.1; B-5.1; C-3.1; C-3.2; C-4.1; C-5.1; C-6.1; C-7.1; A-6.1; A-10.1; A-12.1; A-16.1; A-16.2
- 4. to voluntarily initiate a recognizable verbal approximation to obtain a specific object or activity. [Child produces recognizable approximation spontaneously, e.g., "wa-wa" for water.] (Same as Academic objective A-9.)
Music Therapy Learning Experiences:
  B-3.1; B-4.1; B-5.1; C-4.1; C-5.1; C-6.1; C-7.1; A-5.1; A-6.1; A-10.1; A-12.1; A-16.1; A-16.2
- 5. to produce a recognizable word to obtain a desired response from adult [e.g., "water" instead of "wa-wa" for water. (Verbal cues may be used.)]. (Same as Socialization objective S-8.)
Music Therapy Learning Experiences:
  B-3.1; B-4.1; B-5.1; C-3.1; C-4.1; C-5.1; C-7.1; A-6.1; A-10.1; A-12.1; A-16.1; A-16.2
- 6. to produce a recognizable word to obtain a desired response from another child. [Verbal cues may be used.] (Same as Socialization objective S-9.)

Music Therapy Learning Experiences:
  C-6.1
- 7. to produce a meaningful, recognizable sequence of words to obtain a desired response from adults or children in the classroom. [Bizarre language not acceptable; socially inappropriate word sequences acceptable.]
Music Therapy Learning Experiences:
  B-3.1; B-4.1; B-5.1; C-3.1; C-4.1; C-5.1; C-6.1; C-7.1; A-6.1; A-10.1; A-12.1; A-16.1; A-16.2

STAGE II:
Responding to the Environment with Success

STAGE II COMMUNICATION GOAL: *TO USE WORDS TO AFFECT OTHERS IN CONSTRUCTIVE WAYS*

■ 8. to answer a child's or adult's request with recognizable, meaningful words. [Response does not have to be accurate, correct, or constructive.]
Music Therapy Learning Experiences:
   B-9.2; B-11.1; B-11.2; B-11.4; C-8.1; C-8.2; C-10.1; C-10.2; C-10.3; C-12.1; S-18.1; S-18.3; S-18.5; S-18.6; A-10.1; A-18.1; A-19.1; A-21.1; A-22.1; A-25.1; A-26.1; A-28.1; A-29.1; A-30.1; A-31.1

■ 9. to exhibit a receptive vocabulary no more than two years behind chronological age expectations [as indicated by the Peabody Picture Vocabulary Test or other means].
Music Therapy Learning Experiences:
   B-9.2; B-12.1; C-9.1; C-10.1; C-10.2; C-10.3; C-13.1; S-4.2; S-13.1; S-13.2; S-18.4; A-7.2; A-14.1; A-17.2; A-21.1; A-29.1; A-31.1

■ 10. to label simple feelings in pictures, dramatic play, art, or music: sad, happy, angry, afraid [by gesture or word].
Music Therapy Learning Experiences:
   C-10.1; C-10.2; C-10.3

■ 11. to use simple word sequences to command or request of another child or adult in ways acceptable to classroom procedures. [Bizarre language content or socially inappropriate word sequences are not acceptable; behavior is not a consideration.]
Music Therapy Learning Experiences:
   C-8.1; C-11.1; C-11.2; C-13.1; A-19.1; A-29.2

■ 12. to use words to exchange minimal information with an adult. [Child initiates conversation; requests or questions not applicable.]
Music Therapy Learning Experiences:
   B-9.3; B-11.1; B-11.2; B-14.1; C-12.1; C-16.1; C-20.2; A-18.1; A-19.1; A-22.1; A-23.3; A-26.1

■ 13. to use words spontaneously to exchange minimal information with another child. [Minimal verbal spontaneity with information content; requests or questions are not applicable.]
Music Therapy Learning Experiences:
   B-19.2; C-12.1; C-13.1; C-16.1; C-19.1; C-20.2

STAGE III:
Learning Skills for Successful Group Participation

STAGE III COMMUNICATION GOAL: *TO USE WORDS TO EXPRESS ONESELF IN THE GROUP*

■ 14. to accept praise or success without inappropriate behavior or loss of control.
Music Therapy Learning Experiences:
B-19.6; C-13.1; C-14.1; C-16.1; C-19.1; S-19.2; A-34.1; A-39.2; A-40.1; A-41.1

■ 15. to verbally recall group rules and procedure. (Same as Behavior objective B-13.)
Music Therapy Learning Experiences:
B-11.3; B-11.4; B-13.1; B-14.1; B-14.2; B-15.1; B-16.1; C-19.1; S-18.6; S-19.1; S-19.3; S-20.4; A-33.2; A-35.1; A-44.4

■ 16. to use words spontaneously to describe own ideas, activity, work, or self to another child or adult.
Music Therapy Learning Experiences:
B-14.1; B-14.2; B-15.1; B-16.1; B-19.1; B-19.2; B-19.5; C-16.1; C-20.1; C-20.2; S-20.3; S-21.1; S-22.3; A-38.1; A-44.1; A-44.2; A-48.1

■ 17. to contribute to making group expectations of conduct and procedure. (Same as Behavior objective B-14.)
Music Therapy Learning Experiences:
B-11.4; B-14.1; B-14.2; B-15.1; B-16.1; C-19.1; S-20.2; S-20.4; A-38.1

■ 18. to verbalize consequences if group's expectations are not reached. (Same as Behavior objective B-15.)
Music Therapy Learning Experiences:
B-14.1; B-14.2; B-15.1; B-16.1; C-19.1; S-20.4

■ 19. to use words or nonverbal gestures to show pride in own work, activity, or to make positive statements about self.
Music Therapy Learning Experiences:
B-19.4; B-19.5; B-19.6; C-11.2; C-14.1; C-16.1; C-19.1; C-20.1; C-20.2; S-19.1; S-19.2; S-19.3; S-20.1; S-20.4; S-20.6; S-22.2; A-33.1; A-34.1; A-38.1; A-40.1; A-41.1; A-43.1; A-44.2; A-44.4; A-48.1

■ 20. to use appropriate words or gestures to show feeling responses to environment, materials, people, or animals. [Teacher uses classroom activity to elicit response.]
Music Therapy Learning Experiences:
B-14.1; B-19.5; B-19.6; B-20.1; B-25.1; C-19.1; C-20.1; C-20.2; C-25.1; C-25.2; C-26.1; C-28.1; S-20.5; A-38.1; A-43.1; A-44.1; A-44.2; A-48.1; A-50.1; A-52.1; A-53.1

■ 21. to give simple reasons for group expectations. [Verbal cues from teacher may be used.] (Same as Behavior objective B-16.)
Music Therapy Learning Experiences:
B-14.1; B-14.2; B-15.1; B-16.1; C-19.1

STAGE IV:
Investing in Group Processes

STAGE IV COMMUNICATION GOAL: *TO USE WORDS TO EXPRESS AWARENESS OF RELATIONSHIP BETWEEN FEELINGS AND BEHAVIOR IN SELF AND OTHERS*

■ 22. to verbally recognize feelings in others: sad, happy, angry, afraid [either spontaneously or in response to questions].
Music Therapy Learning Experiences:
  C-26.1; C-28.1; A-52.1

■ 23. to recognize and acknowledge feelings in self: sad, happy, angry, afraid.
Music Therapy Learning Experiences:
  B-25.1; C-25.1; C-25.2; C-26.1; C-28.1; A-50.1; A-52.1; A-53.1

■ 24. to use words to praise or personally support others.
Music Therapy Learning Experiences:
  C-25.1; C-28.1; S-25.1; A-52.1

■ 25. to express experiences and feelings through art, music, dance or drama. [Child does not need to give verbal explanation.]
Music Therapy Learning Experiences:
  B-20.2; B-20.4; C-25.1; C-25.2; C-28.1; S-25.1; S-30.1; A-52.1

■ 26. to use words to express own feelings spontaneously and appropriately.
Music Therapy Learning Experiences:
  B-20.1; B-25.1; C-25.1; C-25.2; C-26.1; C-28.1; S-25.1; A-50.1; A-52.1; A-53.1

■ 27. to use words appropriately to express awareness of feelings in others [peers, adults].
Music Therapy Learning Experiences:
  B-20.1; C-26.1; C-28.1; A-52.1

■ 28. to relate real-life experiences and feelings through stories, art, drama, or music with accompanying verbal expressions.
Music Therapy Learning Experiences:
  C-25.1; C-25.2; C-26.1; C-28.1; A-53.1

■ 29. to verbally express cause and effect relationship between feelings and behavior, between group members, and between individuals [group problem solving]. (Same as Behavior objective B-23.)
Music Therapy Learning Experiences:
  Specific music therapy learning experiences were not planned for this

Developmental Therapy Objective. There should be frequent opportunities to work on this objective during regular Stage Four music activities.

Socialization Objectives

STAGE I:
Responding to the Environment with Pleasure

STAGE I SOCIALIZATION GOAL: *TO TRUST AN ADULT SUFFICIENTLY TO RESPOND TO HIM*

■ 1. to be aware of others. [Child looks at adult or another child when adult or another child speaks directly to child or touches him.]
Music Therapy Learning Experiences:
B-1.1; B-2.1; B-3.1; B-4.2; B-4.3; B-5.1; B-7.1; C-1.1; C-2.1; C-3.1; C-3.2; C-4.1; C-5.1; C-7.1; S-1.1; S-2.1; S-3.1; S-4.1; S-4.2; S-6.1; S-7.1; A-5.1; A-6.1; A-7.1; A-7.2; A-15.1; A-16.1; A-16.2; A-17.2

■ 2. to attend to other's behavior. [Child looks at adult or another child spontaneously.]
Music Therapy Learning Experiences:
B-1.1; B-2.1; B-3.1; B-4.2; B-4.3; B-5.1; B-7.1; C-1.1; C-2.1; C-3.1; C-3.2; C-4.1; C-5.1; C-7.1; S-1.1; S-2.1; S-3.1; S-4.1; S-4.2; S-4.3; S-6.1; S-7.1; A-5.1; A-6.1; A-7.1; A-7.2; A-10.1; A-13.3; A-15.1; A-16.1; A-16.2; A-17.2

■ 3. to respond to adult when child's name is called. [Child looks at adult or away; appropriate or inappropriate response acceptable.]
Music Therapy Learning Experiences:
C-1.1; C-3.1; C-5.1; S-1.1; S-3.1; S-3.2; S-6.1; S-7.1; A-7.2

■ 4. to imitate simple, familiar acts of adults [gesture, words, or activities].
Music Therapy Learning Experiences:
B-1.1; B-2.1; B-4.1; B-4.2; B-4.3; B-5.1; C-1.1; C-2.1; C-3.1; C-3.2; C-5.1; C-7.1; S-1.1; S-2.1; S-3.1; S-3.2; S-4.1; S-4.2; S-4.3; S-6.1; S-11.1; A-5.1; A-6.1; A-7.2; A-12.1; A-13.1; A-13.2; A-13.3; A-16.1; A-16.2; A-17.1; A-17.2

■ 5. to engage in organized solitary play [with direction from teacher if necessary; age-appropriate play not necessary].
Music Therapy Learning Experiences:
B-6.1; S-5.1

■ 6. to respond to adult's verbal and nonverbal requests to come to him. [Child moves next to adult and looks at him, and child accepts adult's touch.]
Music Therapy Learning Experiences:
B-1.1; C-7.1; S-4.3; S-6.1; S-7.1; A-17.1

■ 7. to respond to single verbal request or command given directly to child. [Child follows adult's verbal direction with appropriate physical movement.]

Music Therapy Learning Experiences:
B-1.1; B-4.2; B-4.3; C-1.1; C-2.1; C-4.1; S-3.2; S-4.2; S-4.3; S-6.1; S-7.1; S-11.1; A-7.1; A-11.1; A-12.1; A-15.1; A-15.2; A-16.1; A-17.2

■ 8. to produce a recognizable word to obtain a desired response from adult [e.g., "water" instead of "wa-wa" for water. (Verbal cues may be used.)] (Same as Communication objective C-5.)
Music Therapy Learning Experiences:
B-3.1; B-4.1; B-5.1; C-3.1; C-4.1; C-5.1; C-7.1; A-6.1; A-10.1; A-12.1; A-16.1; A-16.2

■ 9. to produce a recognizable word to obtain a desired response from another child. [Verbal cues may be used.] (Same as Communication objective C-6.)
Music Therapy Learning Experiences:
C-6.1

■ 10. to produce a meaningful, recognizable sequence of words to obtain a desired response from adults or children in the classroom. [Bizarre language not acceptable; socially inappropriate word sequences acceptable.] (Same as Communication objective C-7.)
Music Therapy Learning Experiences:
B-3.1; B-4.1; B-5.1; C-3.1; C-4.1; C-5.1; C-6.1; C-7.1; A-6.1; A-10.1; A-12.1; A-16.1; A-16.2

■ 11. to exhibit a beginning emergence of self [indicated by any one of these: age-approximate human figure drawing; gesturing pleasure at one's work; use of personal pronoun (I, me, my); or looking at self in mirror].
Music Therapy Learning Experiences:
B-9.4; B-12.1; S-3.2; S-11.1

■ 12. to seek contact with adult spontaneously. [Child moves next to adult, touches him, or seeks his attention by word or gesture.]
Music Therapy Learning Experiences:
B-1.1; B-6.1; B-7.1; S-1.1; S-4.3; S-6.1

STAGE II:
Responding to the Environment with Success

STAGE II SOCIALIZATION GOAL: *TO PARTICIPATE IN ACTIVITIES WITH OTHERS*

■ 13. to participate spontaneously in specific parallel activities with another child using similar materials but not interacting.
Music Therapy Learning Experiences:
B-6.1; B-8.1; B-9.2; B-11.1; B-11.2; B-11.3; C-3.1; C-5.1; C-8.1; C-9.1; S-2.1; S-4.3; S-5.1; S-13.1; S-13.2; S-18.4; A-7.2; A-12.1; A-13.1; A-13.3; A-17.1; A-18.1; A-19.2; A-23.1; A-24.1; A-26.1; A-28.1; A-28.2; A-29.1; A-29.2; A-31.1

■ 14. to wait without physical intervention by teachers. [Verbal support or touch may be used.] (Same as Behavior objective B-9.)
Music Therapy Learning Experiences:
B-9.1; B-9.2; B-9.3; B-9.4; B-11.3; B-11.4; B-12.1; C-4.1; C-5.1; C-8.1; C-10.2; C-10.3; C-11.1; C-12.1; C-13.1; S-4.3; S-15.1; S-16.1; S-18.2; S-18.3; S-18.4; S-18.5; S-18.6; S-18.7; A-7.1; A-7.2; A-15.2; A-16.1; A-19.1; A-21.1; A-21.2; A-22.1; A-23.2; A-23.3; A-30.1

■ 15. to initiate appropriate minimal movement toward another child within the classroom routine. [Child, through gesture and action, begins minimal appropriate social interaction with another child.]
Music Therapy Learning Experiences:
C-12.1; C-13.1; S-15.1

■ 16. to participate in a verbally directed sharing activity. [Child passes materials or gives toy to another.]
Music Therapy Learning Experiences:
C-11.1; S-16.1; A-19.1; A-22.1

■ 17. to participate in cooperative activities or projects with another child during play time, indoor or outdoor. [Child is involved actively with another child; verbal support or touch may be used.]
Music Therapy Learning Experiences:
S-17.1; A-39.2

■ 18. to participate in cooperative activities or projects with another child during organized class activities. [Child is involved actively with others; verbal support or touch may be used.]
Music Therapy Learning Experiences:
B-9.2; B-11.1; B-19.1; B-19.2; B-19.5; B-19.6; C-11.1; C-11.2; C-14.1; S-16.1; S-18.1; S-18.2; S-18.3; S-18.4; S-18.5; S-18.6; S-18.7; S-19.3; S-20.3; S-20.4; S-20.5; S-20.6; S-22.3; S-24.1; A-22.1; A-31.1; A-33.2; A-35.1; A-35.2; A-36.1; A-39.2; A-39.3; A-40.1; A-48.1

STAGE III:
Learning Skills for Successful Group Participation

STAGE III SOCIALIZATION GOAL: *TO FIND SATISFACTION IN GROUP ACTIVITIES*

■ 19. to take turns without verbal reminders from teacher.
Music Therapy Learning Experiences:
B-9.1; B-9.2; B-11.4; B-19.2; B-19.4; B-19.5; B-19.6; C-14.1; C-16.1; C-19.1; C-20.2; S-16.1; S-18.2; S-18.4; S-18.5; S-18.6; S-19.1; S-19.2; S-19.3; S-19.4; S-20.1; S-20.2; S-20.4; S-20.5; S-22.2; S-24.1; A-21.1; A-22.1; A-32.1; A-33.1; A-33.2; A-34.1; A-34.2; A-35.2; A-36.1; A-38.1; A-43.1; A-44.3; A-44.4; A-48.1

■ 20. to share materials, activities [minimal verbal reminders from teacher].
Music Therapy Learning Experiences:
B-11.4; B-14.2; B-15.1; B-19.2; B-19.3; B-19.4; B-19.5; B-19.6; C-16.1; C-19.1; C-20.1; C-20.2; S-16.1; S-18.1; S-18.2; S-18.5; S-18.6; S-18.7; S-19.1; S-19.3; S-19.4; S-20.1; S-20.2; S-20.3; S-20.4; S-20.5; S-20.6; S-21.1; S-22.1; S-22.2; S-22.3; S-23.1; S-24.1; A-31.1; A-32.1; A-33.1; A-33.2; A-33.3; A-34.2; A-35.1; A-35.2; A-36.1; A-38.1; A-39.1; A-39.2; A-39.3; A-40.1; A-43.1; A-44.2; A-44.3; A-44.5; A-45.1; A-47.1; A-48.1.

■ 21. to suggest activities or preference for play materials to the teacher for group activity.
Music Therapy Learning Experiences:
C-19.1; S-21.1

■ 22. to participate without inappropriate response to activity suggested by another child.
Music Therapy Learning Experiences:
B-13.1; B-19.2; C-14.1; S-19.1; S-21.1; S-22.1; S-22.2; S-22.3; A-36.1; A-38.1; A-39.3; A-45.1; A-48.1

■ 23. to indicate developing friendship by preference for a particular child or children.
Music Therapy Learning Experiences:
B-19.4; C-20.1; S-21.1; S-22.3; S-23.1; A-34.2; A-36.1; A-39.2

■ 24. to recognize and describe characteristics of others.
Music Therapy Learning Experiences:
S-24.1; A-52.1

STAGE IV:
Investing in Group Processes

STAGE IV SOCIALIZATION GOAL: *TO PARTICIPATE SPONTANEOUSLY AND SUCCESSFULLY AS A GROUP MEMBER*

■ 25. to suggest appropriate group activity directly to peer group [without teacher participation].
   Music Therapy Learning Experiences:
   B-25.1; C-25.1; C-25.2; S-25.1; S-30.1; A-27.1

■ 26. to respond appropriately to choices for leadership in the group [either not being selected or being selected leader]. (Same as Behavior objective B-20.)
   Music Therapy Learning Experiences:
   B-13.1; B-14.2; B-20.1; B-20.2; B-20.3; B-20.4; S-19.1; S-22.1; S-22.2; S-22.3; S-25.1; A-33.2; A-33.3; A-35.1; A-36.1; A-39.1; A-39.3; A-45.1; A-52.1

■ 27. to spontaneously participate in activities previously avoided [without teacher structure]. (Same as Behavior objective B-21.)
   Specific music therapy learning experiences were not planned for this Developmental Therapy Objective. There should be frequent opportunities to work on this objective during regular Stage Four music activities.

■ 28. to verbally indicate preferences among members of the group by differentiating personal characteristics.
   Music Therapy Learning Experiences:
   A-52.1

■ 29. to physically or verbally assist another child in difficult situation; to come to support of another.
   Specific music therapy learning experiences were not planned for this Developmental Therapy Objective. There should be frequent opportunities to work on this objective during regular Stage Four music activities.

■ 30. to participate in group planning and constructive problem solving [with or without minimal teacher participation].
   Music Therapy Learning Experiences:
   B-20.1; B-20.4; B-25.1; C-25.1; C-25.2; S-25.1; S-30.1; A-52.1

Academic Objectives

STAGE I:
Responding to the Environment with Pleasure

STAGE I ACADEMIC GOAL: *TO RESPOND TO THE ENVIRONMENT WITH PROCESSES OF CLASSIFICATION, DISCRIMINATION, BASIC RECEPTIVE LANGUAGE, AND BODY COORDINATION*

■ 1. to respond to sensory stimulus by attending to source of stimulus by body response or by looking directly at object or person [in situations using tactile, kinesthetic, visual, auditory, gustatory, and olfactory modalities]. (Same as Behavior objective B-1.)
Music Therapy Learning Experiences:
   B-1.1; B-2.1; B-3.1; C-1.1; C-3.1; C-3.2; C-4.1; C-5.1; C-7.1; S-2.1; S-7.1; A-6.1; A-7.1; A-7.2

■ 2. to respond to stimulus by sustained attending to source of stimulus [continued looking at object or person after initial stimulus-response has occurred]. (Same as Behavior objective B-2.)
Music Therapy Learning Experiences:
   B-1.1; B-2.1; B-3.1; C-1.1; C-3.1; C-3.2; C-4.1; C-5.1; C-7.1; S-1.1; S-2.1; S-4.1; S-4.2; S-7.1; A-5.1; A-6.1; A-7.1; A-7.2; A-10.1

■ 3. to respond with motor behavior to single environmental stimulus: object, person, sound. (Same as Behavior objective B-3.)
Music Therapy Learning Experiences:
   B-1.1; B-3.1; C-1.1; C-7.1; S-1.1

■ 4. to respond with motor and body responses to complex environmental and verbal stimuli [through imitation "Do this"; through completion of verbal direction; minimal participation in the routine; given physical intervention and verbal cues]. (Same as Behavior objective B-4.)
Music Therapy Learning Experiences:
   B-1.1; B-2.1; B-3.1; B-4.1; B-4.2; B-4.3; B-5.1; C-2.1; C-3.1; C-4.1; C-5.1; C-6.1; C-7.1; S-2.1; S-3.1; S-3.2; S-4.1; S-4.2; S-4.3; S-7.1; S-11.1; A-5.1; A-6.1; A-7.1; A-7.2; A-10.1; A-11.1; A-12.1; A-13.1; A-13.2; A-13.3; A-14.1; A-15.1; A-15.2; A-16.1; A-16.2; A-17.1; A-17.2

■ 5. to respond with rudimentary fine motor skill to simple manipulative tasks associated with two-year level.
Music Therapy Learning Experiences:
   B-3.1; B-5.1; C-1.1; C-4.1; A-5.1; A-6.1; A-15.2; A-16.1

■ 6. to imitate words or action of adult upon request. [Adult gives word and object and says, "This is _____. Say _____." Child imitates with approximation.]

Music Therapy Learning Experiences:
   B-2.1; B-4.1; B-4.2; B-4.3; B-5.1; C-1.1; C-2.1; C-3.1; C-3.2; C-4.1; C-5.1; C-6.1; C-7.1; S-1.1; S-2.1; S-3.1; S-3.2; S-4.1; S-4.2; S-4.3; S-6.1; S-11.1; A-5.1; A-6.1; A-7.2; A-10.1; A-12.1; A-13.2; A-13.3; A-16.1; A-16.2; A-17.1; A-17.2

■ 7. to respond by simple discrimination of objects. [Child gives correct motor or verbal response to the command, "Give me _____." (two different objects presented).]
Music Therapy Learning Experiences:
   A-7.1; A-7.2; A-10.1; A-11.1; A-14.1

■ 8. to respond to verbal stimulus and single object with a recognizable approximation of the appropriate verbal response. [Child gives approximation, by word or gesture, to indicate use or correct answer to question, "What is this?" (object present; function or name acceptable).] (Same as Communication objective C-3.)
Music Therapy Learning Experiences:
   B-4.1; B-5.1; C-3.1; C-3.2; C-4.1; C-5.1; C-6.1; C-7.1; A-6.1; A-10.1; A-12.1; A-16.1; A-16.2

■ 9. to voluntarily initiate a recognizable verbal approximation to obtain a specific object or activity. [Child produces recognizable approximation spontaneously, e.g., "wa-wa" for water.] (Same as Communication objective C-4.)
Music Therapy Learning Experiences:
   B-3.1; B-4.1; B-5.1; C-4.1; C-5.1; C-6.1; C-7.1; A-5.1; A-6.1; A-10.1; A-12.1; A-16.1; A-16.2

■ 10. to indicate short term memory for objects and people. [Child identifies missing objects and missing members of group.]
Music Therapy Learning Experiences:
   A-7.1; A-10.1

■ 11. to respond with classification of similar objects with different attributes.
Music Therapy Learning Experiences:
   A-11.1

■ 12. to indicate short term memory for verbal expressions. [Child repeats appropriate three-word phrases spontaneously. Teacher questions or cues may be used; bizarre repetition of TV commercials or echolalia is not appropriate.]

Music Therapy Learning Experiences:
   B-3.1; C-4.1; C-6.1; C-7.1; A-6.1; A-12.1; A-16.1

■ 13. to perform body coordination activities at the three/four-year level.
Music Therapy Learning Experiences:
   C-1.1; S-3.2; S-4.2; S-4.3; S-6.1; A-12.1; A-13.1; A-13.2; A-13.3

■ 14. to match similar pictures [when presented with both identical and different pictures].
Music Therapy Learning Experiences:
   A-14.1

■ 15. to indicate recognition of color names with the correct response. [Child responds correctly to the command, "Give me _____." (red, blue, and yellow) by picking out correct color from three choices.]
Music Therapy Learning Experiences:
   A-15.1; A-15.2

■ 16. to perform eye-hand coordination activities at the four-year level.
Music Therapy Learning Experiences:
   A-16.1; A-16.2; A-24.1

■ 17. to recognize own body parts [eye, hand, foot, nose, leg, arm, knee]. [Any response appropriate; gesture, word, etc.]
Music Therapy Learning Experiences:
   B-4.3; B-5.1; C-8.1; C-9.1; S-2.1; S-4.1; S-11.1; S-13.1; S-13.2; S-18.3; S-18.4; A-6.1; A-13.3; A-17.1; A-17.2; A-19.2; A-29.2

STAGE II:
Responding to the Environment with Success

STAGE II ACADEMIC GOAL: *TO PARTICIPATE IN CLASSROOM ACTIVITIES WITH LANGUAGE CONCEPTS OF SIMILARITIES AND DIFFERENCES, LABELS, USE, COLOR; NUMERICAL PROCESSES OF ORDERING AND CLASSIFYING; BODY COORDINATION*

■ 18. to recognize uses of objects, toys, etc.
Music Therapy Learning Experiences:
B-6.1; B-8.1; B-9.2; B-11.4; C-13.1; S-5.1; S-18.5; S-18.6; A-18.1; A-22.1; A-23.3; A-30.1

■ 19. to recognize detail in pictures by gesture or word.
Music Therapy Learning Experiences:
C-8.2; C-10.2; A-19.1; A-19.2

■ 20. to rote count to ten.
Music Therapy Learning Experiences:
A-20.1; A-23.1

■ 21. to count with one-to-one correspondence to five.
Music Therapy Learning Experiences:
A-19.2; A-21.1; A-21.2; A-23.1; A-23.2; A-23.3; A-30.1

■ 22. to name colors [black, purple, orange, green]. [Child is able to choose color if given the word; child is able to give approximation of word when presented with color.]
Music Therapy Learning Experiences:
B-11.2; C-10.2; C-13.1; A-22.1

■ 23. to count with one-to-one correspondence to ten.
Music Therapy Learning Experiences:
A-23.1; A-23.2; A-23.3

■ 24. to perform eye-hand coordination activities at the five-year level.
Music Therapy Learning Experiences:
S-18.7; A-24.1

■ 25. to recognize differences among shapes, symbols, numerals, and words. [All forms must be mastered; child need not know how to read words in order to recognize differences among them.]
Music Therapy Learning Experiences:
C-10.3; A-25.1

■ 26. to categorize items which are different but have generally similar characteristics or associations.
Music Therapy Learning Experiences:
A-26.1

■ 27. to write a recognizable approximation of first name, without assistance. [Adult may initiate request; no model used.]
Music Therapy Learning Experiences:
A-27.1

■ 28. to discriminate concepts of opposition [up, down; under, over; big, little; tall, small; hot, cold; first, last]. [Child is able to demonstrate or point, given opposites in pictures.]
Music Therapy Learning Experiences:
B-11.3; B-11.4; C-9.1; C-11.1; S-18.5; A-28.1; A-28.2; A-29.2

■ 29. to perform body coordination activities at the five-year level.
Music Therapy Learning Experiences:
B-12.1; C-9.1; A-29.1; A-29.2

■ 30. to recognize groups of objects to five ["How many?"].
Music Therapy Learning Experiences:
A-30.1; A-32.1; A-36.1

■ 31. to listen to story telling.
Music Therapy Learning Experiences:
C-10.1; C-20.2; S-20.5; A-31.1; A-44.1; A-44.2; A-44.4; A-48.1

STAGE III:
Learning Skills for Successful Group Participation

STAGE III ACADEMIC GOAL: *TO PARTICIPATE IN THE GROUP WITH BASIC EXPRESSIVE LANGUAGE CONCEPTS; SYMBOLIC REPRESENTATION OF EXPERIENCES AND CONCEPTS; FUNCTIONAL, SEMICONCRETE CONCEPTS OF CONSERVATION; BODY COORDINATION*

■ 32. to recognize groups of objects to ten.
Music Therapy Learning Experiences:
  A-32.1; A-36.1; A-40.1

■ 33. to demonstrate left to right orientation for visual motor tasks.
Music Therapy Learning Experiences:
  B-19.6; A-33.1; A-33.2; A-33.3; A-38.1; A-41.1; A-43.1; A-47.1; A-48.1

■ 34. to recognize written names for color words [red, blue, yellow]. [Child selects appropriate color word.]
Music Therapy Learning Experiences:
  A-34.1; A-34.2

■ 35. to recognize written labels [own name, chair, table, part of written schedules].
Music Therapy Learning Experiences:
  B-15.1; B-19.5; B-19.6; S-19.3; S-20.1; S-20.5; S-21.1; A-33.3; A-35.1; A-35.2; A-38.1; A-43.1; A-44.4; A-47.1

■ 36. to recognize and write numerals to represent groupings [1 to 10]. [For mastering this objective, child must be able to accomplish both activities, recognizing numerals and writing numerals to represent groups from 1 to 10.]
Music Therapy Learning Experiences:
  A-36.1; A-40.1

■ 37. to write first and last name and date with written example to copy.
Music Therapy Learning Experiences:
  Specific music therapy learning experiences were not planned for this Developmental Therapy Objective.

■ 38. to perform eye-hand coordination activities at the six-year level.
Music Therapy Learning Experiences:
  B-15.1; B-19.6; C-16.1; S-20.4; A-33.1; A-33.2; A-34.1; A-36.1; A-38.1; A-41.1

■ 39. to perform body coordination activities at the six-year level.
Music Therapy Learning Experiences:
  B-13.1; B-14.2; B-19.3; B-19.6; C-14.1; S-19.2; S-22.1; S-22.2; A-39.1; A-39.2; A-39.3; A-45.1

■ 40. to recognize and write numerals to represent groupings [11 to 20].
Music Therapy Learning Experiences:
  A-40.1

■ 41. to write alphabet or simple words [with or without model].
Music Therapy Learning Experiences:
  S-21.1; A-41.1; A-47.1; A-48.1

■ 42. to do numerical operations of addition and subtraction through ten.
Music Therapy Learning Experiences:
  Specific music therapy learning experiences were not planned for this Developmental Therapy Objective.

■ 43. to use ordinal concepts verbally [first, fifth, last].
Music Therapy Learning Experiences:
  A-32.1; A-33.3; A-43.1

■ 44. to listen to a story and respond with appropriate answers to questions: by comments or gestures.
Music Therapy Learning Experiences:
  C-20.2; S-20.5; A-44.1; A-44.2; A-44.3; A-44.4; A-44.5; A-48.1

■ 45. to read basic primary vocabulary words spontaneously in sentences.
Music Therapy Learning Experiences:
  B-19.6; S-22.3; A-45.1.

■ 46. to do simple numerical operations of addition and subtraction above 10.
Music Therapy Learning Experiences:
  Specific music therapy learning experiences were not planned for this Developmental Therapy Objective.

■ 47. to write basic words from memory or dictation.
Music Therapy Learning Experiences:
  A-47.1; A-48.1; A-50.1; A-53.1

■ 48. to participate in group activity for writing an experience story, dictating to teacher, or working on murals.
Music Therapy Learning Experiences:
  B-19.5; B-25.1; C-20.2; C-25.1; C-25.2; S-20.5; A-48.1

STAGE IV:
Investing in Group Processes

STAGE IV ACADEMIC GOAL: *TO SUCCESSFULLY USE SIGNS AND SYMBOLS IN FORMALIZED SCHOOL WORK AND IN GROUP EXPERIENCES*

- 49. to write full name, address, date, from memory.
  Music Therapy Learning Experiences:
  Specific music therapy learning experiences were not planned for this Developmental Therapy Objective.
- 50. to read and write basic use vocabulary spontaneously in complete sentences.
  Music Therapy Learning Experiences:
  B-25.1; S-22.3; A-50.1; A-53.1
- 51. to read and write quantitative words for measurement of distance, time, money, fractions.
  Music Therapy Learning Experiences:
  B-25.1
- 52. to contribute to group projects requiring expressive skills.
  Music Therapy Learning Experiences:
  B-20.4; B-25.1; C-25.1; C-25.2; S-25.1; S-30.1; A-52.1
- 53. to write individual experience stories. [Child writes own experience story with teacher assistance on difficult words.]
  Music Therapy Learning Experiences:
  A-53.1

chapter 3
MUSIC THERAPY LEARNING EXPERIENCES

Developmental Therapy Objective B-1/to respond to sensory stimulus by attending to source of stimulus by body response or by looking directly at object or person

Type of Activity	Area
Listening	Behavior
(Playing)	
Singing	Stage
Moving	(I)
Creating	II
Verbalizing	III
	IV

MUSIC ACTIVITY

I. Introduction

Direct the children to sit on the floor facing the music therapist. Place the drum in front of them.

II. Implementation

1. Strike the drum and say to the children, "I'm playing the drum!"
2. Tell the children to come play the drum. When all of the children are standing around the drum, begin playing the drum and singing the "Drum Song." Encourage all of the children to strike the drum with their hands.

III. Techniques and Modifications

1. Help all of the children to become involved in the activity. If necessary, take a child's hand and gently move it in striking the drum.
2. Use a drum which is large enough to allow all of the children to stand around it and strike it at the same time.

Resource
large floor drum
"Drum Song": Jennie Purvis (Resource 9)

Cross Reference Objectives
Behavior 2, 3, 4
Communication 1, 2
Socialization 1, 2, 4, 6, 7, 12
Academics 1, 2, 3, 4,

B-2.1 Music Therapy Learning Experience

Developmental Therapy Objective B-2/to respond to stimulus by sustained attending to source of stimulus

Type of Activity	*Area*
Listening	Behavior
Playing	
Singing	*Stage*
(Moving)	Ⓘ
Creating	II
Verbalizing	III
	IV

MUSIC ACTIVITY

I. Introduction

Direct the children to sit on the floor facing the music therapist.

II. Implementation

1. Tell the children to "saw." Begin singing the song and demonstrate the "sawing" action, i.e., push both arms out and back in front of body, parallel to the floor. Verbally encourage the children to imitate the movements.
2. Sing the second verse and demonstrate the "hammering" action, i.e., make hammering motions using the fist of one hand to hit the open palm of the other hand. Direct the children to "hammer."
3. Sing the third verse and show the children the "sanding" movement, i.e., brush palms of hands together in back and forth movement. Tell the children to "sand."

III. Techniques and Modifications

1. If some children do not respond, physically assist them with the movements, e.g., take a child's hands and move them in a "sawing" motion.
2. To aid the children in learning the movements, introduce one action at a time. Be certain that the children are able to do the first movement, i.e., "sawing," before proceeding to the next action.

Resource
"Work Song": Jennie Purvis (Resource 26).

Cross Reference Objectives
Behavior 1, 4
Communication 1, 2
Socialization 1, 2, 4
Academics 1, 2, 4, 6

Developmental Therapy Objective B-3/to respond with motor behavior to single environmental stimulus: object, person, sound

Type of Activity	Area
Listening	Behavior
(Playing)	
Singing	Stage
Moving	(I)
Creating	II
Verbalizing	III
	IV

MUSIC ACTIVITY

I. Introduction

Direct the children to sit on the floor facing the music therapist.

II. Implementation

1. Take a drum out of the box and strike it in front of the children. Tell them that it is a "drum."
2. Hold the drum in front of a child and say, "Do you want the drum?" When the child reaches for the instrument, nods his head, or verbally responds to the question, give him the drum.
3. Repeat step 2 until each child has a drum. Sing "The Band" and play the drums.

III. Techniques and Modifications

1. If a child does not respond when he is asked if he wants the drum, place the drum in his hands and gently assist him in playing it.
2. Give a child an instrument as soon as he makes any type of motor or verbal response which shows that he wants a drum, e.g., as soon as the drum is presented some children may reach for the instrument.

Resource

"The Band": *Music Activities For Retarded Children,* David Ginglend and Winifred Stiles, Abingdon Press, Nashville, Tennessee, 1965, p. 27

hand drums, one for each child and music therapist

one box

Cross Reference Objectives
Behavior 1, 2, 4
Communication 1, 2, 4, 5, 7
Socialization 1, 2, 8, 10
Academics 1, 2, 3, 4, 5, 9, 12

B-4.1 Music Therapy Learning Experience

Developmental Therapy Objective B-4/to respond with motor and body responses to complex environmental and verbal stimuli

Type of Activity	*Area*
Listening	Behavior
(Playing)	
Singing	*Stage*
Moving	(I)
Creating	II
(Verbalizing)	III
	IV

MUSIC ACTIVITY

I. Introduction

Direct the children to sit on the floor in the music area.

II. Implementation

1. Shake the bag of kazoos in front of the children. Take a kazoo out of the bag, telling the children its name.
2. Demonstrate how to play the kazoo by holding it several inches from the mouth. Begin making an "ah" sound, gradually moving the kazoo closer to the mouth until the lips cover the opening and a sound is produced.
3. Ask one child at a time if he wants to play the kazoo, requiring him to make a verbalization in order to obtain the instrument. When he has the kazoo, help him to produce a sound with it. Repeat until all of the children have a kazoo.
4. Begin humming the song on the kazoo. Encourage the children to play the kazoos.

III. Techniques and Modifications

If a child has difficulty producing a sound on the kazoo, face him and repeat step 2.

Resource
"The Band": *Music Activities For Retarded Children,* David Ginglend and Winifred Stiles, Abingdon Press, Nashville, Tennessee, 1965, p. 27
kazoos, one for each child and music therapist
bag

Cross Reference Objectives
Behavior
Communication 3, 4, 5, 7
Socialization 4, 8, 10
Academics 4, 6, 8, 9

Developmental Therapy Objective B-4/to respond with motor and body responses to complex environmental and verbal stimuli

Type of Activity	Area
Listening	Behavior
Playing	
Singing	Stage
(Moving)	I
Creating	II
Verbalizing	III
	IV

MUSIC ACTIVITY

I. Introduction

Instruct the children to sit on the floor.

II. Implementation

1. Begin playing the record. Tell the children to stand up and hold hands to make a circle.
2. Walk around the circle while verbalizing the action to the children, e.g., "Look at us walking." Use various locomotive movements, such as jumping, running, walking toward and away from the center of the circle, etc.

III. Techniques and Modifications

Introduce each action verbally and then begin the action.

Resource
record player
"Gei Gordons": *Happy Folk Dances* (EPA-4129), RCA Victor, Camden, New Jersey

Cross Reference Objectives
Behavior
Communication 1, 2
Socialization 1, 2, 4, 7
Academics 4, 6

B-4.3 Music Therapy Learning Experience

Developmental Therapy Objective B-4/to respond with motor and body responses to complex environmental and verbal stimuli

Type of Activity	Area
(Listening)	Behavior
Playing	
Singing	Stage
(Moving)	(I)
Creating	II
Verbalizing	III
	IV

MUSIC ACTIVITY

I. Introduction

Direct the children to stand up for the "Turn Around" song.

II. Implementation

1. Begin playing the "Turn Around" selection on the record player.
2. As each body movement is named in the words of the song, move accordingly and encourage the children to make the same movement.

III. Techniques and Modifications

1. Some children may need help in making the appropriate movements; e.g., if a child has difficulty with a movement, take his hand and move it as directed in the song.
2. Provide a model for the children and verbally encourage them to watch carefully and to imitate all movements.
3. Use only short segments of the song until the children become familiar with all of the body movements.

Resource
record player
"Turn Around": *Getting to Know Myself* (AR 543), Hap Palmer, Educational Activities, Inc., Freeport, New York

Cross Reference Objectives
Behavior
Communication 1, 2
Socialization 1, 2, 4, 7.
Academics 4, 6, 17

Developmental Therapy Objective B-5/to actively assist in learning self-help skills

Type of Activity	Area
Listening	Behavior
Playing	
Singing	Stage
(Moving)	Ⓘ
Creating	II
(Verbalizing)	III
	IV

MUSIC ACTIVITY

I. Introduction

Direct the children to sit on the floor in the music area.

II. Implementation

1. Hold a wet washcloth in front of each child and tell him to ask for the washcloth. When a child says, "washcloth," "wash," "I want washcloth," etc., give him the washcloth.
2. When all of the children have wash cloths, begin singing the "Washing Song" and lead the children in the appropriate actions.

III. Techniques and Modifications

1. Have a towel available so that the children can dry off after using the wash cloths.
2. If a mirror is available the children may look at themselves as they wash.

Resource
"Washing Song": Jennie Purvis (Resource 25)
wet washcloths, one for each child and music therapist

Cross Reference Objectives
Behavior 4
Communication 1, 2, 3, 4, 5, 7
Socialization 1, 2, 4, 8, 10
Academics 4, 5, 6, 8, 9, 17

B-6.1 Music Therapy Learning Experience

Developmental Therapy Objective B-6/to respond independently to play material

Type of Activity	Area
Listening	Behavior
(Playing)	
Singing	Stage
Moving	(I)
Creating	II
Verbalizing	III
	IV

MUSIC ACTIVITY

I. Introduction

Before the children enter the classroom, place the toys and musical instruments in the play area.

II. Implementation

1. Direct the children to go to the play area. Allow them to move freely among the play materials.
2. As a child picks up a toy or musical instrument, verbally reflect his actions, e.g., "Tim is playing the drum."

III. Techniques and Modifications

1. Use music materials which are colorful and simple to play.
2. Encourage the children to say the names of the toys and instruments as they play with them.

Resource
ukelele
song flute
drum
jingle bells
tambourine
variety of toys with which the children are familiar

Cross Reference Objectives
Behavior 7, 8
Communication
Socialization 5, 12, 13
Academics 18

Developmental Therapy Objective B-7/to respond with recall to the routine spontaneously

Type of Activity	Area
(Listening)	Behavior
Playing	
Singing	*Stage*
(Moving)	(I)
Creating	II
Verbalizing	III
	IV

MUSIC ACTIVITY

I. Introduction

At the end of an activity, tell the children the name of the next activity, e.g., "Art Time is over and now it's Work Time."

II. Implementation

1. Begin singing "Let's Go," substituting the name of the next activity in the song, e.g., "Let's go to Work Time."
2. Move with the children to the part of the room which is designated for the next activity.

III. Techniques and Modifications

1. In a Stage One class it is important to follow the same schedule of activities each day and to designate a certain area in the room for each activity.
2. As each activity is announced (using the "Let's Go" song), allow the children enough time to move independently to the appropriate area in the room. If the children do not initiate the movement, lead them to the designated area.

Resource
"Let's Go": Jennie Purvis (Resource 16)

Cross Reference Objectives
Behavior
Communication 1
Socialization 1, 2, 12
Academics

B-8.1 Music Therapy Learning Experience

Developmental Therapy Objective B-8/to use play materials appropriately, simulating normal play experience

Type of Activity	Area
Listening	Behavior
Playing	
Singing	**Stage**
(Moving)	I
Creating	II
Verbalizing	III
	IV

MUSIC ACTIVITY

I. Introduction

Direct the children to stand in a large circle in the music area.

II. Implementation

1. Show the children the balls and encourage them to talk about various games and activities in which balls are used.
2. Tell the children that they will be able to bounce the balls to music. Give each child a ball and begin playing the record. Demonstrate how to bounce the ball in time to the music and direct the children to begin bouncing the balls.

III. Techniques and Modifications

1. Use large balls which are easy to bounce and catch.
2. Encourage the children to think of other ways to use the balls with the music, e.g., throwing them into the air, bouncing them against the wall, etc.
3. The focus of this activity is the correct use of the ball as a play object. Therefore, do not insist on rhythmic precision while the balls are being bounced. Provide a model for the children, however, by bouncing the ball in rhythm with strong, steady movements.

Resource
record player
"Gentle On My Mind": *Mod Marches* (AR527), Hap Palmer, Educational Activities, Inc., Freeport, New York
large balls, one for each child and music therapist

Cross Reference Objectives
Behavior 11
Communication
Socialization 13
Academics 18

Developmental Therapy Objective B-9/to wait without physical intervention by teachers

Type of Activity	Area
Listening	Behavior
(Playing)	
(Singing)	Stage
Moving	I
Creating	(II)
Verbalizing	III
	IV

MUSIC ACTIVITY

I. Introduction

Direct the children to sit on the floor in a semicircle facing the music therapist.

II. Implementation

1. Ask the children if they know the song, "I've Been Working on the Railroad."
2. Direct the children who know the song to sing it. Sing one verse and accompany the singing by playing the autoharp.
3. Select a child to strum the strings of the autoharp. Press the chord buttons as the child strums and lead the children in singing the song.
4. Repeat this procedure until each child has played the autoharp.

III. Techniques and Modifications

1. Adapt the tempo of the song to correspond to the speed with which each child strums the autoharp strings. The song may be sung, therefore, at a different tempo for each child.
2. Encourage the children to listen to each child as he plays and to comment on the manner in which he plays, e.g., fast or slow, loud or soft, etc.
3. If the children have difficulty waiting for their turns while sitting on the floor, add more structure by using the autoharp at the table.
4. This activity can be modified to include a variety of other familiar songs.

Resource

"I've Been Working on the Railroad": *Making Music Your Own—Book 3* (Teacher's Edition), Silver Burdett Company, Morristown, New Jersey, 1971, pp. 86–87

autoharp

Cross Reference Objectives
Behavior 11
Communication
Socialization 14, 19
Academics

B-9.2 Music Therapy Learning Experience

Developmental Therapy Objective B-9/to wait without physical intervention by teachers

Type of Activity	Area
(Listening)	Behavior
(Playing)	
Singing	**Stage**
Moving	I
Creating	(II)
Verbalizing	III
	IV

MUSIC ACTIVITY

I. Introduction

Direct the children to sit in their chairs in a semicircle facing the music therapist. Place the rhythm instruments on the floor in front of the children.

II. Implementation

1. Ask the children to name the instruments and to discuss how each one is played.
2. Tell the children that they will each be given an instrument. When they hear the words, "Play your instruments and make a pretty sound," everyone is to play his instrument. When they hear, "Listen to the (*name of instrument*)," only the children with that instrument should play.
3. Distribute the rhythm instruments and begin playing the song on the record player.
4. Encourage the children to listen carefully and to play their instruments at the correct time.

III. Techniques and Modifications

1. Before distributing the instruments, be certain that the children understand the directions for the activity by having them repeat the rules and procedures.
2. When only one instrument is being played, direct the other children to listen and/or tap their feet, sway to the music, etc.
3. If the children have difficulty refraining from playing when only one instrument is supposed to be played, instruct them to place their instruments on the floor until it is time for the group to play together for the chorus.
4. When this activity is first introduced, limit the number of instruments

by playing only the first two or three verses of the song. Gradually introduce new verses as the children become familiar with the instruments and the activity.

Resource
record player
"Play Your Instruments and Make a Pretty Sound": *Play Your Instruments and Make a Pretty Sound* (FC 7665) Ella Jenkins, Folkways Records, New York, New York

cowbell

rhythm sticks

maracas

triangle

castanets

tone block

Cross Reference Objectives
Behavior 11
Communication 8, 9
Socialization 13, 14, 18, 19
Academics 18

Developmental Therapy Objective B-9/to wait without physical intervention by teachers

Type of Activity	Area
Listening	Behavior
Playing	
(Singing)	Stage
Moving	I
Creating	(II)
Verbalizing	III
	IV

MUSIC ACTIVITY

I. Introduction

Direct the children to sit in their chairs at the table.

II. Implementation

1. Distribute the paper bag dog puppets which the children made during an art activity.
2. Tell the children to put the puppets on their hands in preparation for the song. Explain that they are to make the dogs go "Woof, Woof" at the end of each line in the song.
3. Begin singing "How Much Is That Doggie in the Window?" and point to the children each time they are to make the dogs bark.
4. Set up a box at the end of the table to serve as a store window.
5. Collect the dog puppets. Pick one and ask the children who owns that dog. Give it to the "owner" and tell him to go behind the box and hold up his puppet as the song is sung. Explain that his dog is to make the "Woofs" at the appropriate time.
6. Begin singing the song. At the end of the song, ask the owner how much his animal costs. Encourage the child to reply with an amount. Tell the other children to pretend that they are collecting money to buy the dog.
7. Repeat steps 5 and 6 for each child's puppet.

III. Techniques and Modifications

1. Vary the "pretend" situation each time so as to make each child feel that his puppet is special.
2. As each child has a turn with his puppet in the store window, encourage the other children to sing along.
3. Discuss the differences in how the "dogs" look and sound.

Resource

"How Much Is That Doggie in the Window?": *Reader's Digest Treasury of Best Loved Songs,* William L. Simon, Reader's Digest Association, Inc., Pleasantville, New York, 1972, pp. 266–267

paper bag hand puppets to represent dogs (made by the children)

large box (with front out) to serve as store window

Cross Reference Objectives
Behavior 11
Communication 12
Socialization 14
Academics

B-9.4 Music Therapy Learning Experience

Developmental Therapy Objective B-9/to wait without physical intervention by teachers

Type of Activity	Area
(Listening)	Behavior
Playing	
Singing	Stage
Moving	I
Creating	(II)
(Verbalizing)	III
	IV

MUSIC ACTIVITY

I. Introduction

Direct the children to sit in a semicircle on the floor.

II. Implementation

1. Tell the children that they will hear a name song in which they will take turns saying their names. Practice by pointing to the children one at a time and asking them to say their names.
2. Begin playing the record and instruct the children to clap their hands. Each time "My name is _____" is heard, point to a child and encourage him to say his name.

III. Techniques and Modification

1. Before using the record with this activity, be certain the children understand that they are to say their names as the music therapist points to them.
2. If necessary use the pause control on the record player or lift the record player arm in order to give a child enough time to respond by saying his name.

Resource
record player
"What Is Your Name": *Learning Basic Skills Through Music—Volume I* (AR514), Hap Palmer, Educational Activities, Inc., Freeport, New York

Cross Reference Objectives
Behavior 11
Communication
Socialization 11, 14
Academics

Developmental Therapy Objective B-10/to participate in activities such as Work Time, Story Time, Talking Time, Juice and Cookie Time without physical intervention by teacher

Type of Activity	Area
(Listening)	Behavior
Playing	
Singing	Stage
(Moving)	I
Creating	(II)
Verbalizing	III
	IV

MUSIC ACTIVITY

I. Introduction

Direct the children to sit on the floor in a circle.

II. Implementation

1. Show the children the popcorn popper. Tell them that they will be able to have popcorn for their Snack Time. Place the popcorn ingredients in the popper and turn it on.
2. Tell the children that while they are waiting for the corn to pop they will listen to a song called "Popcorn."
3. Play a short segment of the music and direct the children to raise their hands when they hear the "corn popping" section (indicated by drums in the music).
4. Instruct them to sit on their knees and gently move up and down with the rhythm of the music. Each time the "corn popping" section is heard, they are to bounce up and down very fast like the corn which is popping.
5. Play the song several times until the actual popcorn is ready to be eaten.
6. Direct the children to return to the table for Snack Time. Put the popcorn into a bowl and pass it to each child.

III. Techniques and Modifications

1. As the children eat the popcorn, encourage them to talk about the corn popping activity. Ask them to name other places where they have eaten popcorn, e.g., movies, home, etc.
2. Plan the Snack Time in such a way that the children will be encouraged to share, e.g., direct each child to pass the bowl of popcorn to the child beside him, allow one child to distribute napkins, etc.

Resource
record player
"Popcorn": *Dance, Sing and Listen Again and Again—Volume III* (D121), Esther Nelson and Bruce Haack, Dimension 5, Bronx, New York
popcorn popper and popcorn ingredients
bowl

Cross Reference Objectives
Behavior 11, 12
Communication
Socialization
Academics

B-11.1 Music Therapy Learning Experience

Developmental Therapy Objective B-11/to participate in activities such as Play Time, Mat Time, Games, Music, Art Time without physical intervention by teacher

Type of Activity	*Area*
Listening	Behavior
Playing	
Singing	*Stage*
(Moving)	I
Creating	(II)
Verbalizing	III
	IV

MUSIC ACTIVITY

I. Introduction

Direct the children to sit on the floor in a circle.

II. Implementation

1. Ask the children questions about railroads. Encourage them to talk about any experiences related to trains which they may have had.
2. Tell the children that they will pretend to be railroad workers who are building train tracks. Demonstrate the hammering motion used in driving spikes into the tracks.
3. Direct the children to stand in the music area. Begin singing the song and lead the children in the actions.
4. During the last verse, assist the children in forming a train, i.e., the children stand one behind the other with each child holding onto the person in front of him.

III. Techniques and Modifications

1. Encourage the children to sing along when they learn the words.
2. Demonstrate how to do the hammering action in rhythm with the music.

Resource
"I've Been Working On the Railroad": *Making Music Your Own—Book 3* (Teacher's Edition), Silver Burdett Co., Morristown, New Jersey, 1971, pp. 86–87

Cross Reference Objectives
Behavior
Communication 8, 12
Socialization 13, 18
Academics

Developmental Therapy Objective B-11/to participate in activities such as Play Time, Mat Time, Games, Music, Art Time without physical intervention by teacher

Type of Activity	Area
Listening	Behavior
Playing	
Singing	Stage
(Moving)	I
Creating	(II)
(Verbalizing)	III
	IV

MUSIC ACTIVITY

I. Introduction

Direct the children to sit on the floor in a semicircle facing the music therapist.

II. Implementation

1. Show the children the box of leaves. Encourage them to talk about the various shapes and colors.
2. Tell the children to pretend that they are leaves falling to the ground. Begin singing the song and lead the children in the movement activity.

III. Techniques and Modifications

1. Pictures related to autumn can be used to stimulate conversation about falling leaves.
2. The leaves which are used in this activity can be collected outdoors by the children or made from various colors of construction paper.
3. Encourage the children to think of different ways to demonstrate falling leaves.
4. If the children have difficulty simulating falling leaves, use props, such as scarves, paper streamers, etc., to create the desired effect.

Resource
"Come, Little Leaves": *Exploring Music—Book K* (Teacher's Edition), Holt, Rinehart and Winston, Inc., New York, New York, 1969, p. 63
box of leaves of different shapes and colors

Cross Reference Objectives
Behavior
Communication 8, 12
Socialization 13
Academics 22

B-11.3 Music Therapy Learning Experience

Developmental Therapy Objective B-11/to participate in activities such as Play Time, Mat Time, Games, Music, Art Time without physical intervention by teacher

Type of Activity	Area
(Listening)	Behavior
(Playing)	
Singing	Stage
Moving	I
Creating	(II)
Verbalizing	III
	IV

MUSIC ACTIVITY

I. Introduction

Direct the children to move their chairs to the music area and sit in a semicircle facing the music therapist.

II. Implementation

1. Tell the children that a selection of music will be played which starts and stops at various times. Instruct them to clap with the music and to stop clapping each time the music stops.
2. Begin the record and direct the children to start clapping. Stop the music at various times by picking up the record player arm.
3. Give each child an instrument. Direct them to play their instruments with the music and to stop playing each time the music stops.
4. Allow the children to take turns operating the record player, starting and stopping it while the others play their instruments.

III. Techniques and Modifications

1. Frequently remind the children to listen carefully to the music so that they will be able to stop clapping or playing as soon as the music stops.
2. To encourage the children to rely on their listening skills, place the record player behind them so that they cannot see the music therapist stop the music.
3. Give the children supervision while they are operating the record player. It may be necessary to precede this activity with a discussion concerning the correct use of the record player.

Resource
record player
"Yellow Submarine": *Mod Marches* (AR527), Hap Palmer, Educational Activities, Inc., Freeport, New York
variety of rhythm instruments, one for each child

Cross Reference Objectives
Behavior 9, 13
Communication 15
Socialization 13, 14
Academics 28

Developmental Therapy Objective B-11/to participate in activities such as Play Time, Mat Time, Games, Music, Art Time without physical intervention by teacher

Type of Activity	Area
(Listening)	Behavior
(Playing)	
Singing	Stage
Moving	I
Creating	(II)
(Verbalizing)	III
	IV

MUSIC ACTIVITY

I. Introduction

Direct the children to sit on the floor in a circle.

II. Implementation

1. Introduce the triangle to the children by asking questions such as, "What does it sound like?" "From what material is it made?" etc.
2. Explain to the children that they will be given an opportunity to play the triangle with the music. Direct them to play loudly or softly depending upon the volume of the music and to stop playing each time the music stops.
3. Encourage the children to recall and make new rules for the activity, e.g., when the music stops, the child should stop playing.
4. Begin playing the record and give the triangle to a child. As the child is playing, vary the volume of the record player between loud and soft and stop the music at various times.
5. After each child's turn, direct him to pass the triangle to the child seated on his right who will have the next turn.

III. Techniques and Modifications

1. When the children have difficulty following directions, it may be helpful to stop the activity and talk about the rules.
2. When one child is playing the triangle, involve the other children through body movement or directed listening.
3. To create a group focus, give each child a rhythm instrument and instruct them to play together. Follow the same procedure as in step 4.

Resource
record player
"Yellow Submarine": *Mod Marches* (AR 527), Hap Palmer, Educational Activities, Inc., Freeport, New York
one triangle

Cross Reference Objectives
Behavior 9, 12, 13, 14
Communication 8, 15, 17
Socialization 14, 16, 19, 20
Academics 18, 28

B-12.1 Music Therapy Learning Experience

Developmental Therapy Objective B-12/to spontaneously participate in routines without physical intervention

Type of Activity	Area
(Listening)	Behavior
Playing	
Singing	Stage
(Moving)	I
Creating	(II)
Verbalizing	III
	IV

MUSIC ACTIVITY

I. Introduction

At the end of the music session, ask the children to name the next activity and to indicate the area of the room where the activity is usually held.

II. Implementation

1. Tell the children to listen carefully to the song. When each child hears his name being sung, he is to go to the designated area using the movement indicated in the song.
2. Begin singing the song, indicating the way in which each child individually is to move, e.g., tiptoe, hop, skip, etc.

III. Techniques and Modifications

1. With a slight modification of the words, this song can be used for the transition between any two classroom activities.
2. Specify where each child is to sit for the new activity.

Resource
"Move On": Jennie Purvis (Resource 19)

Cross Reference Objectives
Behavior 7, 9
Communication 9
Socialization 11, 14
Academics 29

Developmental Therapy Objective B-12/to spontaneously participate in routines without physical intervention

Type of Activity	Area
(Listening)	Behavior
Playing	
Singing	*Stage*
(Moving)	I
Creating	(II)
Verbalizing	III
	IV

MUSIC ACTIVITY

I. Introduction

At the end of the music session, ask the children to name the next activity and to indicate the area of the room where the activity is usually held.

II. Implementation

1. Ask the children if they know how to tiptoe. Have one child demonstrate the movement.
2. Tell the children to tiptoe quietly to the designated area when they hear the song.
3. Begin singing "Hey, Betty Martin" (chorus only) and move with the children as directed in step 2.

III. Techniques and Modifications

1. To set the mood for the song, use a soft, quiet singing voice.
2. Other actions can be substituted for tiptoeing, e.g., jumping, walking, etc.
3. This song can be used for the transition between any two classroom activities.
4. The children's names can be substituted for "Betty Martin," e.g., "Hey, Sue and Jimmy . . ."

Resource
"Hey, Betty Martin": *Making Music Your Own–Book 1* (Teacher's Edition), Silver Burdett Co., Morristown, New Jersey, 1971, pp. 10–11

Cross Reference Objectives
Behavior 7
Communication
Socialization
Academics

B-13.1 Music Therapy Learning Experience

Developmental Therapy Objective B-13/to verbally recall group rules and procedure

Type of Activity	Area
Listening	Behavior
Playing	
Singing	*Stage*
(Moving)	I
Creating	II
(Verbalizing)	(III)
	IV

MUSIC ACTIVITY

I. Introduction

Put three 6-foot strips of masking tape on the floor, parallel to each other and 4 feet apart. Direct the children to divide into two groups. One group should stand side by side on the middle strip of tape and the rest of the children should stand behind them on the third strip of tape, facing the same direction.

II. Implementation

1. Explain the procedures for the activity as follows: 1) both groups should always continue clapping their hands; 2) each group should remain within the bounds of two strips of tape, i.e., the one they are standing on and the one directly in front of them; 3) the children are to listen to and follow the verbal directions for movement which will be given when the music begins.
2. Direct the children to repeat the procedures which have been discussed.
3. Begin playing the record and tell the children to start clapping. Give verbal directions for a movement sequence, e.g., walk forward four steps, walk back four steps, turn around two times, etc.
4. Choose a child to be the leader. Have him stand in front of the two groups and call out directions.
5. Give other children an opportunity to serve as leaders.

III. Techniques and Modifications

1. If the children have difficulty with the activity, stop the music and have them repeat the procedures.
2. Help the leader to give directions which will allow each group to remain within the bounds of their two strips of tape.

Resource
record player
"Save the Country" (895), The Fifth Dimension, Bell Records, New York, New York
masking tape

Cross Reference Objectives
Behavior 12, 19, 20
Communication 15
Socialization 22, 26
Academics 39

Developmental Therapy Objective B-14/to contribute to making group expectations of conduct and procedure

Type of Activity	Area
(Listening)	Behavior
Playing	
Singing	Stage
Moving	I
Creating	II
(Verbalizing)	(III)
	IV

MUSIC ACTIVITY

I. Introduction

Direct the group to sit on the floor in a circle around the record player.

II. Implementation

1. Show the children a record and encourage them to talk about how it should be handled, e.g., hold the outer edge of the record, etc.
2. Demonstrate the use of a record cleaning cloth. Give each child an opportunity to clean a record.
3. Show the children how to use the record player. Ask them questions about various parts of the phonograph, e.g., speed control, on-off-reject, etc.
4. Instruct the group to make some rules for the use of records and the record player. Write down the rules on poster paper as they are dictated by the children.

III. Techniques and Modifications

1. Help the children to state the rules in a positive manner.
2. To follow up this activity, allow the children to put the records on the phonograph and operate the record player.
3. Old, scratched records can be used to demonstrate the improper care of records.

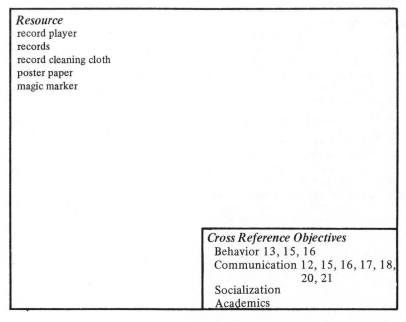

Resource
record player
records
record cleaning cloth
poster paper
magic marker

Cross Reference Objectives
Behavior 13, 15, 16
Communication 12, 15, 16, 17, 18, 20, 21
Socialization
Academics

B-14.2 Music Therapy Learning Experience

Developmental Therapy Objective B-14/to contribute to making group expectations of conduct and procedure

Type of Activity	Area
Listening	Behavior
(Playing)	
Singing	Stage
(Moving)	I
Creating	II
(Verbalizing)	(III)
	IV

MUSIC ACTIVITY

I. Introduction

Direct the children to sit on the floor in a circle.

II. Implementation

1. Tell the children that they will be able to form a marching band.
2. Give each child an opportunity to suggest a rule for the band, e.g., walk in a straight line, follow the band leader, etc.
3. After each child has contributed an idea, discuss the suggestions and decide upon the rules and procedures which will be used.
4. Assign a leader for the band and have each child choose an instrument.
5. Direct the children to stand in line behind the leader and begin marching when they hear the music. Instruct them to follow the leader in all of his movements.

III. Techniques and Modifications

1. The children may need guidance in making rules and procedures which can be used in the activity.
2. If necessary, stop the music and ask the children to restate the rules and procedures which they created.
3. It may be helpful to precede this activity with a music session in which the children learn various marching skills, e.g., marking time, turning, halting, etc.

Resource
record player
"Gentle On My Mind": *Mod Marches* (AR527), Hap Palmer, Educational Activities, Inc., Freeport, New York
variety of rhythm instruments, one for each child

Cross Reference Objectives
Behavior 12, 13, 15, 16, 19, 20
Communication 15, 16, 17, 18, 21
Socialization 20, 26
Academics 39

Developmental Therapy Objective B-15/to verbalize consequences if group's expectations are not reached

Type of Activity	Area
Listening	Behavior
(Playing)	
Singing	Stage
Moving	I
Creating	II
(Verbalizing)	(III)
	IV

MUSIC ACTIVITY

I. Introduction

Direct the children to sit on the floor in a semicircle facing the music therapist.

II. Implementation

1. Show the children an autoharp. Review its name and how it is played.
2. Tell the children that they will be able to play the autoharp to accompany a song.
3. Give each child an autoharp. Have them practice strumming the correct chords as the three cards with the chord names are held up one at a time.
4. After the practice session, tell the children that they need to devise some rules for the group so that the activity will be successful.
5. Encourage each group member to suggest a rule and a reason as to why the rule is needed. Ask the children to think of consequences which may occur if a rule is broken, e.g., music will not sound "good," instruments may be broken, child may not be able to participate, etc.
6. After discussing the rules, tell the children to get ready to play. Begin singing "On Top of Old Smoky" and hold up the cards at the appropriate times to indicate the chord changes.

III. Techniques and Modifications

1. Use this activity only when the children have had previous experience in playing the autoharp.
2. Allow the group members to suggest other songs which they can sing and play on the autoharp.

Resource

"On Top of Old Smoky": *Sigmund Spaeth's Song Session,* Don Wilson, Remick Music Corp., New York, New York, 1958, p. 7

autoharps, one for each child

three 5- by 8-inch cards, each with one of the following chord names: C, F, G^7

Cross Reference Objectives
Behavior 13, 14, 16, 19
Communication 15, 16, 17, 18, 21
Socialization 20
Academics 35, 38

B-16.1 Music Therapy Learning Experience

Developmental Therapy Objective B-16/to give simple reasons for group's expectations

Type of Activity	Area
Listening	Behavior
(Playing)	
Singing	Stage
Moving	I
Creating	II
(Verbalizing)	(III)
	IV

MUSIC ACTIVITY

I. Introduction

Direct the children to sit on the floor in a circle.

II. Implementation

1. Show the children the kazoos and demonstrate how to play them.
2. Tell the children that they will be able to play the kazoos to accompany a record, but that first they need to make some procedures to guide the activity.
3. Encourage the children to suggest rules for the group, e.g., only play the kazoos when the music is playing, play the kazoos at a volume which will permit the record to be heard, etc.
4. Each time a rule is suggested, ask a child to give a reason as to why the rule is needed.
5. Distribute the kazoos and begin playing the record.

III. Techniques and Modifications

1. Help the children to state the rules in a positive manner. Remind them that they are not making the rules to "discipline" each other, but to help in making the activity successful.
2. Encourage the children to think of other songs they can play on the kazoos.

Resource
record player
"When I'm Sixty-Four": *Sgt. Pepper's Lonely Hearts Club Band* (2653), John Lennon and Paul McCartney, Capitol Records, Hollywood, California

kazoos, one for each child and music therapist

Cross Reference Objectives
Behavior 13, 14, 15
Communication 15, 16, 17, 18, 21
Socialization
Academics

Developmental Therapy Objective B-19/to maintain self-control and comply with group procedures

Type of Activity	Area
Listening	Behavior
Playing	
(Singing)	Stage
(Moving)	I
Creating	II
(Verbalizing)	(III)
	IV

MUSIC ACTIVITY

I. Introduction

Direct the children to sit at the table.

II. Implementation

1. Explain to the group that they are going to pretend they are going camping on an island. Pose the question as to how everyone is going to cross the river. When the use of a boat is suggested, explain that they are going to take a rowboat to the island.
2. Ask for a volunteer to sit in the boat. Direct the child to sit on the floor cross-legged.
3. Repeat step 2 until all the children are sitting, one behind the other.
4. Kneel beside the boat with arms stretched forward as if holding oars. Instruct the "crew" to pick up their "oars" and begin rowing together. Provide a model for the action, simultaneously verbalizing "row, row" until everyone is rowing in unison.
5. Tell the children to sing along as soon as they know the words. Begin singing at a moderate tempo.
6. Instruct the children to row faster. Sing the song at a faster tempo.
7. At the end of the song, direct the "crew" to hold the boat steady while each child steps onto the island one at a time.

III. Techniques and Modifications

This activity can be expanded to include other situations for dramatization, e.g., exploring the island, building a fire, setting up tents, etc. Encourage the children to think of additional songs which can be used in the camping trip dramatization.

Resource
"Row, Row, Row Your Boat": Traditional

Cross Reference Objectives
Behavior 11
Communication 16
Socialization 18
Academics

B-19.2 Music Therapy Learning Experience

Developmental Therapy Objective B-19/to maintain self-control and comply with group procedures

Type of Activity	*Area*
Listening	Behavior
Playing	
Singing	*Stage*
(Moving)	I
Creating	II
(Verbalizing)	(III)
	IV

MUSIC ACTIVITY

I. Introduction

Direct the group to sit on the floor in a semicircle facing the music therapist.

II. Implementation

1. Explain to the group that they are to pretend they are hunters camping in the woods. Encourage them to discuss the kinds of foods hunters try to find in the woods to cook for their meals as well as how they might catch their "food."
2. Direct two children to each be an animal that was suggested by the group, e.g., bears. Have them sit in a corner of the room pretending to eat their own food.
3. Tell the "hunters" that they are going to sneak up on the animals very quietly, catch them, and bring them back to the campsite to tie them up.
4. Tell the "hunters" to start searching for the animals. Begin singing the song. Intersperse verbal directions between the lines of the song to enable continuous action on the part of the children.
5. Repeat steps 2 to 4 selecting two other children to be other animals. Continue until all of the children have been both hunters and animals.

III. Techniques and Modifications

Verbal directions through the activity are important for cuing the actions of the children. Comments such as "Sneak up slowly and quietly," or "The animals are very heavy so pull them slowly," can minimize random running and the possible hurting of each other. These statements should be made within the context of the action rather than as commands or rules.

Resource
"A-Hunting We will Go": *Heritage Songster,* Leon and Lynn Dollin, Wm. C. Brown Co., Dubuque, Iowa, 1972, p. 17

Cross Reference Objectives
Behavior 11
Communication 13, 16
Socialization 18, 19, 20, 22
Academics

Developmental Therapy Objective B-19/to maintain self-control and comply with group procedures

Type of Activity	*Area*
Listening	Behavior
Playing	
Singing	*Stage*
(Moving)	I
Creating	II
Verbalizing	(III)
	IV

MUSIC ACTIVITY

I. Introduction

Divide the class into two groups. Place two strips of masking tape on the floor side by side and direct each group to stand on a strip of tape, all facing the same direction.

II. Implementation

1. Begin playing the record and show the children how to bob up and down to the music (bend at waist with arms stretched out to the side).
2. Direct the first group to bob up and down eight times. Then the first group stops and the second group bobs eight times. Then, the first group bobs up and down four times while the second group stands motionless. As soon as the first group finishes this movement, the second group follows it. This same procedure (first group moves while second group stands still, then second groups imitates the movements while first group stands still) is followed for a series of two bobs and then one bob.
3. Repeat step 2 using backward bobs.
4. Demonstrate how to combine forward bobs and backward bobs, i.e., eight forward bobs, eight backward bobs, four forward bobs, four backward bobs, etc. Lead the groups in these movements.

III. Techniques and Modifications

1. Before the two groups begin alternating movements, lead them in practicing together until they become familiar with the movements and rhythmic sequence.
2. Encourage the group members to suggest other movement sequences.

Resource
record player
"H$_2$ Overture": *Deliver the Word,* War, United Artists, Inc., Los Angeles, California
masking tape

Cross Reference Objectives
Behavior
Communication
Socialization 20
Academics 39

B-19.4 Music Therapy Learning Experience

Developmental Therapy Objective B-19/to maintain self-control and comply with group procedures

Type of Activity	Area
Listening	Behavior
Playing	
Singing	Stage
(Moving)	I
(Creating)	II
Verbalizing	(III)
	IV

MUSIC ACTIVITY

I. Introduction

Direct the group to sit on the floor in a semicircle.

II. Implementation

1. Ask the children to think of different ways to move from "here to there," designating a starting point and ending point.
2. Show the children the boundaries for a large, open area and instruct each child to choose a place to sit within the area. Direct the children to sit so that they are not touching another person or object in the room.
3. Explain that as the music is playing each child will have a chance to move in the spaces between the children. Begin playing the record and demonstrate by moving in various ways in the spaces.
4. Ask for a volunteer to try the movement activity. After the child has had a turn moving in the spaces, direct him to select someone else to have a turn.
5. Continue with step 4 until all of the children have had turns.

III. Techniques and Modifications

1. While each child is moving, verbally reflect his actions, e.g., "Jim is crawling so slowly," or "Mary left a small space when she moved around Kim."
2. If the children are having difficulty moving in different ways, suggest movements that involve different body parts or different directions and heights.
3. If the group is large, more than one child can move in the spaces at one time.

Resource
record player
"The Easy Winners": *Scott Joplin: The Red Back Book* (S-2-36060), Gunther Schuller (conductor), Angel Records, New York, New York

Cross Reference Objectives
Behavior
Communication 19
Socialization 19, 20, 23, 27
Academics

Developmental Therapy Objective B-19/to maintain self-control and comply with group procedures

Type of Activity	Area
Listening	Behavior
(Playing)	
Singing	Stage
Moving	I
(Creating)	II
(Verbalizing)	(III)
	IV

MUSIC ACTIVITY

I. Introduction

Instruct the children to sit at the table.

II. Implementation

1. Show the children one instrument and ask them its name.
2. Show them two word cards, one of which is the name of the instrument just displayed, and have them indicate the word card which corresponds to the instrument.
3. Select a child to place the card on the wall in a designated position and the instrument on the floor below it.
4. Repeat steps 1 to 3 for the remaining instruments, tape recorder, and radio. Each new word card should be placed on the wall to the right of the card which preceded it so that the cards will appear in a horizontal line from left to right across the wall and the corresponding instruments will be on the floor underneath the cards. The tape recorder should be the last instrument in the line.
5. Explain the following procedure. When a child's name card is held up, he is to move to the beginning of the line of instruments and play each instrument in sequence. When he reaches the tape recorder (at the end of the line of instruments), he is to say, "This is (name of child) saying, 'A-O.K. and signing off.'" He should then return to his chair.
6. Begin the tape recorder and hold up the first name card. Hold up each subsequent name card as the previous child in the line begins playing the third instrument. As each child finishes speaking into the tape recorder, direct him back to the table.
7. Replay the tape. Encourage the children to discuss what they hear.

III. Techniques and Modifications

1. Instrument name cards should be taped to the wall approximately one to two feet apart.
2. The word card for radio should be next to last (the radio is played by turning it on and off) and the tape recorder should be at the end of the line. The support teacher can be stationed by the tape recorder to assist the children as they speak into it. If necessary, a sign with the designated verbalization, i.e., *This is (child's name) saying, "A-O.K. and signing off,"* can be placed by the tape recorder.
3. The instruments used should be those which will be interesting and motivating for the children.
4. If the written labels for the instruments are familiar to the children, eliminate steps 1 and 2. Instead, show each word card individually and have the group read them.

Resource
tape recorder
radio
glockenspiel
tone bells
conga drum
bongo drums
six 9- by 12-inch word cards (construction paper), one for each instrument, radio, and tape recorder
5- by 8-inch cards, one for each child's name
masking tape

Cross Reference Objectives
Behavior
Communication 16, 19, 20
Socialization 18, 19, 20
Academics 35, 48

B-19.6 Music Therapy Learning Experience

Developmental Therapy Objective B-19/to maintain self-control and comply with group procedures

Type of Activity	Area
Listening	Behavior
(Playing)	
(Singing)	Stage
Moving	I
Creating	II
Verbalizing	(III)
	IV

MUSIC ACTIVITY

I. Introduction

Direct the children to sit in their chairs at the table.

II. Implementation

1. Give each child an instrument which he has learned how to play in previous sessions. Allow the group to "warm up," playing the instruments as they wish.
2. Tell the children that they will be able to play "Joy to the World" on the instruments. Show the children the chart with the words and color symbols.
3. Explain that the color symbols on the chart correspond to the colors with which certain chords or notes have been marked on the instruments.
4. Point to the various colors on the chart and have the children practice playing the corresponding chords or notes on their instruments.
5. Introduce the first line of the song. As the first line is sung, the children play the appropriate chords or notes as designated by the color symbols.
6. After the children are able to play the first line, introduce the second line of the song.
7. Tell the children that they will be able to learn the rest of the song in subsequent sessions. It will probably require several music therapy sessions to complete this music learning experience.

III. Techniques and Modifications

1. Before introducing this activity, be certain that each child is able to play one of the instruments which will be used.
2. Mark only two or three notes or chords on each instrument.

Resource
"Joy to the World": *Joy to the World and Other Big Hits,* Hoyt Axton, Big 3 Music Corporation, New York, New York, pp. 4–6
chord organ
autoharp
guitaro
tone bells
glockenspiel
(Each instrument has small colored pieces of paper on it to indicate chords or notes)
chart with words to "Joy to the World" and color symbols underneath the words to indicate chord changes

Cross Reference Objectives
Behavior
Communicaton 14, 19, 20
Socialization 18, 19, 20
Academics 33, 35, 38, 39, 45

Developmental Therapy Objective B-20/to respond appropriately to choices for leadership in the group

Type of Activity	Area
(Listening)	Behavior
Playing	
Singing	Stage
Moving	I
Creating	II
(Verbalizing)	III
	(IV)

MUSIC ACTIVITY

I. Introduction

Direct the children to sit on the floor in a circle.

II. Implementation

1. Tell the group that they will play a listening game. Direct them to choose a leader for the group.
2. Explain that various sounds will be played on the tape recorder. As each sound is heard, the group members are to discuss it and give the answer to the team captain. Only the team captain can say the answer to the music therapist. If the group correctly identifies the sound, they get one point. If they are wrong, the "invisible" team gets the point.
3. Play the tape. Stop after each sound and give the group a few minutes to discuss what they hear. Ask the team captain for the answer.
4. At the completion of the tape, tell the group the total number of points they won. Compare this score with that of the "invisible" team.

III. Techniques and Modifications

Playing against an "invisible" team will motivate the children to work together as a group. Remind them that only the team captain can say the answer, so they must discuss their ideas and reach a decision which will be agreeable to all group members.

Resource
tape recorder

tape with the following sounds: 1) autoharp, 2) footsteps, 3) water running in a sink, 4) spoon hitting pan, 5) turning on shower, 6) brushing teeth, 7) electric razor, 8) toilet flushing, 9) car starting, 10) dog chewing food, 11) cat meowing, 12) guitar, 13) hair dryer, 14) spraying a spray can, 15) drawers shutting, 16) shuffling cards, 17) television program, 18) jingling keys, 19) shutting door, 20) blowing across coke bottle, 21) blowing up and popping a paper bag

Cross Reference Objectives
Behavior 19
Communication 20, 26, 27
Socialization 26, 30
Academics

B-20.2 Music Therapy Learning Experience

Developmental Therapy Objective B-20/to respond appropriately to choices for leadership in the group

Type of Activity	Area
Listening	Behavior
Playing	
Singing	Stage
(Moving)	I
Creating	II
Verbalizing	III
	(IV)

MUSIC ACTIVITY

I. Introduction

Direct the children to choose a place to stand within the music area. They should be at least an arm's length from one another.

II. Implementation

1. Select a leader for the activity.
2. Tell the group that they are to begin moving when the music begins. They can move or dance in any way that they desire, but when the music stops they must immediately "freeze" in position.
3. Direct the leader to choose the record that he wishes to use for the activity and have him decide upon the method he will use for stopping and starting the music, e.g., he can choose a child to start and stop the record player as he gives verbal or visual cues, he can ask the music therapist to do this task, etc.
4. Begin playing the music and encourage the children to start moving. The leader watches the children move and then stops the music as decided upon in step 3. The leader verbally indicates those children who are "caught by the music," i.e., do not stop moving as soon as the music stops. These children are directed to sit on the floor.
5. The leader continues with this procedure until almost all of the children are sitting on the floor. The leader then chooses another child to become the next leader.

III. Techniques and Modifications

1. Encourage the children to suggest rules and procedures for the activity.
2. Some children may have difficulty accepting the decision of the leader as he indicates those children who do not "freeze" as soon as the music stops. It may be necessary, therefore, to guide the children in solving this problem, e.g., suggest that the leader's decision is final, ask the leader to select a panel of judges for the activity, etc.
3. Give the children who are eliminated from the game something to do while they are sitting on the floor, e.g., clapping with the music, playing rhythm instruments, etc.
4. A modification of this activity could be a game of "musical tag" in which the children move with the music and then run to a "base" when the music stops. The leader attempts to catch those children off base when the music stops. The child who is caught becomes the new leader.

Resource
record player
variety of records

Cross Reference Objectives
Behavior 19
Communication 25
Socialization 26
Academics

Developmental Therapy Objective B-20/to respond appropriately to choices for leadership in the group

Type of Activity	*Area*
Listening	Behavior
Playing	
Singing	*Stage*
(Moving)	I
(Creating)	II
Verbalizing	III
	(IV)

MUSIC ACTIVITY

I. Introduction

Direct the group to sit at the table.

II. Implementation

1. Show the chart to the children. Point to each arrow and ask them which way they would be moving if they were standing in front of the chart.

2. Have one child tape the chart to the wall.

3. Instruct the group to line up one next to the other, in one or more rows, facing the chart. Explain that the leader is to follow the directions for movement as indicated by the arrows on the chart. The rest of the group is to imitate his movements.

4. Begin playing the record. Stand in front of the group facing the chart. Begin the movement sequence using various locomotive movements and changes in the height of the movement and using many body parts, e.g., squat low while moving around in the circle and shake hands above head. Verbalize changes in the movements as they occur in the sequence.

5. Choose a child to be the leader. Direct the group to watch their leader and to follow his suggestions for movements.

6. Repeat step 5 until all group members who want to have a turn have led the group.

III. Techniques and Modifications

1. When leading the children, continue a particular movement until all are doing the action in unison.

2. If no child volunteers to be a leader, select the child who has the least difficulty being a leader. If necessary, give the leader verbal cues for movement changes, e.g., "What's another way you can walk?" or "What can you do with your arms?"

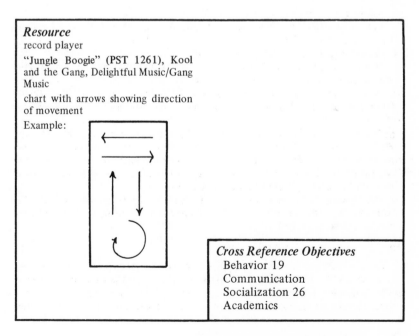

Resource

record player

"Jungle Boogie" (PST 1261), Kool and the Gang, Delightful Music/Gang Music

chart with arrows showing direction of movement

Example:

Cross Reference Objectives
Behavior 19
Communication
Socialization 26
Academics

B-20.4 Music Therapy Learning Experience

Developmental Therapy Objective B-20/to respond appropriately to choices for leadership in the group

Type of Activity	Area
Listening	Behavior
(Playing)	
Singing	Stage
Moving	I
(Creating)	II
(Verbalizing)	III
	(IV)

MUSIC ACTIVITY

I. Introduction

Direct the group to sit on the floor in a semicircle. Place the rhythm instruments in front of them.

II. Implementation

1. Show the children a chart of instrument symbols. Ask them to name the instrument which they think corresponds to each symbol ($\bigcirc$ = hand drum; $*$ = tambourine; $\bigwedge\bigvee$ = guiro; $\triangle$ = triangle; $+$ = claves).
2. Distribute the instruments to the children. Direct them to strike their instrument once each time the corresponding symbol is pointed to on the chart.
3. Begin playing the music and point to the symbols, one at a time, in any order and as many times as desired. Synchronize pointing to the symbols with the rhythm of the music.
4. Select a leader and provide him with poster paper and a magic marker. Instruct him to write sequences of instrument symbols from left to right across the paper as they are dictated by group members. The symbols can be placed in any order on the paper and can be used as many times as necessary to create the sounds desired by the group.
5. After the leader has notated the sound sequences, have him select accompanying music from the available records. Direct him to point to the symbols, one at a time, moving left to right across the page, while the group members play their instruments accordingly.

III. Techniques and Modifications

1. After giving the basic instructions, allow the children to direct the activity as much as possible.

2. Encourage the children to share their ideas concerning the sound sequences.
3. Allow the children to suggest other instruments and corresponding symbols which might be used in the activity.
4. A sequel to this activity might be to create several lines of instrument symbols to be played simultaneously.

Resource
record player
variety of popular records
hand drums
tambourines
guiros
triangles
claves
(at least one
instrument per
child)
chart with following symbols:

$\bigcirc \quad * \quad \bigwedge\bigvee \quad \triangle \quad +$

poster paper
magic marker

Cross Reference Objectives
Behavior 19
Communication 25
Socialization 26, 30
Academics 52

Developmental Therapy Objective B-25/to respond to suggestions of a new, real-life experience, or change with appropriate verbal and body control

Type of Activity	*Area* Behavior
Listening	
Playing	*Stage*
Singing	I
Moving	II
Creating	III
(Verbalizing)	(IV)

MUSIC ACTIVITY

I. Introduction

Direct the children to sit at the table.

II. Implementation

1. Tell the group that they will have an opportunity to take a field trip to a musical event in the community.
2. Distribute several newspapers to be shared by the group members and instruct them to find the announcements of forthcoming musical events, e.g., rock concerts, modern dance programs, school musicals, etc.
3. Encourage the children to discuss the possible choices for the field trip and to make a group decision about which musical event the class will attend.
4. After a choice has been made, discuss concerns related to the event, such as time of the concert, appropriate dress, expectations for behavior, etc. Guide the children in making decisions related to these concerns and help them in preparing for the field trip.
5. After the field trip, assist the children in writing a group experience story about the musical event.

III. Techniques and Modifications

1. Encourage the children to make their own decisions concerning the field trip, but give ideas and suggestions when necessary.
2. Prepare the children for the musical event by providing a framework for directed listening, e.g., give background information on the music to be performed.

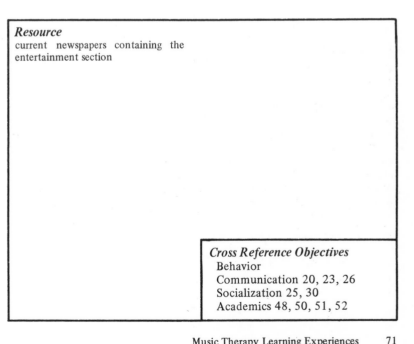

Resource
current newspapers containing the entertainment section

Cross Reference Objectives
Behavior
Communication 20, 23, 26
Socialization 25, 30
Academics 48, 50, 51, 52

C-1.1 Music Therapy Learning Experience

Developmental Therapy Objective C-1/to attend to person speaking

Type of Activity	Area
Listening	Communication
Playing	
Singing	Stage
(Moving)	I
Creating	II
Verbalizing	III
	IV

MUSIC ACTIVITY

I. Introduction

Direct the children to sit on the floor facing the music therapist.

II. Implementation

1. Hold the bag in front of the children and take out the yarn ball. Tell the children what it is and hold it in front of each child so that he can touch it.

2. Begin playing the record, simultaneously tossing the yarn ball up in the air. Throw it to a child, verbalizing his name and the action, e.g., "I'm throwing the yarn ball to David," or "Catch the yarn ball, Judy." Then, instruct him to throw it back. Repeat for all of the children.

III. Techniques and Modifications

1. If a child does not direct his throw, give the yarn ball back to him and repeat the directions. Assistance may be necessary.

2. As a sequel to this activity, direct each child to throw the yarn ball to another child in the group. The children may need aid in recognizing other children in the group; e.g., point to the child to whom the throw should be directed and say, "Here is (child's name). Throw the yarn ball to (child's name)."

Resource

record player

"Save the Country" (895), The Fifth Dimension, Bell Records, New York, New York

one brightly colored yarn ball, approximately 6 inches in diameter

bag

Cross Reference Objectives

Behavior 1, 2, 3, 8
Communication 2
Socialization 1, 2, 3, 4, 7
Academics 1, 2, 3, 5, 6, 13

Developmental Therapy Objective C-2/to respond to verbal stimulus with a motor behavior

Type of Activity	Area
(Listening)	Communication
Playing	
Singing	Stage
(Moving)	(I)
Creating	II
Verbalizing	III
	IV

MUSIC ACTIVITY

I. Introduction

Direct the children to sit on the floor in a semicircle facing the music therapist.

II. Implementation

1. Give the children directions for pointing to a specific body part, e.g., "Point to your leg." Assist the children in finding the correct body part; e.g., point to a child's body part, take a child's hand and place it on the correct body part.
2. Repeat step 1 using other body parts, e.g., arms, head, feet, etc.
3. Begin singing the "Body Part Song" and lead the children in touching the body parts as directed in the song.

III. Techniques and Modifications

1. Praise the children for any attempts they make at touching the various body parts.
2. If some children have difficulty finding their own body parts, help them to point to the body parts on another child.

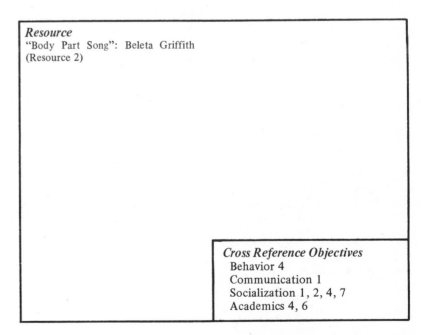

Resource
"Body Part Song": Beleta Griffith
(Resource 2)

Cross Reference Objectives
Behavior 4
Communication 1
Socialization 1, 2, 4, 7
Academics 4, 6

C-3.1 Music Therapy Learning Experience

Developmental Therapy Objective C-3/to respond to verbal stimulus and single object with a recognizable approximation of the appropriate verbal response

Type of Activity	Area
Listening	Communication
(Playing)	
Singing	Stage
Moving	(I)
Creating	II
(Verbalizing)	III
	IV

MUSIC ACTIVITY

I. Introduction

Direct the children to sit on the floor in a semicircle facing the music therapist.

II. Implementation

1. Show the bells (sleigh bells) to the children and ask them the name of the instrument. If they do not respond, tell them what it is called.
2. Direct each child to ask for the bells.
3. When a child says, "bells," "I want the bells," etc., give him the instrument.
4. When all of the children are holding their instruments, sing the song ("Play the Bells") and lead the children in playing the bells "high" or "low" as indicated in the words of the song.

III. Techniques and Modifications

1. To help some children become involved in the activity, it may be necessary to take a child's hand/bells and move it in the actions for the song.
2. The verbalization which is required for individual children should be determined by each child's language level. Some children may be expected to say a sentence, while with others, only a word or approximation of a word is necessary. In some cases only eye contact may be required.
3. Encourage the children to play the bells independently rather than focusing upon whether they are playing "high" or "low" at the appropriate times.

Resource
"Play the Bells": Jennie Purvis (Resource 22)
sleigh bells (bells), one for each child and music therapist

Cross Reference Objectives
Behavior 1, 2, 4
Communication 1, 2, 5, 7
Socialization 1,2, 3, 4, 8, 10
    13
Academics, 1, 2, 4, 6, 8

Developmental Therapy Objective C-3/to respond to verbal stimulus and single object with a recognizable approximation of the appropriate verbal response

Type of Activity	*Area*
Listening	Communication
Playing	
Singing	*Stage*
Moving	Ⓘ
Creating	II
Ⓥerbalizing	III
	IV

MUSIC ACTIVITY

I. Introduction

Direct the children to sit on the floor facing the music therapist.

II. Implementation

1. Hold up the first picture and ask the children the name of the animal. If they do not respond, say the name.
2. Make the sound that is associated with the animal, e.g., cat—meow, and encourage the children to imitate.
3. Tell the children that they are going to sing a song about animals on a farm. Begin singing while holding up the first picture.
4. Repeat step 2 when presenting each new animal and then sing the song substituting the new animal name and sound.

III. Techniques and Modifications

1. Use animals with which the children are familiar.
2. When possible, bring actual dogs, cats, etc., into the classroom for the children to see.
3. This activity may have to be done several times before the children begin to make verbal responses. Praise them for any attempts which they make at approximating the animal names and sounds.

Resource
"Animal Song": Shelley Samet (Resource 1)
pictures of animals to be used in the song

Cross Reference Objectives
Behavior 1, 2
Communication 1
Socialization 1, 2, 4
Academics 1, 2, 6, 8

C-4.1 Music Therapy Learning Experience

Developmental Therapy Objective C-4/to voluntarily initiate a recognizable verbal approximation to obtain a specific object or activity

Type of Activity	*Area*
Listening	Communication
(Playing)	
Singing	*Stage*
Moving	(I)
Creating	II
(Verbalizing)	III
	IV

MUSIC ACTIVITY

I. Introduction

Direct the children to sit on the floor in a semicircle facing the music therapist. Place the toy piano in front of them.

II. Implementation

1. Play the toy piano. Tell the children its name.
2. Give the children enough time to make spontaneous verbalizations, e.g., "piano," "I want to play the piano," etc. As a child makes a verbalization, such as "piano" or an approximation of the word, allow him to play the piano.
3. If a child does not produce a spontaneous verbalization, then give him a verbal cue, i.e., tell the child to say "piano." Then permit him to play the piano.

III. Techniques and Modifications

1. To encourage the children to make spontaneous verbalizations, use new, "exciting" instruments which they have not seen, or familiar music materials which have been successful in previous music sessions.
2. As one child plays the piano, listen for spontaneous verbalizations from the other children.

Resource
toy piano

Cross Reference Objectives
Behavior 1, 2, 4, 9
Communication 1, 2, 3, 5, 7
Socialization 1, 2, 7, 8, 10, 14
Academics 1, 2, 4, 5, 6, 8, 9, 12

Developmental Therapy Objective C-5/to produce a recognizable word to obtain a desired response from adult

Type of Activity	*Area*
Listening	Communication
(Playing)	
Singing	*Stage*
Moving	(I)
Creating	II
(Verbalizing)	III
	IV

MUSIC ACTIVITY

I. Introduction

Direct the children to sit on the floor in a semicircle facing the music therapist. Place the box of rhythm instruments in front of them.

II. Implementation

1. Direct one of the children to look into the box and point to the instrument he wants to play.
2. Hold the instrument in front of the child and request that he say the name. When he responds, give him the instrument.
3. Repeat steps 1 and 2 until each child is holding an instrument.
4. Sing "Play the Band" and lead the children in playing the instruments.

III. Techniques and Modifications

1. Some children may have difficulty in choosing an instrument. For these children it may be helpful to show them just two instruments and tell them to point to the one they want.
2. The verbal response required of a child before he is given an instrument should be determined by his language ability, e.g., sentence, word, word approximation.

Resource
"Play the Band": Clementine Gigliotti (Resource 21)
variety of familiar rhythm instruments, one for each child and music therapist
box

Cross Reference Objectives
Behavior 1, 2, 4, 9
Communication 1, 2, 3, 4, 7
Socialization 1, 2, 3, 4, 8, 10, 13, 14
Academics, 1, 2, 4, 6, 8, 9

C-6.1 Music Therapy Learning Experience

Developmental Therapy Objective C-6/to produce a recognizable word to obtain a desired response from another child

Type of Activity	*Area*
Listening	Communication
(Playing)	
Singing	*Stage*
Moving	(I)
Creating	II
(Verbalizing)	III
	IV

MUSIC ACTIVITY

I. Introduction

Direct the children to sit on the floor in a semicircle facing the music therapist.

II. Implementation

1. Show the children the drum and ask them its name. If they do not respond, tell them the name of the instrument.
2. Choose one child to sit in front of the other children. Give him the drum.
3. Direct another child to ask him for the drum. When the child says "drum," "I want the drum," etc.. help the child with the drum to hand the instrument to the other child.
4. Allow the child who receives the drum to strike it several times. Then give the drum back to the child who is sitting in front of the group and direct another child to ask him for the drum.

III. Techniques and Modifications

1. Give the children verbal cues to indicate how they should ask for the drum, e.g., "John, tell Susan that you want the drum."
2. Encourage the child who is holding the drum to give it to the other child as soon as he asks for it. It may be necessary to physically assist the child in handing it to the other child.
3. Verbally reflect the children's actions, e.g., "Susan is giving the drum to John."

Resource
one hand drum

Cross Reference Objectives
Behavior 4
Communication 3, 4, 7
Socialization 9, 10
Academics 4, 6, 8, 9, 12

Developmental Therapy Objective C-7/to produce a meaningful, recognizable sequence of words to obtain a desired response from adults or children in the classroom

Type of Activity	Area
Listening	Communication
(Playing)	
Singing	Stage
Moving	(I)
Creating	II
(Verbalizing)	III
	IV

MUSIC ACTIVITY

I. Introduction

Direct the children to sit on the floor in a semicircle facing the music therapist.

II. Implementation

1. Show the children the autoharp. Tell them that it is a "harp."
2. Say to the children, "Who wants to play the harp?" When a child says, "I want to play," "I want the harp," etc., allow him to strum the strings.
3. Repeat step 2 until each child has had a turn playing the autoharp.

III. Techniques and Modifications

1. Push the chord buttons as each child strums the strings. Allow the child to push the buttons if he indicates a desire to do so.
2. As each child strums the strings, a simple song can be sung, e.g., "Row, Row, Row," "Old MacDonald," etc.
3. When each child is having a turn playing the autoharp, give the other children something to do, e.g., clap, play other instruments, etc.
4. When using a modificaton of this activity for a Stage Two class, the correct name of the instrument (autoharp) can be substituted for "harp."

Resource
autoharp (harp)

Cross Reference Objectives
Behavior 1, 2, 3, 4
Communication 1, 3, 4, 5
Socialization 1, 2, 4, 6, 8, 10
Academics 1, 2, 3, 4, 6, 8, 9, 12

C-8.1 Music Therapy Learning Experience

Developmental Therapy Objective C-8/to answer a child's or adult's request with recognizable, meaningful words

Type of Activity	Area
Listening	Communication
Playing	
Singing	Stage
(Moving)	I
Creating	(II)
(Verbalizing)	III
	IV

MUSIC ACTIVITY

I. Introduction

Direct the children to sit on the floor in a circle.

II. Implementation

1. Sing the "Wiggle Song," using the thumb as the body part which is moved. Tell the children to wiggle their thumbs.
2. Ask a child to name another body part which can be wiggled. Sing the song using the body part which is suggested by the child.
3. Repeat step 2 until each child has had a turn in suggesting a body part.

III. Techniques and Modifications

Some children may need assistance in thinking of a body part to suggest for the song. Encourage the children to think of body parts which have not already been mentioned.

Resource
"Wiggle Song": *This Is Music—Book K,* Allyn and Bacon, Inc.. Boston, Massachusetts, 1971, p. 77

Cross Reference Objectives
Behavior 9, 11
Communication 11
Socialization 13, 14
Academics 17

Developmental Therapy Objective C-8/to answer a child's or adult's request with recognizable, meaningful words

Type of Activity	Area
(Listening)	Communication
Playing	
(Singing)	Stage
Moving	I
Creating	(II)
(Verbalizing)	III
	IV

MUSIC ACTIVITY

I. Introduction

Direct the children to sit on the floor in a semicircle facing the music therapist.

II. Implementation

1. Show the children the picture of the turkey. Ask them questions, such as, "What do you see in the picture?," "Have you ever seen a turkey?," "What color is a turkey?," "What kind of sound does he make?," etc.
2. Tell the children to listen to the song and to raise their hands when they hear the turkey gobble.
3. Begin playing the song. Praise the children when they raise their hands at the correct time.
4. Play the song again and encourage the children to sing along.

III. Techniques and Modifications

1. If the children are not able to sing all of the words of the song, direct them to make the "gobble" sound at the appropriate time.
2. An art activity involving drawing turkeys might be used in conjunction with this music learning experience.

Resource
record player
"I'm a Very Fine Turkey": *Making Music Your Own—Book K, Record IV,* Silver Burdett Co., Morristown, New Jersey
picture of a turkey

Cross Reference Objectives
Behavior 11, 12
Communication
Socialization
Academics 19

C-9.1 Music Therapy Learning Experience

Developmental Therapy Objective C-9/to exhibit a receptive vocabulary no more than two years behind chronological age expectations

Type of Activity	*Area*
(Listening)	Communication
Playing	
Singing	*Stage*
(Moving)	I
(Creating)	(II)
Verbalizing	III
	IV

MUSIC ACTIVITY

I. Introduction

Direct the children to stand in a circle in the music area.

II. Implementation

1. Say to the children, "Listen to the music and try to do everything the song says to do."
2. Begin playing the record. As specific directions are given, such as "bend something," encourage the children to use various parts of their bodies. Tell them that the movement can be done in many different ways and that no one way is "correct."
3. Verbally reflect the various movements which the children make, e.g., "Bob is bending his foot; Pam is bending her arm."

III. Techniques and Modifications

It may be necessary to give some children suggestions as to how they can do a specific movement which is called for in the song.

Resource
record player
"Shake Something": *Getting to Know Myself* (AR543), Hap Palmer, Educational Activities, Inc., Freeport, New York

Cross Reference Objectives
Behavior 11, 12
Communication
Socialization 13
Academics 17, 28, 29

Developmental Therapy Objective C-10/to label simple feelings in pictures, dramatic play, art, or music: sad, happy, angry, afraid

Type of Activity	Area
Listening	Communication
Playing	
(Singing)	Stage
Moving	I
Creating	(II)
(Verbalizing)	III
	IV

MUSIC ACTIVITY

I. Introduction

Direct the children to sit in their chairs at the table.

II. Implementation

1. Ask the children questions about Halloween. Encourage them to talk about things which make them feel afraid.
2. Direct the children to make sounds to demonstrate how the wind might sound on Halloween night. Explain that they are to make the wind sound each time the tone bells are played. (Play bells in the following descending sequence: B, A, G, E.)
3. Sing the song "Skin and Bones" and accompany the last four notes of each verse with the tone bell sequence, B, A, G, E. Direct the children to make the wind sound as the tone bells are played.
4. Sing the song slowly and use the voice to heighten the suspense. At the end of the song, shout "boo" very loudly for a surprise ending.
5. Sing the song again and allow the children to shout "boo" at the end.

III. Techniques and Modifications

1. To prompt a discussion of things that make the children afraid, it may be necessary to suggest situations and ask if they would feel afraid.
2. At the end of the song, ask the children to talk about the feelings they experienced when they heard the "surprise ending."
3. When the children know the song, allow them to invite someone to the classroom to hear them perform it.
4. After the children are familiar with the activity, allow them to play the tone bell sequence as the other children sing.
5. Any descending tone bell sequence which has the same pattern as B, A, G, E can be used, e.g., E, D, C, A; G, F, E♭, C. However, the tone bells used

should correspond with the key in which the song is sung, i.e., the four tone bells should match the last four notes in the song.

Resource
"Skin and Bones": *Making Music Your Own—Book 3* (Teacher's Edition), Silver Burdett Co., Morristown, New Jersey, 1971, p. 44
four tone bells (B, A, G, E) to form a descending melodic sequence

Cross Reference Objectives
Behavior 11
Communication 8, 9
Socialization
Academics 31

C-10.2 Music Therapy Learning Experience

Developmental Therapy Objective C-10/to label simple feelings in pictures, dramatic play, art, or music: sad, happy, angry, afraid

Type of Activity	*Area*
(Listening)	Communication
Playing	
(Singing)	*Stage*
Moving	I
Creating	(II)
Verbalizing	III
	IV

presenting them with two situations from which they select the appropriate situation may be more successful for them (step 6 above).

MUSIC ACTIVITY

I. Introduction

Direct the children to sit in a semicircle on the floor.

II. Implementation

1. Hold up the happy face and sad face. Ask the children which one is happy. Tell them to smile and make a happy face.
2. Direct one child to tape the happy face to the wall in a designated area.
3. Repeat steps 1 and 2 until all four faces have been described and taped to the wall.
4. Explain to the children that they are going to play a game called "Match the Face." Instruct them to listen carefully to the song because it mentions things that make them happy, sad, etc. They have to correctly match the face to the characteristic mentioned in the song.
5. Play the autoharp and begin singing, directing one child to select the correct face by pointing to or stating the color of the card.
6. After each child has had a turn, present each child with two alternative situations and ask which one makes him sad, e.g., "Are you sad when it's raining outside or when you are eating ice cream?" Sing the verse using the words of the child's answer and direct that child to select another member of the group to "match the face."
7. Repeat step 6 until all the children have chosen words for the song.

III. Techniques and Modifications

1. The use of a mirror may help the children to make a face. Provide them with a model and then let them see themselves in the mirror.
2. For a modification of this activity, ask the children to describe situations which make them feel sad, happy, etc. Many children, however, may not be able to state what makes them happy or sad. Consequently,

---

Resource

"Match the Face": Shelley Samet (Resource 18)

autoharp

four 6- by 9-inch pieces of different colored construction paper, "happy," "sad," "scared," or "mad" face drawn on each

masking tape

Cross Reference Objectives

Behavior 9
Communication 8, 9
Socialization 14
Academics 19, 22

Developmental Therapy Objective C-10/to label simple feelings in pictures, dramatic play, art, or music: sad, happy, angry, afraid

Type of Activity	Area
Listening	Communication
(Playing)	
Singing	Stage
Moving	I
(Creating)	(II)
(Verbalizing)	III
	IV

MUSIC ACTIVITY

I. Introduction

Direct the children to sit in their chairs in a semicircle facing the music therapist. Place the snare drum on the stand in front of them.

II. Implementation

1. Show the "face" cards, one at a time, to the children. Ask them to describe the face shown on each card.
2. Ask the children to discuss ways in which they could play the snare drum to show that they are happy, sad, angry, or afraid.
3. Select a child to play the snare drum. Show him one of the picture cards without permitting the other children to see it.
4. Tell the child to play the snare drum in such a way that he will demonstrate the emotion shown by the card. Encourage him to accompany the drum playing with a facial expression which will correspond with the feeling shown on the picture card.
5. Direct the other children to listen and watch the child as he plays the drum. Ask them to name the feeling he is demonstrating.
6. Repeat steps 3 to 5 until each child has had a turn.

III. Techniques and Modifications

1. Before introducing the snare drum, assist the children in becoming familiar with the four facial expressions. Use demonstration, a mirror, etc.
2. The pictures for this activity can be found in magazines or drawn by the children.
3. A modification of this activity might be the use of rhythm instruments and/or moving to the music to portray the feelings represented on the picture cards.

Resource
snare drum
snare drum stand
pair of drum sticks
four 5- by 8-inch cards, each with a drawing of a face to describe happy, sad, angry, or afraid

Cross Reference Objectives
Behavior 9, 11
Communication 8, 9
Socialization 14
Academics 25

C-11.1 Music Therapy Learning Experience

Developmental Therapy Objective C-11/to use simple word sequences to command or request of another child or adult in ways acceptable to the classroom procedures

Type of Activity	*Area*
Listening	Communication
(Playing)	
Singing	*Stage*
Moving	I
Creating	(II)
(Verbalizing)	III
	IV

MUSIC ACTIVITY

I. Introduction

Direct the children to sit on the floor in a semicircle facing the music therapist.

II. Implementation

1. Show the children the autoharp. Demonstrate how to play it by pressing the chord buttons with the left hand and crossing the right hand over the left to strum the strings.
2. Choose one child to play the autoharp. Tell him that he can press any of the chord buttons as he strums the strings.
3. Repeat step 2 until each child has had a turn.
4. Demonstrate how to strum the autoharp fast and slow. Direct the children to listen and to raise their hands each time they hear fast strums.
5. When all of the children seem to be able to differentiate between fast and slow, choose one child to be the leader. Tell the leader that he will give each child verbal instructions for playing fast or slow.
6. Direct the leader to sit in front of the other children. Choose one child to play the autoharp. Instruct the leader to tell that child how to play the autoharp, i.e., either fast or slow.
7. Direct the child playing the autoharp to pass it to the next child. Instruct the leader to give the new child directions for playing the autoharp fast or slow. Continue in this manner until each child has had a turn playing either fast or slow.
8. Repeat step 4, demonstrating the difference between loud and soft. Continue with steps 5 to 7 until each child has had a turn in playing the autoharp loud or soft.

III. Techniques and Modifications

1. In this activity it is important for the children to explore the variety of sounds which can be produced on the autoharp. Guide the children in discussing the different sounds which are heard.
2. Some children may have difficulty playing the autoharp as directed by the leader. It may be necessary to again demonstrate the various ways to play or to give the child physical assistance.
3. As a sequel to this activity, have the children play the autoharp using various combinations of the fast/slow, loud/soft concepts, e.g., play fast and loud; slow and loud; fast and soft, etc.

Resource
autoharp

Cross Reference Objectives
Behavior 9, 11, 12
Communication
Socialization 14, 16, 18
Academics 28

Developmental Therapy Objective C-11/to use simple word sequences to command or request of another child or adult in ways acceptable to the classroom procedures

Type of Activity	*Area*
Listening	Communication
Playing	
Singing	*Stage*
(Moving)	I
(Creating)	(II)
(Verbalizing)	III
	IV

MUSIC ACTIVITY

I. Introduction

Direct the children to stand in a line, one behind the other.

II. Implementation

1. Explain that they are to follow "Mr. Piper" (music therapist) around the room and do whatever he does. Tell them that Mr. Piper will wear the streamers around his neck.
2. Stand in front of the line (with streamers hanging from neck) and begin playing the record. Walk, jump, etc., around the room saying, "Mr. Piper says (*name of action*)."
3. After several actions, place the streamers on the floor and say, "Mr. Piper says, 'Jump over the river.'" After all of the children have done this, hold the streamers up and tell the children (as above) to walk under the bridge.
4. Place the streamers around the neck of one of the children and direct the group to follow the new Mr. Piper. Tell the leader to verbalize the actions he wants the group to imitate.

III. Techniques and Modifications

1. To prevent the children from losing interest in the activity, make each leader's turn very brief. It may be necessary to have only two or three children be leaders during each music session.
2. Assist each leader in the following manner:
    1) While the group is moving around the room, say, "Mr. Piper, what should we do?" If the child makes no response, suggest an action.
    2) Verbalize what the leader is doing and encourage the group to imitate him, i.e., "Mr. Piper is (*action*), so let's do that too."

3) If the leader verbalizes an action he wants the group to imitate, state that "Mr. Piper wants us to (*action*)." This will reinforce the child's leadership position.

Resource
record player

"1st Movement—Allegro ma non troppo": *Symphony No. 6 in F Major,* Op. 68 ("Pastoral") (Everest 3074). L. van Beethoven, Everest Records, Hollywood, California

four crepe paper streamers (two colors), each approximately 3 feet long; twisted individually and all four fastened together at each end

Cross Reference Objectives
Behavior 11, 12
Communication 19
Socialization 18
Academics

C-12.1 Music Therapy Learning Experience

Developmental Therapy Objective C-12/to use words to exchange minimal information with an adult

Type of Activity	Area
Listening	Communication
Playing	
(Singing)	Stage
Moving	I
Creating	(II)
(Verbalizing)	III
	IV

MUSIC ACTIVITY

I. Introduction

Direct the children to sit on the floor in a circle.

II. Implementation

1. Ask the children to talk about their plans for the Christmas holidays.
2. Tell the children that a song will be sung to wish each child a merry Christmas. Direct one child to choose another child to sing about.
3. Sing "We Wish You a Merry Christmas," substituting the name of the child who was selected, i.e., "We wish (*child's name*) a merry Christmas . . ."
4. Ask the child who was selected to choose another child to sing about. Repeat step 3.
5. Continue with the activity until each child has an opportunity to select another child for the song.

III. Techniques and Modifications

1. If the children have difficulty talking about their plans for the holidays, ask them questions to stimulate conversation.
2. If a child has difficulty selecting another child for the activity, give him suggestions concerning possible choices, e.g., tell him that a certain child has not had a turn, suggest that he choose the child who is beside him, etc.

Resource
"We Wish You a Merry Christmas":
Making Music Your Own—Book 2
(Teacher's Edition), Silver Burdett
Co., Morristown, New Jersey, 1971,
p. 79

Cross Reference Objectives
Behavior 9, 11, 12
Communication 8, 13
Socialization 14, 15
Academics

Developmental Therapy Objective C-13/to use words spontaneously to exchange minimal information with another child

Type of Activity	Area
(Listening)	Communication
Playing	
Singing	Stage
Moving	I
Creating	(II)
(Verbalizing)	III
	IV

MUSIC ACTIVITY

I. Introduction

Direct the children to sit in their chairs at the table.

II. Implementation

1. Hold up one rhythm instrument at a time, reviewing its name.
2. Tell the children that they are going to play a guessing game. Choose one child to cover his eyes.
3. Direct another child to look at one of the rhythm instruments and to give verbal clues about it to the child who has his eyes closed, e.g., color of the instrument, size, sound, etc.
4. Tell the child who has his eyes covered to listen carefully and to try to name the instrument which is being described.
5. Repeat this procedure until each child has an opportunity to participate.

III. Techniques and Modifications

1. Use instruments which are very different in terms of size, color, etc. Only use instruments with which the children are familiar.
2. The child who is giving the clues may need help in describing the instrument.
3. If a child cannot guess the name of an instrument, allow the child who described it to help him by making some sounds on the instrument.

Resource
variety of familiar rhythm instruments

Cross Reference Objectives
Behavior 9, 11, 12
Communication 9, 11, 14
Socialization 14, 15
Academics 18, 22

C-14.1 Music Therapy Learning Experience

Developmental Therapy Objective C-14/to accept praise or success without inappropriate behavior or loss of control

Type of Activity	Area
(Listening)	Communication
(Playing)	
Singing	Stage
Moving	I
(Creating)	II
Verbalizing	(III)
	IV

MUSIC ACTIVITY

I. Introduction

Direct the children to sit in a semicircle on the floor.

II. Implementation

1. Explain that each child will play different rhythm patterns on the bongo drums for the group to imitate.
2. Give each child a set of bongo drums. Play a simple rhythm pattern on the bongo drums and direct the class to repeat it.
3. Select one child to play a rhythm pattern for the other children to imitate. Praise him for creating the rhythm pattern and for leading the group.
4. Repeat step 3 until each of the children has been a leader of the group.

III. Techniques and Modifications

1. Encourage those children who act as leaders to begin with short, simple rhythm patterns which will not be difficult for the group to imitate.
2. Direct the group to listen carefully until the leader finishes the rhythm pattern. Then, help them to begin playing the rhythm pattern together by giving a verbal and/or visual cue.

Resource
bongo drums, one set for each child and music therapist

Cross Reference Objectives
Behavior 19
Communication 19
Socialization 18, 19, 22
Academics 39

Developmental Therapy Objective C16/to use words spontaneously to describe own ideas, activity, work, or self to another child or adult

Type of Activity	Area
Listening	Communication
Playing	
Singing	Stage
Moving	I
(Creating)	II
(Verbalizing)	(III)
	IV

MUSIC ACTIVITY

I. Introduction

Direct the group to stand around the table.

II. Implementation

1. Show the children the materials which they can use to make musical instruments.
2. Tell the children that they will each be able to make an instrument using the materials on the table.
3. After the instruments are completed, direct each child to play his instrument and to describe how he made it.

III. Techniques and Modifications

1. Provide enough materials so that the children will have a variety of items from which they can make their instruments.
2. If problems arise over the distribution of the materials, give suggestions as to how the items can be shared.
3. Tell the children when their time is almost over so that they will be able to complete their instruments.
4. As a sequel to this activity, divide the children into pairs to make instruments or instruct the whole group to make one "group instrument" which they can play together.

Resource
cigar boxes, variety of other small boxes; cans and other empty containers; rice, macaroni, etc.; sandpaper; small pieces of wood; bottle caps; nails; rubber bands; string; scissors; masking tape; glue; hammer

Cross Reference Objectives
Behavior 11
Communication 12, 13, 14, 19
Socialization 19, 20
Academics 38

C-19.1 Music Therapy Learning Experience

Developmental Therapy Objective C-19/to use words or nonverbal gestures to show pride in own work, activity, or to make positive statements about self

Type of Activity	Area
(Listening)	Communication
(Playing)	
(Singing)	**Stage**
Moving	I
Creating	II
Verbalizing	(III)
	IV

MUSIC ACTIVITY

I. Introduction

Direct the group to move to a semicircle on the floor.

II. Implementation

1. Explain that each child in the group will have an opportunity to be taped for 1 minute. The "performance" may include playing rhythm instruments and/or singing a song.
2. Encourage the children to discuss procedures for the activity, e.g., suggestions for group behavior when one child is being taped, method for deciding which child will have the first turn, etc.
3. Start the tape recorder and direct the first child to begin his performance. After one minute give him a signal to stop.
4. Repeat step 3 for each child.
5. Play back the tape for the group to hear. Encourage the children to talk about the performances.

III. Techniques and Modifications

1. When playing back the tape, point out the positive aspects of each child's contribution.
2. Direct the children to listen for specific things as they hear the tape, e.g., "What instrument do you hear?" "Is he playing loud or soft?" "Do you know that song?"

Resource
tape recorder
variety of rhythm instruments

Cross Reference Objectives
Behavior 13, 14, 15, 16, 19
Communication 13, 14, 15, 17,
   18, 20, 21
Socialization, 19, 20
Academics

Developmental Therapy Objective C-20/to use appropriate words or gestures to show feeling responses to environment, materials, people, or animals

Type of Activity	*Area*
(Listening)	Communication
(Playing)	
Singing	*Stage*
Moving	I
Creating	II
(Verbalizing)	(III)
	IV

MUSIC ACTIVITY

I. Introduction

Direct the group to sit in a semicircle on the floor.

II. Implementation

1. Tell the children that they are going to make a tape recording.
2. Distribute the instruments and have the group play together with the record for a practice session.
3. Direct the children to each choose another child with whom they can exchange instruments. After they have exchanged instruments, begin playing the record and cue the children to start playing. Begin tape recording as soon as the music begins.
4. Play back the tape and ask the children for comments as to how it sounds and how it might be improved.
5. Make another tape recording repeating step 3. Before beginning the recording, remind the children of their suggestions for improvement.
6. Play back the tape and encourage the children to comment upon what they heard.

III. Techniques and Modifications

1. Before beginning the activity, discuss how sharing and cooperation will be essential for the success of the recording session.
2. Some children may need assistance in choosing another child for the exchanging of instruments.
3. If the children have difficulty commenting upon the tape recording, ask questions which refer to the speed of the playing, volume, whether all of the instruments could be heard, etc.

Resource
cassette tape recorder
record player
"Raindrops Keep Falling On My Head": *Butch Cassidy and the Sundance Kid* (SP 4227), Burt Bacharach, A & M Records, Hollywood, California
instruments with which the children are familiar, one per child

Cross Reference Objectives
Behavior 19
Communication 16, 19
Socialization 20, 23
Academics

C-20.2 Music Therapy Learning Experience

Developmental Therapy Objective C-20/to use appropriate words or gestures to show feeling responses to environment, materials, people, or animals

Type of Activity	*Area*
(Listening)	Communication
(Playing)	
Singing	*Stage*
Moving	I
(Creating)	II
(Verbalizing)	(III)
	IV

MUSIC ACTIVITY

I. Introduction

Direct the group to sit on the floor in a circle.

II. Implementation

1. Tell the children that they are going to create a sound story which will be tape recorded.
2. Have the children work together to create a story which will involve many environmental sounds, e.g., birds chirping, dogs barking, car horns, sirens, footsteps, etc. Write down the story as it is dictated by the group members.
3. Place the instruments in the center of the circle. Direct the children to determine which instruments can be used to produce the sound effects for the story. Have the group members decide who will play each instrument and the sound effect which will be represented by each instrument. Tell the children to practice making each sound effect.
4. Turn on the tape recorder. Begin reading the story and direct the children to make the sound effects at the appropriate times.
5. Play back the tape and encourage a group discussion of the story.

III. Techniques and Modifications

1. Encourage the children to work together in finding instruments to use for the various sound effects.
2. When playing back the tape, point out contributions of various group members.

Resource
tape recorder
variety of rhythm instruments, at least one per child
pencil and paper

Cross Reference Objectives
Behavior 19
Communication 12, 13, 16, 19
Socialization 19, 20
Academics 31, 44, 48

Developmental Therapy Objective C-25/to express experiences and feelings through art, music, dance, or drama

Type of Activity	*Area* Communication
Listening	
(Playing)	*Stage*
Singing	I
Moving	II
(Creating)	III
(Verbalizing)	(IV)

MUSIC ACTIVITY

I. Introduction

Direct the group to sit at the table.

II. Implementation

1. Explain to the group that they are going to tape record a story and create the sound effects for it using instruments of their choice.
2. Tell the group to suggest a topic and have them elaborate upon it. Ask them to determine where the sound effects should be and who will make those sound effects. Distribute the instruments.
3. Begin the tape recorder and the narration.
4. Replay the tape. Upon completion, ask for comments from the group.

III. Techniques and Modifications

Provide the group with topics for the story if they cannot suggest one, e.g., a 40-foot monster invades a town, sunny day evolves into a storm, a huge wave is approaching a surfer, etc.

Resource
tape recorder
variety of rhythm instruments, such as gong, bongo drum, castanets, bells, tambourines
autoharp

Cross Reference Objectives
Behavior
Communication 20, 23, 24, 26, 28
Socialization 25, 30
Academics 48, 52

C-25.2 Music Therapy Learning Experience

Developmental Therapy Objective C-25/to express experiences and feelings through art, music, dance, or drama

Type of Activity	*Area*
Listening	Communication
(Playing)	
Singing	*Stage*
Moving	I
(Creating)	II
(Verbalizing)	III
	(IV)

MUSIC ACTIVITY

I. Introduction

Direct the group to sit on the floor in a circle. Place the instruments in the center of the circle.

II. Implementation

1. Tell the children that they are going to use the musical instruments to give their interpretation of a tornado.
2. Encourage the group members to discuss the environmental sounds associated with a tornado, e.g., wind, rain, thunder, etc. Tell the children to decide which musical instruments can be used to represent the various sounds.
3. Direct the children to discuss the procedures which will be followed in tape recording the "tornado," e.g., which instruments will begin, how the activity will end, who will operate the tape recorder, etc.
4. After the children have decided upon the procedures for the activity, direct them to begin with their interpretation of the tornado. Tape record their performance.
5. Play the tape for the group to hear. Encourage the group members to comment on the sounds which are heard.

III. Techniques and Modifications

1. Encourage the children to share any experiences which they may have had related to tornadoes, hurricanes, thunder storms, etc.
2. Ask the children to give suggestions for other events which could be interpreted using musical instruments.

Resource
tape recorder
variety of rhythm instruments, at least one per child

Cross Reference Objectives
Behavior 19
Communication 20, 23, 26, 28
Socialization 25, 30
Academics 48, 52

Developmental Therapy Objective C-26/to use words to express own feelings spontaneously and appropriately

Type of Activity	Area
(Listening)	Communication
Playing	
Singing	Stage
Moving	I
Creating	II
(Verbalizing)	III
	(IV)

MUSIC ACTIVITY

I. Introduction

Direct the group to sit on the floor in a circle.

II. Implementation

1. Explain to the group that they are going to listen to several musical selections. While listening they are to think about how the music makes them feel or what it makes them think of or feel like doing.
2. Play the first selection and encourage the group members to share their ideas and feelings.
3. Repeat step 2 for the remaining musical selections.

III. Techniques and Modifications

If some children have difficulty expressing their ideas about a selection, provide them with suggestions as to what the composer might have intended his music to portray.

Resource

tape recorder

tape composed of short segments of the following selections:

American in Paris (LM-2367), George Gershwin, RCA Victor Records, New York, New York

"Sunrise": *Grand Canyon Suite* (SDBR 3044), Ferde Grofé, Everest Records, Hollywood, California.

Billy the Kid (LM-2195), Aaron Copland, RCA Victor Records, New York, New York

"Ballet of the Unhatched Chicks": *Pictures at an Exhibition* (ML5401), Modeste Moussorgsky, Columbia Records, New York, New York

"Sweet Creek's Suite": *Sea Train* (SP4171), Sea Train, A & M Records, Hollywood, California

"Cloudburst": *Grand Canyon Suite* (SDBR 3044), Ferde Grofé, Everest Records, Hollywood, California

Cross Reference Objectives

Behavior
Communication 20, 22, 23, 27, 28
Socialization
Academics

C-28.1 Music Therapy Learning Experience

Developmental Therapy Objective C-28/to relate real-life experiences and feelings through stories, art, drama, or music with accompanying verbal expressions

Type of Activity	*Area*
(Listening)	Communication
Playing	
Singing	*Stage*
Moving	I
(Creating)	II
(Verbalizing)	III
	(IV)

MUSIC ACTIVITY

I. Introduction

Direct the children to sit at the table.

II. Implementation

1. Instruct the children to listen to the musical selection and to think of something that has recently happened to them which the music brings to mind.
2. After listening to the music, give each child a sheet of drawing paper and colored chalk. Direct the children to create a picture which describes the experience they thought of while listening to the music. Play the musical selection again as the children work on the pictures.
3. When the pictures are completed, ask each child to show his picture to the group and to describe the experience he has related through the art. Encourage a discussion of the characteristics of the music (rhythm patterns, tempo, instruments, etc.) which may have influenced each picture.

III. Techniques and Modifications

1. A wide variety of musical selections may be used with this activity.
2. A sequel to this activity could involve a group mural in which all the children work together on a large sheet of paper. This could consist of drawings to represent individual ideas or a single theme with group members contributing to one creation.
3. Other art materials may be used with this activity, e.g., finger paint, water colors, etc.

Resource
record player
The Planets (M31125), Gustav Holst, Columbia Masterworks, New York, New York
drawing paper and colored chalk, enough for each child in the group

Cross Reference Objectives
Behavior
Communication 20, 22, 23, 24, 25, 26, 27
Socialization
Academics

Developmental Therapy Objective S-1/to be aware of others

Type of Activity	Area
Listening	Socialization
Playing	
Singing	Stage
(Moving)	I
Creating	II
Verbalizing	III
	IV

MUSIC ACTIVITY

I. Introduction

Direct the children to sit on the floor facing the music therapist.

II. Implementation

1. Shake hands with each child and say "hello."
2. Begin singing the song. While singing, shake each child's hand.

III. Techniques and Modifications

1. When directing attention to a particular child to shake his hand, cue him by holding one hand in a "shake hands" position and wait for him to hold out his hand. If the child does not initiate the response, take his hand and move it in the "shaking hands" action.
2. Sing a complete phrase of the song without stopping while shaking hands with different children.
3. To modify this activity for a Stage Two class, direct the children to shake hands with each other.

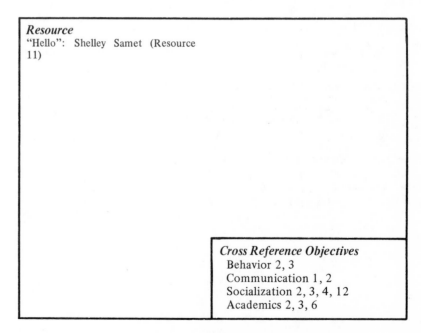

Resource
"Hello": Shelley Samet (Resource 11)

Cross Reference Objectives
Behavior 2, 3
Communication 1, 2
Socialization 2, 3, 4, 12
Academics 2, 3, 6

S-2.1 Music Therapy Learning Experience

Developmental Therapy Objective S-2/to attend to other's behavior

Type of Activity	Area
Listening	Socialization
Playing	
Singing	Stage
(Moving)	I
Creating	II
Verbalizing	III
	IV

MUSIC ACTIVITY

I. Introduction

Instruct the children to sit in a circle on the floor.

II. Implementation

1. Begin playing the record. Say to the children, "Let's clap hands."
2. When all of the children are clapping their hands, introduce another movement, e.g., slap knees. Verbally reflect the new action, e.g., "We're slapping our knees."
3. Continue with the activity using other body movements, e.g., slap legs, tap toes, shake head, etc.

III. Techniques and Modifications

1. It may be necessary to physically assist a child with the movements, e.g., take a child's hands and move them in a clapping motion.
2. Wait until all of the children are involved in a specified body movement before beginning the next movement.
3. Do not require rhythmic precision in clapping, etc., but praise the children for all attempts at participation.
4. Use simple verbalizations to reflect the ongoing activity, e.g., "We're clapping," "We're tapping our toes," etc.

Resource
record player
"Save the Country" (895), The Fifth Dimension, Bell Records, New York, New York

Cross Reference Objectives
Behavior 1, 2, 4
Communication 1, 2
Socialization 1, 4, 13
Academics 1, 2, 4, 6, 17

Developmental Therapy Objective S-3/to respond to adult when child's name is called

Type of Activity	Area
Listening	Socialization
Playing	
Singing	*Stage*
(Moving)	①
Creating	II
Verbalizing	III
	IV

MUSIC ACTIVITY

I. Introduction

Instruct the support teacher to make a bridge with one of the children. All of the other children stand up and hold hands to form a line with the music therapist as the leader.

II. Implementation

1. Tell the children that they are going to play a game called "London Bridge." Lead the children in walking under the bridge and begin singing the song.
2. At the end of the song, a child is caught under the bridge (support teacher and child lower their arms to enclose one of the children in the line.) Substitute that child's name instead of "lady" for the last word of the song, e.g., ". . . my fair David." He then becomes the support teacher's partner.
3. Continue playing until all children have had an opportunity to be part of the bridge.

III. Techniques and Modifications

1. Use a moderate singing tempo to coincide with the children's walking tempo. Vary the tempo at the end of the song so as to allow time for different children to be caught under the bridge.
2. After several children have been caught under the bridge, direct one child to lead the group under the bridge.

Resource
"London Bridge": *Teacher's Guide to the Open Court Kindergarten Music Program,* Betty N. Smith, T. C. Harter, and Mary W. Walter, Open Court Publishing Co., La Salle, Illinois, 1973, p. 103

Cross Reference Objectives
Behavior 4
Communication
Socialization 1, 2, 4
Academics 4, 6

S-3.2 Music Therapy Learning Experience

Developmental Therapy Objective S-3/to respond to adult when child's name is called

Type of Activity	Area
(Listening)	Socialization
Playing	
Singing	Stage
(Moving)	(I)
Creating	II
Verbalizing	III
	IV

MUSIC ACTIVITY

I. Introduction

Instruct the children to stand up and hold the circle (hula hoop) with both hands. The circle should be held out horizontally at a height where all the children can hold on comfortably.

II. Implementation

1. Direct the children to begin walking while holding the circle.
2. Begin singing the song. When beginning the fourth line, hold the circle vertically so the child whose name is sung can walk through it.
3. Repeat all four lines until each child has had a turn walking through the circle.

III. Techniques and Modifications

1. If the children are of varying heights, direct the taller children to stand on one side and the shorter children on the other. This will enable the tilting of the circle for the second line such that the circle will be above each child's head.
2. When doing this activity for the first time, instruct one of the teachers to go through the circle (fourth line) to provide a model for imitation.

Resource
"Let's Walk the Circle All Around":
Shelley Samet (Resource 17)

one hula hoop (circle)

Cross Reference Objectives
Behavior 4
Communication
Socialization 4, 7, 11
Academics 4, 6, 13

Developmental Therapy Objective S-4/to imitate simple, familiar acts of adults

Type of Activity	Area
Listening	Socialization
Playing	
Singing	*Stage*
(Moving)	Ⅰ
Creating	Ⅱ
(Verbalizing)	Ⅲ
	Ⅳ

MUSIC ACTIVITY

I. Introduction

Direct the children to sit on the floor facing the music therapist.

II. Implementation

1. Instruct the children to clap their hands while providing a model for the action. Say to them, "Do what I do."
2. Begin singing the song, using familiar movements, such as nod your head, touch your nose, stamp your feet, etc. Include sounds in addition to movements as part of the song, e.g., "If you're happy and you know it, say "Oooo," "Oooo," etc.

III. Techniques and Modifications

1. For those children who do not imitate the movements, encourage them by using verbal cues or by helping them move the appropriate body part for the action.
2. Be certain that each child has attempted the movement specified in the song before introducing a new action.
3. When doing this activity with Stage Two children, ask them if they can think of any other actions. Verbal cues, such as, "What else can we do with our hands?" may be necessary. Also, guitar or autoharp accompaniment may be used.

Resource
"If You're Happy and You Know It": *Teacher's Guide To the Open Court Kindergarten Music Program,* Betty N. Smith, T. C. Harter, and Mary M. Walter, Open Court Publishing Co., La Salle, Illinois, 1973, p. 100

Cross Reference Objective
Behavior 2, 4
Communication 1, 2
Socialization 1, 2
Academic 2, 4, 6, 17

S-4.2 *Music Therapy Learning Experience*

Developmental Therapy Objective S-4/to imitate simple, familiar acts of adults

Type of Activity	*Area*
Listening	Socialization
Playing	
Singing	*Stage*
(Moving)	I
Creating	II
Verbalizing	III
	IV

MUSIC ACTIVITY

I. Introduction

Direct the children to stand and hold hands to form a circle.

II. Implementation

1. Instruct the children to begin walking. Then begin singing "Let everybody walk..," ending the song with "...and now let's all sit down."
2. Before introducing each new movement, stop the children and tell them to do the new action (run, jump, etc.) and then continue singing as they start the new movement. Use movements that the children can do, such as running, jumping, tiptoeing, sliding, etc.

III. Techniques and Modifications

When doing this activity with Stage Two children, the same manner of presentation should be employed. In addition, the children should be asked, after several movements, what other movements the group can make. If no response is given, provide a lead-in to a response such as, "What can we do with our hands?"

Resource
"Let Everybody Walk": Shelley Samet (Resource 15)

Cross Reference Objectives
Behavior 2, 4
Communication 1, 2, 9
Socialization 1, 2, 7
Academics 2, 4, 6, 13

Developmental Therapy Objective S-4/to imitate simple, familiar acts of adults

Type of Activity	*Area*
Listening	Socialization
Playing	
Singing	*Stage*
(Moving)	I
Creating	II
Verbalizing	III
	IV

MUSIC ACTIVITY

I. Introduction

Direct the children to sit on the floor facing the music therapist.

II. Implementation

1. Begin playing the record and say that everyone is going to learn to do the twist.
2. Direct one child to stand up. Face the child and hold both of his hands. Begin moving his arms: one in a forward motion and one in a backward motion. Move your body in a side to side manner to provide a model for the twisting action.
3. Tell the child to "twist" and give him an opportunity to attempt the movement without physical assistance.
4. Direct the child to sit down. Repeat steps 2 and 3 for each child.
5. After each child has "twisted" with the music therapist, tell all of the children to stand up and twist.

III. Techniques and Modifications

1. It may be necessary to move a child's hips to help him with the "twisting" action.
2. Direct the other children to watch as each child "twists." Make each child's turn brief so as to minimize the length of time the other children must wait.

Resource
record player
"The Twist" (811), Chubby Checker,
Parkway Records, Inc.

Cross Reference Objectives
Behavior 4, 9
Communication
Socialization 2, 6, 7, 12, 13, 14
Academics 4, 6, 13

S-5.1 Music Therapy Learning Experience

Developmental Therapy Objective S-5/to engage in organized solitary play

Type of Activity	Area
Listening	Socialization
(Playing)	
Singing	Stage
(Moving)	I
Creating	II
Verbalizing	III
	IV

MUSIC ACTIVITY

I. Introduction

Place the music materials and toys in the play area. Direct the children to go to the play area for Play Time.

II. Implementation

1. Allow the children to move around freely in the play area.
2. As a child picks up a toy or musical instrument, verbally reflect his action, e.g., "Tommy has the bells." Encourage the child to use the object in the play situation.

III. Techniques and Modifications

Use music materials which the children have had experience with in previous music sessions.

Resource
variety of toys and rhythm instruments

Cross Reference Objectives
Behavior 6, 7, 8
Communication
Socialization 13
Academics 18

Developmental Therapy Objective S6/to respond to adult's verbal and nonverbal requests to come to him

Type of Activity	Area
Listening	Socialization
Playing	
Singing	Stage
(Moving)	I
Creating	II
Verbalizing	III
	IV

MUSIC ACTIVITY

I. Introduction

Direct the children to sit on the floor. Place the rope on the floor to form a circle in front of them.

II. Implementation

1. Stand in the circle and call one child by name to come to the circle.
2. As the child comes forward, take his hand and jump with him in and out of the circle. Sing the "Jumping" song, using the child's name.
3. Repeat steps 1 and 2 until each child has had a turn.

III. Techniques and Modifications

1. If a child is not able to jump, stand behind him and hold him around the chest, physically moving him through the jumping action.
2. Other movements such as hopping or walking can be substituted for jumping.

Resource
"Jumping": Shelley Samet (Resource 13)
rope

Cross Reference Objectives
Behavior
Communication 1, 2
Socialization 1, 2, 3, 4, 7, 12
Academics 3, 6, 13

S-7.1 Music Therapy Learning Experience

Developmental Therapy Objective S-7/to respond to single verbal request or command given directly to child

Type of Activity	Area
(Listening)	Socialization
Playing	
Singing	Stage
(Moving)	(I)
Creating	II
Verbalizing	III
	IV

MUSIC ACTIVITY

I. Introduction

Direct the children to sit on the floor in a semicircle facing the music therapist.

II. Implementation

1. Shake the tambourine inside the box where the children cannot see it. Ask the children, "What do you hear?" If they do not answer, show them the instrument and have them attempt to verbalize "tambourine."
2. While the children are watching, put the tambourine in an obvious place in the room, e.g., on table, in a corner, etc. Say to the children, "I'm hiding the tambourine."
3. Tell one child to find the tambourine and bring it back to the group. As the child goes to get the instrument, clap and sing. "Go find the tambourine, (child's name)," etc. When the child picks up the instrument, begin singing, "Bring back the tambourine, (child's name)," etc.
4. Allow the child to play the tambourine when he brings it back to the group.
5. Repeat steps 2 to 4 for each child.

III. Techniques and Modifications

1. It may be necessary to go with the child to help him retrieve the tambourine.
2. As the instrument is being hidden in the room, remind the children to watch. If necessary, turn their heads in the direction of the instrument.
3. When one child is being directed to find the instrument, encourage the other children to watch and clap.
4. Use other simple instruments with which the children are familiar.

5. As a sequel to this activity, place two instruments in different areas of the room and direct each child to retrieve one of the two instruments.

Resource
"Go Find It": Jennie Purvis (Resource 10)

one tambourine
one box

Cross Reference Objectives
Behavior 1, 2, 4
Communication 1, 2
Socialization 1, 2, 3, 6
Academics 1, 2, 3, 4

Developmental Therapy Objective S-11/to exhibit a beginning emergence of self

Type of Activity	Area
(Listening)	Socialization
Playing	
Singing	Stage
(Moving)	(I)
Creating	II
Verbalizing	III
	IV

MUSIC ACTIVITY

I. Introduction

Direct the children to stand facing the mirror.

II. Implementation

1. Tell the children to look in the mirror and point to their nose. After all of the children are pointing to their nose, direct them to point to their mouth. Repeat this procedure for ears, eyes, etc.
2. Begin singing "I Can Touch." Lead the children in touching the correct body parts.

III. Techniques and Modifications

Some children may need physical assistance in finding the correct body parts; e.g., take a child's hand and place it on the designated body part.

Resource
"I Can Touch": Beleta Griffith (Resource 12)
mirror

Cross Reference Objectives
Behavior 4
Communication 2
Socialization 4, 7
Academics 4, 6, 17

S-13.1 Music Therapy Learning Experience

Developmental Therapy Objective S-13/to participate spontaneously in specific parallel activities with another child using similar materials but not interacting

Type of Activity	*Area*
(Listening)	Socialization
Playing	
Singing	*Stage*
(Moving)	I
Creating	(II)
Verbalizing	III
	IV

MUSIC ACTIVITY

I. Introduction

Direct the children to stand in a circle in the music area.

II. Implementation

1. Ask the children to demonstrate clapping their hands; stamping their feet; tapping their toes.
2. Tell them to listen to the music and to do each action as directed by the words of the song.
3. Begin playing the record and perform each body movement at the appropriate time.

III. Techniques and Modifications

1. Since only the chorus of the song suggests body movements, it is important to give the children verbal directions to specify their involvement during the verses.
2. Before demonstrating each action, allow the children enough time to perform the movement independently.

Resource
record player
"Clapping Land": *Folk Song Carnival* (AR524), Hap Palmer, Educational Activities, Inc., Freeport, New York

Cross Reference Objectives
Behavior 11
Communication 9
Socialization
Academics 17

Developmental Therapy Objective S-13/to participate spontaneously in specific parallel activities with another child using similar materials but not interacting

Type of Activity	Area
(Listening)	Socialization
Playing	
Singing	*Stage*
(Moving)	I
Creating	(II)
Verbalizing	III
	IV

MUSIC ACTIVITY

I. Introduction
Direct the children to stand in a circle in the music area.

II. Implementation
1. Tell the children to listen to the music and to do what the words of the song say to do.
2. Begin playing the record. Perform the body movements as indicated in the song and verbally encourage the children to participate.

III. Techniques and Modifications
Participate in all of the movements with the children. After each new direction is given, however, give the children enough time to attempt the action on their own. Praise those children who are able to follow the directions for movement without imitating the music therapist's actions.

Resource
record player
"Clap Your Hands": *American Folk Songs For Children* (FC7601), Pete Seeger, Folkways Records, New York, New York

Cross Reference Objectives
Behavior 11
Communication 9
Socialization
Academics 17

S-15.1 Music Therapy Learning Experience

Developmental Therapy Objective S-15/to initiate appropriate minimal movement toward another child within the classroom routine

Type of Activity	Area
Listening	Socialization
Playing	
(Singing)	*Stage*
Moving	I
Creating	(II)
(Verbalizing)	III
	IV

MUSIC ACTIVITY

I. Introduction

Direct the children to sit on the floor in a semicircle facing the music therapist.

II. Implementation

1. Ask the children if they know the song, "He's Got the Whole World." Begin singing the song, using the autoharp for accompaniment. Encourage them to sing along.
2. Tell the children that they will each have a turn choosing another child to sing about. Ask one child to select another child by name.
3. Sing the song, substituting the name of the child who was selected, i.e., "He's got (*child's name*) in his hands . . ."
4. Ask the child who was selected to choose another child to sing about. Repeat step 3.
5. Continue with the activity until each child has had an opportunity to select another child for the song.

III. Techniques and Modifications

1. If a child has difficulty selecting another child for the activity, give him suggestions concerning possible choices, e.g., tell him that a certain child has not had a turn, suggest that he choose the child who is beside him, etc.
2. A modification of this activity might be to allow the child who chooses another child to accompany the singing on the autoharp, i.e., the music therapist pushes the chord buttons and the child strums the strings.

Resource
"He's Got the Whole World": *Music Activities For Retarded Children,* David Ginglend and Winifred Stiles, Abingdon Press, Nashville, Tennessee, 1965, p. 61
autoharp

Cross Reference Objectives
Behavior 9, 11, 12
Communication
Socialization 14
Academics

Developmental Therapy Objective S-16/to participate in a verbally directed sharing activity

Type of Activity	Area
(Listening)	Socialization
(Playing)	
(Singing)	Stage
Moving	I
Creating	(II)
Verbalizing	III
	IV

MUSIC ACTIVITY

I. Introduction

Direct the children to move their chairs to the music area and sit in a semicircle facing the music therapist.

II. Implementation

1. Instruct the children to listen to the song and raise their hands as soon as they discover what kind of animal is mentioned in the words of the song (rabbit). Play a brief segment of the selection on the record player.
2. Direct the children to sing "oh, yes" each time that phrase occurs in the song (it appears after each short solo section). Play the complete selection on the record player.
3. Tell the children that the selection will be played a third time and that they are to strike the tambourine on each "oh, yes" phrase.
4. Give the tambourine to one child and repeat the instructions in step 3. Direct him to pass the tambourine to the next child when given a verbal cue ("pass") by the music therapist.
5. Continue with the activity until each child has had several opportunities to play the "oh, yes" phrase on the tambourine.

III. Techniques and Modifications

A sequel to this activity would be to have several children play tambourines or other instruments for step 4.

Resource
record player
"John the Rabbit": *Silver Burdett Music—Book 2, Record 9,* General Learning Corporation, Morristown, New Jersey
one tambourine

Cross Reference Objectives
Behavior 9, 11
Communication
Socialization 14, 18, 19, 20
Academics

S-17.1 Music Therapy Learning Experience

Developmental Therapy Objective S-17/to participate in cooperative activities or projects with another child during play time, indoor or outdoor

Type of Activity	*Area*
Listening	Socialization
Playing	
Singing	*Stage*
(Moving)	I
Creating	(II)
Verbalizing	III
	IV

MUSIC ACTIVITY

I. Introduction

During a free play situation suggest that the children pretend to be a train.

II. Implementation

1. Ask for a volunteer to be the train engine.
2. Tell the other children to line up behind the engine. Have each child put his hands on the shoulders of the child in front of him.
3. Direct the children to move around the play area. Begin singing the song. Encourage the children to make train sounds and to slide their feet as they move around the room.

III. Techniques and Modifications

1. Encourage the children to take turns being the train engine. Have each child suggest a name for his train car, e.g., coal car, passenger coach, caboose, etc.
2. Assist the children in thinking of ways to modify this play activity, e.g., one child can run the train station, several children can build a railroad crossing, etc.

Resource
"Down At The Station": *Making Music Your Own—Book 3* (Teacher's Edition), Silver Burdett Co., Morristown, New Jersey, 1971, p. 89

Cross Reference Objectives
Behavior 11, 12
Communication
Socialization
Academics

Music Therapy Learning Experience S-18.1

Developmental Therapy Objective S-18/to participate in cooperative activities or projects with another child during organized class activities

Type of Activity	Area
Listening	Socialization
Playing	
Singing	**Stage**
(Moving)	I
Creating	(II)
Verbalizing	III
	IV

MUSIC ACTIVITY

I. Introduction

Instruct the group to sit at the table.

II. Implementation

1. Tell the children that they are going to pretend they are taking a train to the zoo to see the animals.
2. Ask for a volunteer to be the conductor. Choose the other children to be the train cars, instructing them (one at a time) to stand in a straight line behind the conductor with hands on each other's hips.
3. Tell the conductor that he can go all around the room, designating the zoo (music area) as the stopping point. Begin playing the record. When the children stop at the music area, instruct them to sit down.
4. Make a train, as explained above, to leave the zoo (music area) to go back to the table.

III. Techniques and Modifications

1. Make statements such as "The train is coming 'round the bend," while the children are moving around the room.
2. Verbally guide the conductor around the room if he does not know where to move.

Resource
record player
"Get On Board": *Silver Burdett Music—Book 1, Record 3,* General Learning Corp., Morristown, New Jersey

Cross Reference Objectives
Behavior 11, 12
Communication 8
Socialization 20
Academics

S-18.2 Music Therapy Learning Experience

Developmental Therapy Objective S-18/to participate in cooperative activities or projects with another child during organized class activities

Type of Activity	*Area*
Listening	Socialization
(Playing)	
Singing	*Stage*
Moving	I
Creating	(II)
Verbalizing	III
	IV

MUSIC ACTIVITY

I. Introduction

Direct the children to sit in their chairs in a circle.

II. Implementation

1. Show the children two cards, one with *Pass* written on it and the other with *Stop*. Ask them the meaning of the two words.
2. Instruct the children to say the word on each card as it is held up in front of them.
3. Hold up the cards one at a time in front of the children until they are able to recognize the words.
4. Give the hand drum to a child and direct him to begin playing the instrument when the music starts and to continue playing until the *Pass* card or *Stop* card is presented. Each time the *Stop* card is held up he is to stop playing, and when the *Pass* card is presented he must pass the drum to the child on his right.
5. Continue this activity until the drum has been passed around the circle.
6. Ask various children to direct the activity by holding up the cards for the class.

III. Techniques and Modifications

1. It is important to help the children learn to recognize the two words before beginning the activity. It may be helpful to: 1) introduce the written words during other activities before using them in the music session, and/or 2) color code the words on the cards to aid in their recognition.
2. Children who serve as leaders may need help in deciding when to hold up the two cards.

Resource
record player
"Yellow Submarine": *Mod Marches* (AR527), Hap Palmer, Educational Activities, Inc., Freeport, Long Island, New York
one hand drum
two 5- by 8-inch cards, one for each word: *Pass, Stop*

Cross Reference Objectives
Behavior 9, 11
Communication
Socialization 14, 19, 20
Academics

Developmental Therapy Objective S-18/to participate in cooperative activities or projects with another child during organized class activities

Type of Activity	Area
Listening	Socialization
Playing	
Singing	Stage
(Moving)	I
(Creating)	(II)
Verbalizing	III
	IV

MUSIC ACTIVITY

I. Introduction

Direct the children to sit in their chairs in a semicircle facing the music therapist.

II. Implementation

1. Ask the children, "What is a steady beat?" Guide them in discussing various ways to produce a steady beat, e.g., clapping hands, stamping feet, snapping fingers, etc., and demonstrate the suggestions.
2. Begin playing the record and keep a steady beat with the music as discussed in step 1. Direct the children to imitate these actions.
3. Give each child an opportunity to serve as the leader. The leader is directed to sit in front of the group and keep a steady beat, using his own ideas for movement. The other children are instructed to follow the leader's movements.

III. Techniques and Modifications

1. Frequently direct the children's attention to the child who is serving as the leader.
2. Some children may have difficulty maintaining a steady beat with the music. It is not necessary to focus on this, but it will probably help the child to sit close to him and clap, stamp, etc., with a loud, strong beat.
3. When children have difficulty thinking of movements, provide prompts, such as, "Use your head to keep a steady beat," etc.
4. Praise the leaders for originality in movement.

Resource
record player
"Happy Together": *Mod Marches* (AR527), Hap Palmer, Educational Activities, Inc., Freeport, New York

Cross Reference Objectives
Behavior 9, 11
Communication 8
Socialization 14
Academics 17

S-18.4 Music Therapy Learning Experience

Developmental Therapy Objective S-18/to participate in cooperative activities or projects with another child during organized class activities

Type of Activity	*Area*
(Listening)	Socialization
Playing	
Singing	*Stage*
(Moving)	I
Creating	(II)
Verbalizing	III
	IV

MUSIC ACTIVITY

I. Introduction

Direct the children to stand in a straight line facing the music therapist.

II. Implementation

1. Instruct the children to put their hands on their heads, simultaneously demonstrating the action for them. Do the same for shoulders, knees, toes; touch eyes, ears, mouth, and nose.
2. Instruct the children to listen to the song and to imitate the actions.
3. Sing the song at a moderately slow tempo and lead the children in the actions.
4. Assign the children to work as partners and designate one child in each pair to touch the body parts of the other child when the song tells them to. Sing the song again.
5. Direct the second child in each pair to touch the body parts of his partner while the song is sung again.

III. Techniques and Modifications

1. Sequence visual and verbal cues as follows for successive sessions: 1) demonstrate action before the appropriate word in the song is heard; 2) simultaneously present verbal and visual cues; 3) present only verbal cues of the song.
2. Pace the song to the children's movements, eventually increasing the speed in successive sessions.
3. When working as partners, encourage the children to touch each other "gently." It may be necessary, however, to explain and demonstrate the word "gently" or substitute the word "softly." Also, verbally reflect this behavior. Physically assist those children who do not touch each other gently.

Resource
"Head, Shoulders, Knees and Toes": *Teacher's Guide to the Open Court Kindergarten Music Program,* Betty N. Smith, T. C. Harter, and Mary W. Walter, Open Court Publishing Co., La Salle, Illinois, 1973, pp. 72–73

Cross Reference Objectives
Behavior 9, 11
Communication 9
Socialization 13, 14, 19
Academics 17

Developmental Therapy Objective S-18/to participate in cooperative activities or projects with another child during organized class activities

Type of Activity	Area
Listening	Socialization
(Playing)	
Singing	Stage
Moving	I
Creating	(II)
Verbalizing	III
	IV

MUSIC ACTIVITY

I. Introduction

Direct the children to sit on the floor in a semicircle facing the music therapist.

II. Implementation

1. Ask the children questions about the various instruments, such as, "What is this called?" "How is it played?" etc.
2. Distribute rhythm instruments to the children and select one child to be the leader.
3. As the music begins, direct the leader to play the snare drum and tell the other children that this is a signal for them to begin playing their instruments. Instruct the leader to cue the children to stop playing by raising his sticks in the air. The record player should also be stopped when the leader raises his sticks.
4. After each child has had a turn being the leader, instruct the children to exchange rhythm instruments.

III. Techniques and Modifications

Frequently remind the children to watch the leader and follow his directions.

Resource
record player
"Yellow Rose of Texas": *Popular and Folk Tunes For Dancing and Rhythmic Movements* (HLP-4074), Elizabeth Polk, Hoctor Dance Records, Waldwick, New Jersey
snare drum and drum sticks
variety of rhythm instruments, one for each child

Cross Reference Objectives
Behavior 9, 11, 12
Communication 8
Socialization 14, 19, 20
Academics 18, 28

S-18.6 Music Therapy Learning Experience

Developmental Therapy Objective S-18/to participate in cooperative activities or projects with another child during organized class activities

Type of Activity	Area
Listening	Socialization
(Playing)	
Singing	*Stage*
Moving	I
(Creating)	(II)
(Verbalizing)	III
	IV

MUSIC ACTIVITY

I. Introduction

Direct the children to move their chairs to the music area and sit in a semicircle facing the music therapist.

II. Implementation

1. Show a kazoo to the children and ask questions, such as: "What color is it?" "From what material is it made?" "How is it played?" etc.
2. Explain the rules for the kazoo band as follows. 1) When the conductor is moving the conducting stick, all the children play the kazoos. 2) When the conductor touches the floor with the stick, all stop playing (place kazoos in laps). 3) When the conductor points to one child, that child plays alone (other children place kazoos in their laps).
3. After explaining the rules, begin playing the music and serve as the first conductor for the children. The conductor stands in front of the children and moves his stick as indicated by the above rules. The children watch the conductor and play the kazoos accordingly.
4. Give each child an opportunity to be the conductor for the kazoo band.

III. Techniques and Modifications

1. Before beginning the activity, be certain that the children understand the rules for the kazoo band.
2. Encourage the children to create other rules for the activity.

Resource
record player
"Wake Me, Shake Me": *Silver Burdett Music—Book 2, Record 1,* General Learning Corporation, Morristown, New Jersey
kazoos, one for each child
conducting stick

Cross Reference Objectives
Behavior 9, 11, 13
Communication 8, 15
Socialization 14, 19, 20
Academics 18

Developmental Therapy Objective S-18/to participate in cooperative activities or projects with another dhild during organized class activities

Type of Activity	Area
Listening	Socialization
(Playing)	
Singing	Stage
Moving	I
(Creating)	(II)
(Verbalizing)	III
	IV

MUSIC ACTIVITY

I. Introduction

Direct the children to sit on the floor in a semicircle facing the music therapist. Place the nine tone bells in front of the children.

II. Implementation

1. Tell the children that they will learn to play a "Chinese Song." Using two mallets, one in each hand, demonstrate how to keep a steady beat on two bells, playing D_3# and A_3# simultaneously in a repetitive manner. (D_3# and A_3# will be the lowest in pitch of the nine bells used in this activity.)
2. Select a child to play this steady beat pattern on the bells. Sit on the right of the child as he plays the bells. Begin playing the other tone bells using two mallets, one in each hand. Play the bells in any order and as many times as desired. Almost any sequence of bells will sound "correct" as the child maintains the steady beat "bass" on the tone bells.
3. Direct the other children to listen and to discuss the sound of the "Chinese Song."
4. Repeat steps 2 and 3 until each child has had a turn.
5. Have two children play the song together: one child plays the steady beat section while the other child creates an accompanying part on the remaining bells.
6. Repeat step 5 until each child has had a turn playing the accompanying melody section.

III. Techniques and Modifications

1. Maintaining a steady beat in this activity is essential. It may be necessary, therefore, to introduce this concept in other activities, e.g., clapping, playing rhythm instruments, etc., before introducing this music learning experience.

2. Set a time limit for each pair of children to play the song. Tell them when their time is almost over so they will be able to bring their song to an end.
3. A sequel to this activity might involve using a tape recorder to record the songs created by the children. The tape could be played back in order to discuss the various sounds which are produced.

Resource
nine tone bells, D_3#, A_3#, C_4#, D_4#, F_4#, G_4#, A_4#, C_5#, D_5# (the subscript numbers indicate that the tone bells progress in pitch from the lowest, D_3#, to the highest, D_5#.)

Cross Reference Objectives
Behavior 9, 11
Communication
Socialization 14, 18, 20
Academics 24

S-19.1 Music Therapy Learning Experience

Developmental Therapy Objective S-19/to take turns without verbal reminders from teacher

Type of Activity	*Area*
Listening	Socialization
(Playing)	
Singing	*Stage*
Moving	I
Creating	II
Verbalizing	(III)
	IV

MUSIC ACTIVITY

I. Introduction

Direct the children to sit in their chairs in a semicircle.

II. Implementation

1. Choose a child to be the "music policeman." Tell him to move his arms (like a traffic policeman) to signal when the other children should play the drums. He is to stop moving his arms to direct the children to stop playing.
2. Have the children review the procedures for the activity.
3. Distribute the drums and instruct the music policeman to stand in front of the group. As he starts moving his arms, begin playing the record. Stop the record when he stops moving his arms.
4. Have the children exchange drums. Repeat step 3 until each child has had a turn being the music policeman.

III. Techniques and Modifications

1. This activity can be preceded by a discussion of policemen and law enforcement.
2. As a modification of this activity, the music policeman can use a whistle to signal the group to stop and start.

Resource
record player
"Yellow Rose of Texas": *Popular and Folk Tunes For Dancing and Rhythmic Movements* (HLP-4074), Elizabeth Polk, Hoctor Dance Records, Waldwick, New Jersey
drums (bongo drums, hand drums, etc.), one for each child

Cross Reference Objectives
Behavior 13, 19, 20
Communication 15, 19
Socialization 20, 22, 26
Academics

Developmental Therapy Objective S-19/to take turns without verbal reminders from teacher

Type of Activity	*Area*
Listening	Socialization
Playing	
Singing	*Stage*
(Moving)	I
Creating	II
Verbalizing	(III)
	IV

MUSIC ACTIVITY

I. Introduction

Direct the group to sit on the floor in a semicircle.

II. Implementation

1. Ask how many of the children have done the limbo. Demonstrate the dance as follows. 1) Have two children hold the pole horizontally at the height of the music therapist's shoulders. 2) Walk under the pole, bending backward so that the body forms a "C" shape. 3) State that only the feet can touch the floor and that the head has to be thrown back.
2. Direct the children to line up one behind the other. Hold the pole horizontally at the height of the tallest child. Explain that after each child has gone under the pole, he is to go to the end of the line.
3. Begin playing the music. Direct the children to start moving under the pole one at a time.
4. For each successive round, lower the pole so that the children have to bend more to get underneath.

III. Techniques and Modifications

If some children have difficulty getting under the pole, suggest that they stretch their arms out in front of them and pretend that their arms are pulling them under the pole.

Resource
record player
current rock records
one long pole or stick

Cross Reference Objectives
Behavior 11, 12
Communication 14, 19
Socialization
Academics 39

S-19.3 Music Therapy Learning Experience

Developmental Therapy Objective S-19/to take turns without verbal reminders from teacher

Type of Activity	Area
Listening	Socialization
(Playing)	
Singing	Stage
Moving	I
(Creating)	II
Verbalizing	(III)
	IV

MUSIC ACTIVITY

I. Introduction

Instruct the group to sit at the table.

II. Implementation

1. Give the green cards to one child and instruct him to pass them to the left around the table until everyone has a card.
2. Give the magic marker to one child. Instruct him to write his name on the card and then to pass the marker to the next person as in step 1 above.
3. Direct the group to pass their completed name cards to the music therapist.
4. Explain to the group that they are going to make their own musical composition. Hold up one name card and ask who will be playing while that card is being held up by the "conductor." Repeat this until all the cards (including *STOP*) have been read by the group.
5. Distribute the materials for the homemade instruments, one set per child, and instruct them to practice making as many different sounds as they can with their instruments.
6. Set up the tape recorder and explain that their composition will be tape recorded.
7. Hold up the *STOP* card. When everyone has stopped playing, state that the "conductor" is ready to record. Begin holding up the name and *STOP* cards in various combinations and sequences.
8. Instruct the children to place their instruments in the bag while the tape rewinds.
9. Play the recording of the composition created by the group.

III. Techniques and Modifications

1. The household items can be combined in any manner as long as the children will be able to easily produce a sound, e.g., can-macaroni-rubber band; box-paper clip-rubber band.
2. While the tape recording is playing, point to individual children as their instruments/sounds are heard to acknowledge their contribution to the composition.
3. "Store-bought" instruments can be substituted for the homemade instruments.
4. Individual children can be conductors after the music therapist has provided the model.

Resource
tape recorder

materials for homemade instruments, one set of materials per child (each set consists of a can, circular carton, or small box in combination with several of the following items: spoons, macaroni, paper clips, rubber bands)

6- by 9-inch green cards (construction paper), one per child; one 6- by 9-inch red card, *STOP* written on it

one magic marker

large plastic bag

Cross Reference Objectives
Behavior 11, 13, 19
Communication 15, 19
Socialization 18, 20
Academics 35

Developmental Therapy Objective S-19/to take turns without verbal reminders from teacher

Type of Activity	Area
(Listening)	Socialization
(Playing)	
Singing	Stage
Moving	I
Creating	II
Verbalizing	(III)
	IV

MUSIC ACTIVITY

I. Introduction

Direct the children to sit on the floor in a circle.

II. Implementation

1. Show the group the harmonica. Play it and talk about its sound.
2. Tell the children to listen to the "Motorcycle Song" and to raise their hands when they hear a harmonica. Begin playing the record and help the children to recognize the sound of the harmonica.
3. Tell the children that they will each have a turn playing the harmonica. Each child is to play the harmonica, wipe it clean with a cloth, and then pass it to the next child. Explain that each child who plays the harmonica will be responsible for deciding when to pass it to the next child. They should attempt to pass it all the way around the circle before the song ends.
4. Give the harmonica and cleaning cloth to the first child. Begin playing the record.

III. Techniques and Modifications

1. If problem situations arise, help the children to devise some rules and procedures which will aid them in the remainder of the activity.
2. Keep the group informed as to how much of the song remains so that they can pass around the harmonica before the music is completed.

Resource
record player
"Motorcycle Song": *Alice's Restaurant* (6267), Arlo Guthrie, Reprise Records, New York, New York
harmonica
cloth

Cross Reference Objectives
Behavior 19
Communication
Socialization 20
Academics

S-20.1 Music Therapy Learning Experience

Developmental Therapy Objective S-20/to share materials, activities

Type of Activity	Area
Listening	Socialization
Playing	
Singing	Stage
(Moving)	I
(Creating)	II
(Verbalizing)	(III)
	IV

MUSIC ACTIVITY

I. Introduction

Direct the group to sit in a circle on the floor.

II. Implementation

1. Sing "I Saw Three Ships" and encourage those children who know the song to participate in the singing.
2. Tell the children that they will be able to play a game to guess what toys are aboard the three ships.
3. Explain that there are ten picture cards, each with a drawing and the name of a toy.
4. Select a child to look at one of the picture cards. Instruct him to act out the toy while the other children sing the song.
5. When the song is over, direct the other children to guess the name of the toy on the card. Then show them the card and point to the toy name, telling them to read it aloud.
6. Repeat this procedure until each child has had a turn to act out a toy.

III. Techniques and Modifications

1. Structure a "time to answer," e.g., children must wait until the song is over to guess the toy and/or raise their hand to answer.
2. A sequel to this activity could involve having the children use words to describe the toys without using any hand or body movements.

Resource
"I Saw Three Ships": *Making Music Your Own—Book 1* (Teacher's Edition), Silver Burdett Co., Morristown, New Jersey, 1971, p. 57
ten 5- by 8-inch cards, each with one of the following pictures and corresponding written labels: *dog, cat, football, jack-in-the-box, train, car, robot, ariplane, yo-yo, motorcycle*

Cross Reference Objectives
Behavior 19
Communication 19
Socialization 19
Academics 35

Developmental Therapy Objective S-20/to share materials, activities

Type of Activity	Area
Listening	Socialization
(Playing)	
Singing	Stage
Moving	I
Creating	II
(Verbalizing)	(III)
	IV

MUSIC ACTIVITY

I. Introduction

Direct the group to sit on the floor in a semicircle. Place the instruments, which are in a closed box, in front of the children.

II. Implementation

1. Explain to the group that the shapes on the cards match the instruments in the box and that they are to guess which instruments they are.
2. Hold up one card and ask the group to name the shape and to state which instruments look like that shape, e.g.. circle = drum, tambourine. As the children mention an instrument, hold it up for the group to see.
3. Repeat step 2 until all instruments have been matched to a shape.
4. Distribute the instruments by holding up one at a time and asking who would like to play it. If several children want to play the same instrument, assist the group in deciding how to share it.
5. Explain that different cards will be held up and only the instruments that match the shapes should be played. Hold up the *STOP* card and ask the group what they are supposed to do when that card is held up; similarly, the *PASS* card, designating a direction in which to pass the instruments.
6. Hold up the *STOP* card and then begin playing the record. Hold up the shape cards singly and in combination. At various times, hold up the *PASS* card and the *STOP* card

III. Techniques and Modifications

If the group cannot guess the instrument by the shape on the card, give clues such as how it should be held, played, etc.

Resource
record player
"Spanish Flea": *Music for Movement Exploration* (L.P. 5090), Karol Lee, Educational Activities and Kimbo Educational Records
cymbals
finger cymbals
triangle
rhythm sticks
maracas
guiro
wood block
six 6- by 9-inch cards (construction paper) with the following words and shapes, one per card:

1) △   3) ▭   5) *STOP*
2) ○   4) ⬭   6) *PASS*

Cross Reference Objectives
Behavior 14
Communication 17
Socialization 19
Academics

S-20.3 Music Therapy Learning Experience

Developmental Therapy Objective S-20/to share materials, activities

Type of Activity	Area
(Listening)	Socialization
Playing	
Singing	Stage
(Moving)	I
(Creating)	II
Verbalizing	(III)
	IV

MUSIC ACTIVITY

I. Introduction

Direct the group to sit on the floor in a semicircle.

II. Implementation

1. Draw an imaginary circle in the air and ask the group what shape it is. Direct them to make their own circles as many different ways as they can. Imitate at least one shape created by each child.
2. Ask the group what other shapes they can make in the air and direct them to make the same shape in different ways. Suggest a square and a triangle.
3. Explain that some records will be played and that each one mentions an object. When the group determines what the object is, they are to stand up and work together to form the shape of the object. Give them an example, e.g., "If the song talks about a chair, what shape would you make?" (a square).
4. Play one record at a time directing the group to listen carefully. Listen for a few seconds until the object is mentioned, raise the needle, and ask the group to name the object mentioned and its shape.
5. Direct the group to stand and to work together to form the shape. Give clues, when necessary, as to how this can be done. After the shape has been made once, ask the group if they can think of another way to create the same shape.
6. Instruct them to sit on the floor and listen to the next record. Repeat steps 4 and 5.

III. Techniques and Modifications

Encourage the children to name songs which might be used in this activity. Talk about the object and direct the group to form the shape.

Resource
record player

"Does Your Chewing Gum Lose Its Flavor?" (45-15911), Lonnie Donegan, Dot Records, Inc., Hollywood, California

"Catch a Falling Star" (47-7128), Perry Como, RCA Victor, Camden, New Jersey

"Mashed Potato Time" (C-212), Dee Dee Sharp, Cameo Records

Cross Reference Objectives
Behavior 19
Communication 16
Socialization 18
Academics

Developmental Therapy Objective S-20/to share materials, activities

Type of Activity	Area
Listening	Socialization
(Playing)	
Singing	**Stage**
Moving	I
Creating	II
(Verbalizing)	

MUSIC ACTIVITY

I. Introduction

Instruct the group to sit at the

II. Implementation

1. Direct the group to name
the group is going to play to
2. Point out the color-co
organ, glockenspiel, tone
cards.
3. Direct the children to
procedure they will follo
4. Designate the area in
organize themselves, e
they will sit or stand, e
5. Begin the following
up the color cards in
direct their playing
particular card is h
Simultaneously en
rhythm combo ins
To practice when
to, first state tha
conductor stand
slightly upward
their instrumen
can play what
up the color card
in the "attention" posit

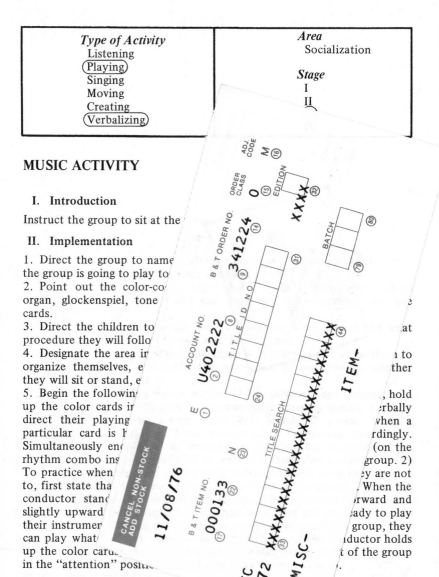

6. Stand in front of the group. Begin playing the record and hold up the cards according to the chord changes in the song. After several verses, have the children exchange instruments.
7. Repeat step 6 until all of the children have played several instruments.

III. Techniques and Modifications

1. On the glockenspiel and tone bells (both of which have moveable keys), group together the notes which compose each chord and slightly separate the three chords.
2. When practicing the "play/not play" aspect of conducting, express nonverbally an attitude of "I'm going to catch you," to create a game-like situation.
3. Present cue cards slightly before the chord changes need to be made.
4. If the group is not able to organize a system for exchanging instruments, it may be necessary to designate a procedure before the activity begins.

Resource
record player
"I Can't Help Myself": *Four Tops Greatest Hits—Volume I* (M5-662), Four Tops, Motown Record Co., Detroit, Michigan
chord organ
glockenspiel
tone bells
rhythm combo: large conga drum, tambourine, bongo drum
three 6- by 9-inch cards (construction paper), three different colors
small pieces of colored paper (the colors corresponding to the larger pieces) taped to the following groups of instrument keys: CEG = color 1; DFA = color 2; GBDF = color 3
Note: Do not use more than one color on a key.

Cross Reference Objectives
Behavior 11, 13, 14, 15, 19
Communication 15, 17, 18, 19
Socialization 18, 19
Academics 38

S-20.5 Music Therapy Learning Experience

Developmental Therapy Objective S-20/to share materials, activities

Type of Activity	Area
(Listening)	Socialization
Playing	
Singing	Stage
Moving	I
(Creating)	II
Verbalizing	(III)
	IV

MUSIC ACTIVITY

I. Introduction

Direct the group to sit on the floor in a circle.

II. Implementation

1. Explain to the children that they are going to create their own sound effects for a story.
2. Describe the six sound effects which are needed and ask for volunteers for each part. Tell the children that they can use rhythm instruments and/or vocal sounds to produce the sound effects. Also, a child can ask other group members to assist him in making a particular sound.
3. Have each child demonstrate how he will make his assigned sound effect.
4. Explain that cue cards will be used to indicate when each sound effect should occur. Show the cue cards and have the children read each one aloud.
5. Turn on the tape recorder. Hold up the first cue card and begin reading the story as the sound effect is heard.
6. Play back the tape and encourage the group members to discuss the sounds which are heard.

III. Techniques and Modifications

1. Hold up each cue card just before the sound is to be heard in order to give the child enough time to read the card.
2. If the children have difficulty reading the cue cards, point to each child when it is his turn to provide a sound effect.

Resource
tape recorder
"The Dream": Shelley Samet (Resource 7)
variety of rhythm instruments
six 6- by 9-inch cards (construction paper), one for each of the following: *birds; pounding; dogs; slam door; scream; "What is it? Where is it coming from?"*

Cross Reference Objectives
Behavior 11, 19
Communication 20
Socialization 18, 19
Academics 31, 35, 44, 48

Developmental Therapy Objective S-20/to share materials, activities

Type of Activity	*Area*
Listening	Socialization
Playing	
(Singing)	*Stage*
Moving	I
Creating	II
Verbalizing	(III)
	IV

MUSIC ACTIVITY

I. Introduction

Direct the group to sit on the floor in a circle.

II. Implementation

1. Show the children the chart on which is written the words of "Hey, Ho! Nobody Home." Sing the song several times and encourage the children to sing along.
2. Explain to the children what a musical round is and how it is sung. To demonstrate a round, begin playing the tape of "Hey, Ho! Nobody Home," which will serve as the first voice. Start singing at the point on the tape where the second voice of the round should enter. In this way, the children will be able to hear a round being sung.
3. Rewind the tape. Divide the children into two groups. One group will sing with the tape and the other group will sing with the music therapist. Start the tape and direct the first group to begin singing. Bring in the second group at the correct time.
4. Have the two groups attempt to sing the round without using the tape.

III. Techniques and Modifications

1. A mark can be placed on the word chart to indicate when the second group should begin singing.
2. To aid in the singing of the round, a leader can be designated for each group.
3. Suggest other rounds which the children can sing.

Resource

tape recorder

tape recording of "Hey, Ho! Nobody Home": *Songs For Fun And Fellowship—#2,* William Reynolds and Cecil McGee, Broadman Press, Nashville, Tennessee, 1961, p. 17

chart with words of "Hey, Ho! Nobody Home"

Cross Reference Objectives
Behavior 19
Communication 19
Socialization 18
Academics

S-21.1 Music Therapy Learning Experience

Developmental Therapy Objective S-21/to suggest activities or preference for play materials to the teacher for group activity

Type of Activity	Area
Listening	Socialization
(Playing)	
Singing	Stage
Moving	I
Creating	II
(Verbalizing)	(III)
	IV

MUSIC ACTIVITY

I. Introduction

Direct the children to sit on the floor in a circle.

II. Implementation

1. Tell the children that they will be able to suggest records and instruments to use in the music activity.
2. Encourage the group to discuss the possible choices for materials. Direct them to make suggestions concerning instruments and records to be used.
3. When the children have decided on the instruments which will be used, direct them to list them on the chalk board.
4. Using the group's suggestions, assign a different instrument to each child. Distribute cards and magic markers, directing the children to each write the name of his assigned instrument on his card.
5. Collect the magic markers and completed cards. Place the cards face down on the floor and instruct the children to each select one. Each child is to find the actual instrument which matches the name of the instrument on his card.
6. Begin playing the record which was selected by the group. Direct the children to play their instruments.
7. When the music stops, tell the children to trade cards and instruments with a child of their choice. Play the record again and direct the children to play their instruments.

III. Techniques and Modifications

The children may need assistance in making decisions about records and instruments to be used, e.g., suggest that the group members vote to settle a disagreement, etc.

Resource
record player
variety of familiar records
5- by 8-inch cards, one for each child
magic markers, one for each child
chalk board and chalk
variety of rhythm instruments

Cross Reference Objectives
Behavior
Communication 16
Socialization 20, 22, 23
Academics 35, 41

Developmental Therapy Objective S-22/to participate without inappropriate response to activity suggested by another child

Type of Activity	Area
Listening	Socialization
Playing	
Singing	Stage
(Moving)	I
Creating	II
Verbalizing	(III)
	IV

MUSIC ACTIVITY

I. Introduction

Direct the children to stand in a circle in the music area. They should be at least an arm's length from each other.

II. Implementation

1. Discuss with the children what is meant by moving in rhythm with the music. Tell them that they will each be able to lead the group in some exercises done in rhythm to the music.
2. Begin playing the record and lead the children in some movement exercises, e.g., jumping jacks, knee bends, etc. Help the children to keep a steady rhythm by counting as follows: "Jump-2-3-4-Jump-2-3-4" or "Bend-2-3-4-Bend-2-3-4."
3. Choose a child to lead the group in exercises of his choice. Encourage the other children to imitate his movements.
4. Give each child an opportunity to be the leader.

III. Techniques and Modifications

1. Encourage the leader to maintain a steady rhythm in his movements and to continue with each exercise until all of the children are doing it together.
2. Praise the group members for imitating movements suggested by the leader.
3. Encourage the leaders to create original movement sequences.

Resource
record player

"When I'm Sixty-Four": *Sgt. Pepper's Lonely Hearts Club Band* (2653), John Lennon and Paul Mc-Cartney, Capitol Records, Hollywood, California

Cross Reference Objectives
Behavior 12, 19, 20
Communication
Socialization 20, 26
Academics 39

S-22.2 Music Therapy Learning Experience

Developmental Therapy Objective S-22/to participate without inappropriate response to activity suggested by another child

Type of Activity	*Area*
(Listening)	Socialization
(Playing)	
Singing	*Stage*
(Moving)	I
(Creating)	II
Verbalizing	(III)
	IV

MUSIC ACTIVITY

I. Introduction

Instruct the group to sit at the table. Sit at the head of the table holding the drum.

II. Implementation

1. Ask for suggestions as to how different sounds can be made on the drum. If no suggestions are made, demonstrate such sounds as hitting the drum head, tapping the side, etc.
2. Ask for two volunteers to be leaders: one to lead the group around the room, "group leader"; and the other to conduct using the drum, "conductor." State that each child will have a chance to be a leader.
3. Explain that the conductor will play different sounds on his drum; when the group leader hears changes in the sound, he is to change his movement, e.g., walk, then slide, etc. The group is to imitate him. The conductor also has the option of not playing, in which case the group stops moving.
4. Demonstrate step 3.
5. Direct the group to line up behind the group leader and the conductor to stand away from the group. Instruct the conductor to begin playing the drum when the group is lined up.
6. Repeat step 5 until everyone has a turn being a group leader and/or conductor.

III. Techniques and Modifications

1. As the group is moving, suggest changes that the group leader can make, e.g., changes in direction of movement, type of movement, etc.
2. The order of turns can be determined at the beginning of the activity to minimize delay.

Resource
one conga drum

Cross Reference Objectives
Behavior 19, 20
Communication 19
Socialization 19, 20, 26
Academics 39

Developmental Therapy Objective S-22/to participate without inappropriate response to activity suggested by another child

Type of Activity	Area
Listening	Socialization
Playing	
Singing	Stage
Moving	I
(Creating)	II
(Verbalizing)	(III)
	IV

MUSIC ACTIVITY

I. Introduction

Direct the children to sit at the table while waiting for directions for the activity.

II. Implementation

1. Tell the children that they will have an opportunity to plan and pose for snapshots of music activities.
2. Show them slips of paper on which are written directions for the snapshots, e.g., *take a picture of children playing rhythm instruments, take a picture of a child playing the autoharp, etc.*
3. One at a time, each child chooses a slip of paper and plans the snapshot based on the instructions. The child tells the other children what to do in order to pose for the picture.
4. Snap the picture with the camera when the children are in the pose called for by the child who planned the picture.

III. Techniques and Modifications

1. Some children may need suggestions to help them decide how to arrange the other children for the snapshot.
2. Since this activity involves so many instruments and a wide variety of equipment, leave all music materials outside of the room and bring them in as they are needed for snapshots.
3. After the film has been developed, use the pictures to stimulate class discussion concerning the activity.

Resource
record player
camera
variety of rhythm instruments, at least one for each child
autoharp
guitar
tone bells
snare drum
slips of paper, each with instructions for a snapshot

Cross Reference Objectives
Behavior 19, 20
Communication 16
Socialization 18, 20, 23, 26
Academics 45, 50

S-23.1 Music Therapy Learning Experience

Developmental Therapy Objective S-23/to indicate developing friendship by preference for a particular child or children

Type of Activity	Area
Listening	Socialization
(Playing)	
Singing	Stage
Moving	I
Creating	II
(Verbalizing)	(III)
	IV

MUSIC ACTIVITY

I. Introduction

Direct the children to sit on the floor in a circle.

II. Implementation

1. Show the group the three types of drums. Encourage them to talk about the similarities and differences between the drums.
2. Tell the children that they are going to play the drums to accompany a record. Each time the music stops they are to choose a child with whom they can exchange drums.
3. Direct each child to take one of the drums. Begin playing the record.
4. Stop the music at various times and remind the children to exchange drums.
5. Continue with the activity until all of the children have had an opportunity to play the three different types of drums.

III. Techniques and Modifications

1. If the children have difficulty with the exchanging of drums, help them to develop procedures for the activity which will aid in this process.
2. Encourage the children to suggest other instruments and records which could be used in this activity.

Resource
record player
"Batman Theme": *The Batman Theme* (WS 1642), The Marketts, Warner Brothers Records, Hollywood, California
barrel drums
conga drums
bongo drums

Cross Reference Objectives
Behavior 12
Communication
Socialization 20
Academics

Developmental Therapy Objective S-24/to recognize and describe characteristics of others

Type of Activity	Area
(Listening)	Socalization
Playing	
(Singing)	*Stage*
Moving	I
Creating	II
(Verbalizing)	(III)
	IV

MUSIC ACTIVITY

I. Introduction

Direct the children to sit in their chairs at the table.

II. Implementation

1. Ask the children questions about echoes, such as "What are echoes?" "Where can you hear echoes?" etc.
2. Direct the children to raise their hands when they hear the echo part (hoo! hoo!) as the song is sung.
3. Sing the song again and ask the children to sing the echo part.
4. Tell the children that they will each have a turn being the echo and that the other children will try to determine who is the echo.
5. Blindfold one child who is seated at the table.
6. Point to another child who then walks quietly to the corner of the room.
7. Sing the song and at the echo part point to the child in the corner to sing the words "hoo! hoo!"
8. Ask the blindfolded child to describe the voice and to guess who was singing the echo part.
9. Repeat the procedure until each child has had a turn being blindfolded and being the echo.

III. Techniques and Modifications

1. Encourage the children to sing or say the echo part in their natural voice, and do not emphasize accurate intonation or rhythmic precision. Praise them for their individual responses.
2. Besides asking the blindfolded child to describe the voice of the child who is the echo, he might also be directed to describe how the child looks before saying his name.

> **Resource**
> "Hoo! Hoo!": *Making Music Your Own—Book K* (Teacher's Edition), Silver Burdett Co., Morristown, New Jersey, 1971, p. 25
> scarf for blindfold

> **Cross Reference Objectives**
> Behavior 19
> Communication
> Socialization 18, 19, 20
> Academics

S-25.1 Music Therapy Learning Experience

Developmental Therapy Objective S-25/to suggest appropriate group activity directly to peer group

Type of Activity	*Area*
Listening	Socialization
Playing	
Singing	*Stage*
Moving	I
(Creating)	II
(Verbalizing)	III
	(IV)

MUSIC ACTIVITY

I. Introduction

Direct the group to sit on the floor in a circle.

II. Implementation

1. Tell the children that they are going to plan their own music activities. Discuss the music materials which they will be able to use.
2. Give each child a turn in planning and directing a short music activity.

III. Techniques and Modifications

1. Present ideas and suggestions and guide the children in establishing procedures to facilitate the implementation of their activities.
2. Setting a time limit for each activity will encourage the children to make efficient use of their allotted time and will assure each child of having a turn.
3. Encourage the children to modify and build upon activities with which they are familiar.

Resource
record player
tape recorder
variety of records
variety of rhythm instruments
poster paper
magic markers

Cross Reference Objectives
Behavior 19, 20, 25
Communication 24, 25, 26
Socialization 26, 30
Academics 52

Developmental Therapy Objective S-30/to participate in group planning and constructive problem solving

Type of Activity	Area
Listening	Socialization
Playing	
Singing	*Stage*
(Moving)	I
(Creating)	II
(Verbalizing)	III
	(IV)

MUSIC ACTIVITY

I. Introduction

Direct the group to sit on the floor in a circle.

II. Implementation

1. Lead the children in a discussion about machines, e.g., name different types of machines, talk about components of machines, etc.
2. Tell the children that they will use members of the group to create "music machines."
3. Instruct the children to stand in a circle. Begin playing the music and form the first "music machine" by giving each child a specific repetitive movement to perform with the music. The movements should be planned in such a way that the group members will seem to be working together as "parts of a machine," e.g., children stand in a circle with their hands on the shoulders of the children on either side of them; every alternate child is directed to bend his knees in an up and down movement while the other children move their heads from side to side in rhythm with the music.
4. Direct the group to work together to create other "music machines." Allow them to select the music which they wish to use for each machine.

III. Techniques and Modifications

1. Encourage all of the children to make suggestions and help them to build on each other's ideas.
2. Allow the children to select music for the activity from a variety of records, e.g., popular, classical, etc.

Resource
record player
variety of familiar records

Cross Reference Objectives
Behavior 19
Communication 25
Socialization 25
Academics 52

A-5.1 Music Therapy Learning Experience

Developmental Therapy Objective A-5/to respond with rudimentary fine motor skill to simple manipulative tasks associated with two-year level

Type of Activity	*Area*
Listening	Academics
Playing	
Singing	*Stage*
Moving	Ⓘ
(Creating)	II
Verbalizing	III
	IV

MUSIC ACTIVITY

I. Introduction

Direct the children to sit at the table.

II. Implementation

1. Place a piece of drawing paper on the table in front of each child.
2. Hold a magic marker in front of a child and give it to him as he makes a verbal response, reaches for the marker, or gives some other indication that he wants the marker.
3. Repeat step 2 until each child has a magic marker.
4. Show the children how to make lines on the paper with vertical strokes.
5. Begin singing the "Drawing Song" while helping each child to make vertical strokes on his paper.

III. Techniques and Modifications

1. Praise the children for any attempts made at drawing lines. The quality of the response is not as important as is an independent response.
2. Provide a model for the children by moving around the table and drawing lines on each child's paper.
3. If a child does not hold the magic marker or make any attempt to use it, place the marker in his hand and gently move it in drawing lines on the paper.
4. This activity can also include drawing circular lines.

Resource
"Drawing Song": Jennie Purvis (Resource 6)

drawing paper, several sheets for each child and music therapist

magic markers, one for each child and music therapist

Cross Reference Objectives
Behavior 2, 4
Communication 1, 2, 4
Socialization 1, 2, 4
Academics 2, 4, 6, 9

Developmental Therapy Objective A-6/to imitate words or action of adult upon request

Type of Activity	*Area*
Listening	Academics
(Playing)	
Singing	*Stage*
Moving	(I)
Creating	II
(Verbalizing)	III
	IV

MUSIC ACTIVITY

I. Introduction

Direct the children to sit on the floor facing the music therapist.

II. Implementation

1. Show the children how to play the tambourine by striking various body parts, e.g., hand, knee, elbow, etc.
2. Hold a tambourine in front of a child and tell him to say, "tambourine." Give the child the instrument when he says "tambourine" or an approximation of the word.
3. Repeat step 2 for each child. When all of the children have received tambourines, sing the "Tambourine Song" and lead the children in using various body parts to play the tambourine as directed by the words of the song.

III. Techniques and Modifications

1. If a child does not have the language skills which will enable him to make a verbal response, give him the tambourine when he reaches for it or when he makes some other motor response which indicates that he wants the instrument.
2. When singing the "Tambourine Song," be certain that each child is hitting his instrument with the correct body part before moving to the next verse.
3. Before beginning each verse of the song, verbally direct the children to point to the body part which will be used in the next verse. Say the name of the body part while showing the children its location.

Resource
"Tambourine Song": Jennie Purvis
(Resource 23)

tambourines, one for each child and music therapist

Cross Reference Objectives
Behavior 1, 2, 4
Communication 1, 2, 3, 4, 5, 7
Socialization 1, 2, 4, 8, 10
Academics 1, 2, 3, 4, 5, 8, 9,
12, 17

A-7.1 Music Therapy Learning Experience

Developmental Therapy Objective A-7/to respond by simple discrimination of objects

Type of Activity	Area
(Listening)	Academics
Playing	
Singing	Stage
Moving	(I)
Creating	II
Verbalizing	III
	IV

MUSIC ACTIVITY

I. Introduction

Direct the children to sit on the floor in a semicircle facing the music therapist. Place the shaker (maraca) and triangle on the floor in front of the children.

II. Implementation

1. Point to each instrument and ask the children what it is called. If they do not respond, tell them the name of each instrument.
2. Pick up both instruments and hold them in front of a child. Say, "Point to the shaker." If the child does not respond or points to the wrong instrument, help him to make the correct choice by placing the shaker close to him and saying, "Here is the shaker, point to it." When the child points to the instrument, allow him to play it.
3. Use this same procedure for each child, requesting the child to point to either the shaker or the triangle.
4. Repeat steps 1 to 3 using other familiar rhythm instruments.

III. Techniques and Modifications

1. Use only instruments with which the children have had previous experience. In order for this activity to be successful, the children must know the name of each instrument which is used.
2. To demonstrate the "pointing" motion: 1) provide a model by having a teacher discriminate between the instruments by pointing, or 2) take a child's hand and place it on the instrument in a pointing motion.

Resource
maraca (shaker)
triangle
variety of rhythm instruments with which the children are familiar

Cross Reference Objectives
Behavior 1, 2, 4, 9
Communication 1, 2
Socialization 1, 2, 7, 14
Academics 1, 2, 4, 10

Developmental Therapy Objective A-7/to respond by simple discrimination of objects

Type of Activity	Area
(Listening)	Academics
(Playing)	
Singing	Stage
Moving	(I)
Creating	II
Verbalizing	III
	IV

MUSIC ACTIVITY

I. Introduction

Instruct the children to sit on the floor facing the music therapist. Place the box of instruments (jingle bells and tambourines) in front of the children.

II. Implementation

1. Hold up a set of jingle bells and ask the children what instrument it is. When a child correctly names the instrument, repeat his answer to the group. Return the jingle bells to the box.
2. Put the box of jingle bells and tambourines on the floor in front of a child. Tell him to look into the box and find a set of jingle bells.
3. Repeat step 2 until each child has a set of jingle bells.
4. Tell the children to play their jingle bells over their heads, simultaneously demonstrating the action. Begin singing the song, playing the jingle bells "up in the air" or "down on the floor" as the song indicates.
5. Instruct the children to put their instruments back in the box. Repeat steps 1 to 4 using the tambourines.

III. Techniques and Modifications

1. If a child is not able to discriminate between the two types of instruments, help him to make the correct choice by placing his hand on the appropriate instrument.
2. When changing the position of the instrument (up in the air/down on the floor), modify the song tempo so that each child will have enough time to do the appropriate action.
3. If a child does not move his instrument up and down when given the verbal and visual cues, move his arms accordingly.

Resource
"Up in the Air": Shelley Samet (Resource 24)

jingle bells, one for each child and music therapist

tambourines, one for each child and music therapist

box

Cross Reference Objectives
Behavior 1, 2, 4, 9
Communication 1, 2, 9
Socialization 1, 2, 3, 4, 13, 14
Academics 1, 2, 4, 6

A-10.1 Music Therapy Learning Experience

Developmental Therapy Objective A-10/to indicate short term memory for objects and people

Type of Activity	Area
Listening	Academics
(Playing)	
Singing	**Stage**
Moving	(I)
Creating	II
(Verbalizing)	III
	IV

MUSIC ACTIVITY

I. Introduction

Direct the children to sit on the floor facing the music therapist.

II. Implementation

1. Show the children the sand blocks and ask them what they are called. If they do not respond, tell them to say "sand blocks." Repeat this procedure using the drum.
2. Put the sand blocks and drum on the floor in front of the children. Cover one of the instruments with the handkerchief while saying to the children, "Look! I'm hiding something!"
3. Ask one child what is under the handkerchief. As the child says the name of the instrument, remove the handkerchief and allow him to play it.
4. Repeat steps 2 and 3 for each child.

III. Techniques and Modifications

1. Use instruments with which the children are familiar.
2. If a child is not able to say what is hidden, remove the handkerchief and ask him to name the instrument.
3. A sequel to this activity might be to have the children close their eyes as one instrument is covered with the handkerchief.

Resource
one pair of sand blocks
one hand drum
one large handkerchief

Cross Reference Objectives
Behavior 2, 4
Communication 3, 4, 5, 7, 8
Socialization 2, 8, 10
Academics 2, 4, 6, 7, 8, 9

Developmental Therapy Objective A-11/to respond with classification of similar objects with different attributes

Type of Activity	Area
Listening	Academics
(Playing)	
Singing	*Stage*
Moving	I
Creating	II
Verbalizing	III
	IV

MUSIC ACTIVITY

I. Introduction

Direct the children to sit in a semicircle on the floor. Place the rhythm instruments in the middle of the semicircle.

II. Implementation

1. Hold up a picture of an instrument and select a child to pick up the rhythm instrument which corresponds to the drawing.
2. Repeat step 1 until all of the children are holding an instrument.
3. Direct the children to begin playing together while singing "Play the Band."

III. Techniques and Modifications

1. Use rhythm instruments with which the children are familiar.
2. After a child has picked up the correct instrument, encourage the other children to say its name. If the child has difficulty selecting the matching instruments, cue him by saying the name of the instrument.

Resource
"Play the Band": Clementine Gigliotti (Resource 21)
triangle
maracas
rhythm sticks
cow bell
other rhythm instruments with which the children are familiar
cards, each with a drawing of one of the instruments used in the activity (number of cards should correspond to the number of instruments used)

Cross Reference Objectives
Behavior 4
Communication 2
Socialization 7
Academics 4, 7

A-12.1 Music Therapy Learning Experience

Developmental Therapy Objective A-12/to indicate short term memory for verbal expressions

Type of Activity	Area
Listening	Academics
(Playing)	
Singing	Stage
(Moving)	(I)
Creating	II
(Verbalizing)	III
	IV

MUSIC ACTIVITY

I. Introduction

Direct the children to sit on the floor in a semicircle facing the music therapist.

II. Implementation

1. Hold a drum in front of each child and say, "What do you want?" As the child says "I want drum," give him the instrument.
2. When each child has a drum, stand up and begin playing the drum while moving the feet in a marching movement (marching in place). Tell the children to stand up and play the drum.
3. When all of the children are standing begin marching around the roon while playing the drum. Encourage the children to follow the movements.
4. Lead the children back to where they were sitting on the floor.

III. Techniques and Modifications

1. If in step 1 a child does not respond with the correct verbal expression, tell him what to say by verbalizing the exact words he is to imitate.
2. Introduce this learning experience after the children have had practice in both marching and in playing the drum as separate activities.
3. Marching music can be used to accompany this activity.

Resource
hand drums, one for each child and
music therapist

Cross Reference Objectives
Behavior 4
Communication 3, 4, 5. 7
Socialization 4, 7, 8, 10, 13
Academics 4, 6, 8, 9, 13

Developmental Therapy Objective A-13/to perform body coordination tasks at the three/four year level

Type of Activity	Area
(Listening)	Academics
Playing	
Singing	Stage
(Moving)	(I)
Creating	II
Verbalizing	III
	IV

MUSIC ACTIVITY

I. Introduction

Direct the children to stand up for the "Train Song."

II. Implementation

1. Ask each teacher to place his hands on the shoulders of a child while standing behind the child.
2. When the music begins, encourage the children to slide their feet and make train sounds. Each adult should guide a child around the room while keeping his hands on the child's shoulders.
3. Verbally reflect the children's actions, e.g., "We're making a train."
4. When the music stops, direct the children back to their seats.

III. Techniques and Modifications

1. As the children become familiar with this activity, several children can form a "train" together.
2. When moving with a child around the room, frequently change direction of movement and verbally reflect the child's actions in order to keep him alert and aware of his movements.

Resource
record player

"Train Song": *More Learning As We Play* (FC 7658), David Ginglend and Winifred Stiles, Folkways Records, New York, New York

Cross Reference Objectives
Behavior 4
Communication
Socialization 4, 13
Academics 4

A-13.2 Music Therapy Learning Experience

Developmental Therapy Objective A-13/to perform body coordination tasks at the three/four-year level

Type of Activity	Area
Listening	Academics
Playing	
Singing	Stage
(Moving)	I
Creating	II
Verbalizing	III
	IV

MUSIC ACTIVITY

I. Introduction

Direct the children to stand in a circle and hold hands.

II. Implementation

1. Sing the words of the song while leading the children in the designated actions. Movements include going around in a circle, standing on one foot, and jumping up and down.
2. After each new movement, repeat the first verse, i.e., going 'round the circle.

III. Techniques and Modifications

1. If a child has difficulty with a movement, physically assist him with the action.
2. Adapt the tempo of the song to match the speed at which the children are able to perform the movements.

Resource
"Circle Song": Clementine Gigliotti
(Resource 4)

Cross Reference Objectives
Behavior 4
Communication 2
Socialization 4
Academics 4, 6

Developmental Therapy Objective A-13/to perform body coordination tasks at the three/four-year level

Type of Activity	*Area*
Listening	Academics
Playing	
Singing	*Stage*
(Moving)	①
Creating	II
Verbalizing	III
	IV

MUSIC ACTIVITY

I. Introduction

Direct the children to stand in a circle.

II. Implementation

1. Begin playing "Johnny Comes Marching Home" on the record player. Demonstrate how to march in place while verbalizing, "I'm marching."
2. Direct the children to begin marching in place. Encourage them to pick up their feet very high and swing their arms.
3. Continue marching in place until the end of the music.

III. Techniques and Modifications

1. It may be necessary to help some children by picking up their legs and moving them in a marching motion.
2. Frequently remind the children to pick up their feet and swing their arms. Also encourage them to stamp their feet as they march in order to emphasize the marching movements.
3. Verbally reflect the children's actions, e.g., "We're marching."
4. After the children have practiced marching in place, lead them in marching around the room.

Resource
record player

"Johnny Comes Marching Home":
More Learning As We Play (FC 7658), David Ginglend and Winifred Stiles, Folkways Records, New York, New York

Cross Reference Objectives
Behavior 4
Communication 1, 2
Socialization 2, 4, 13
Academics 4, 6, 17

A-14.1 Music Therapy Learning Experience

Developmental Therapy Objective A-14/to match similar pictures

Type of Activity	Area
Listening	Academics
Playing	
Singing	Stage
(Moving)	Ⓘ
Creating	II
Verbalizing	III
	IV

MUSIC ACTIVITY

I. Introduction

Direct the children to sit at the table.

II. Implementation

1. Give a set of cards with instrument pictures (drums, triangles, bells) to each child.
2. Place a card with the picture of a drum in front of the children and say, "Find all of the pictures like this."
3. Assist each child in finding all of the drum pictures in his set of cards. Show the children how to sort the cards so that all of the drum pictures are together.
4. Repeat steps 2 and 3 using the picture of the triangle or the bells.

III. Techniques and Modifications

Introduce this activity after the children have had experience using the actual instruments and are able to match the pictures with the corresponding instruments.

Resource
3- by 5-inch instrument picture cards, one set for each child and music therapist (each set consists of nine cards: three pictures of drums, three pictures of triangles, three pictures of bells).

Cross Reference Objectives
Behavior 4
Communication 9
Socialization
Academics 4, 7

Developmental Therapy Objective A-15/to indicate recognition of color names with the correct response

Type of Activity	Area
(Listening)	Academics
(Playing)	
Singing	Stage
Moving	(I)
Creating	II
Verbalizing	III
	IV

MUSIC ACTIVITY

I. Introduction

Direct the children to sit on the floor facing the music therapist.

II. Implementation

1. Show the children the red rhythm sticks. Say, "What color are the sticks?" If the children do not respond, tell them the color of the sticks and direct them to say, "red."
2. Repeat step 1 using the green rhythm sticks.
3. Hold both pairs of sticks (red and green) in front of one child. Direct him to take the red sticks.
4. Repeat step 3 until each child has a pair of red rhythm sticks.
5. Play the sticks and sing "Play the Band."

III. Techniques and Modifications

If a child is not able to choose the red rhythm sticks, put his hands on the red sticks and say, "Here are the red sticks."

Resource
"Play the Band": Clementine Gigliotti (Resource 21)
red rhythm sticks, one pair for each child and music therapist
one pair of green rhythm sticks

Cross Reference Objectives
Behavior 4
Communication 1, 2
Socialization 1, 2, 7
Academics 4

A-15.2 Music Therapy Learning Experience

Developmental Therapy Objective A-15/to indicate recognition of color names with the correct response

Type of Activity	Area
Listening	Academics
(Playing)	
Singing	Stage
Moving	(I)
Creating	II
Verbalizing	III
	IV

MUSIC ACTIVITY

I. Introduction

Direct the children to sit on the floor in a semicircle around the toy piano.

II. Implementation

1. Point to the red keys on the toy piano. Direct the children to say "red."
2. Play the red piano keys while verbalizing, "I'm playing the red keys."
3. Direct each child to play the red keys.

III. Techniques and Modifications

1. Space the red keys so that several white keys are between each red key. In this way, the children will need to look over the entire keyboard to find the red keys.
2. When the children are able to recognize the red keys, introduce other colors, e.g., blue keys, yellow keys, etc.
3. After the children are familiar with this activity, use two or more colors at the same time, e.g., red, blue, and yellow keys. This will make it necessary for the children to discriminate between the colors.

Resource
toy piano
five red note-shaped pieces of paper taped over five of the white keys on the piano
tape

Cross Reference Objectives
Behavior 4, 9
Communication 2
Socialization 7, 14
Academics 4, 5

Developmental Therapy Objective A-16/to perform eye-hand coordination activities at the four-year level

Type of Activity	Area
Listening	Academics
(Playing)	
Singing	Stage
Moving	(I)
Creating	II
(Verbalizing)	III
	IV

MUSIC ACTIVITY

I. Introduction

Direct the children to sit on the floor in a semicircle. Place the tone bells in front of them. (Put the bells side by side, leaving approximately 1 inch between each bell.)

II. Implementation

1. Ask the children to name the instrument in front of them. If they do not respond, tell them to say "bells."
2. Play each bell and sing "bong," matching the pitch of the bell.
3. Tell the children to ask for the bells. When a child says "bells," "I want the bells," etc., give him the mallet and place the five tone bells in front of him.
4. After the child has had an opportunity to play the bells in any manner that he wishes, point to each bell and say, "Play this one." As the child strikes each bell, sing "bong," matching the pitch of the bell.
5. Repeat steps 3 and 4 until each child has had a turn.

III. Techniques and Modifications

1. If a child has difficulty hitting the tone bells with the mallet, take his hand/mallet and guide it slowly to a bell. Repeat this several times until the child is able to strike the bell.
2. Sing "bong" at the same tempo with which a child strikes each tone bell.
3. Any attempt made by the children to sing "bong" should be praised. The correctness of the response is not the primary concern for this stage of therapy.

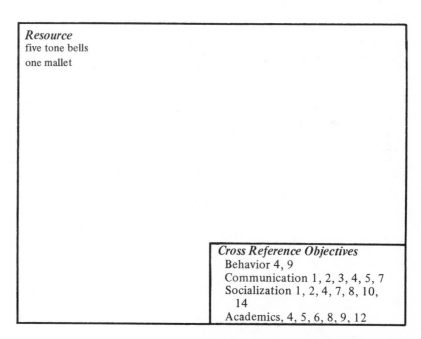

Resource
five tone bells
one mallet

Cross Reference Objectives
Behavior 4, 9
Communication 1, 2, 3, 4, 5, 7
Socialization 1, 2, 4, 7, 8, 10, 14
Academics, 4, 5, 6, 8, 9, 12

A-16.2 Music Therapy Learning Experience

Developmental Therapy Objective A-16/to perform eye-hand coordination activities at the four-year level

Type of Activity	Area
Listening	Academics
Playing	
Singing	**Stage**
(Moving)	Ⓘ
Creating	II
(Verbalizing)	III
	IV

MUSIC ACTIVITY

I. Introduction

Direct the children to sit on the floor in the music area.

II. Implementation

1. Show the children the shirts. Direct each child to ask for a shirt. When a child makes the required verbalization, give him a shirt.
2. When all of the children have shirts, say to them, "Let's put on our shirts!" If necessary, assist them in putting on the shirts.
3. Say to the children, "Let's button our shirts." Begin singing the "Button-Up Song" and demonstrate how to button a shirt. Encourage the children to button their shirts. Give physical assistance when necessary.
4. When all of the children have their shirts buttoned, tell them to unbutton the shirts.
5. Sing the song again, repeating step 3.

III. Techniques and Modifications

1. Use shirts which have large buttons and buttonholes. Try to find shirts which are large enough to fit easily over the children's regular clothes.
2. If a child has difficulty buttoning, hold each buttonhole open so that he can easily slip the buttons through the holes.

Resource
"Button-Up Song": Jennie Purvis (Resource 3)

shirts (with buttons and button-holes), one for each child and music therapist

Cross Reference Objectives
Behavior 4, 5
Communication 1, 2, 3, 4, 5, 7
Socialization 1, 2, 4, 8, 10
Academics 4, 6, 8, 9

Developmental Therapy Objective A-17/to recognize own body parts

Type of Activity	*Area*
(Listening)	Academics
Playing	
Singing	*Stage*
(Moving)	(I)
Creating	II
Verbalizing	III
	IV

MUSIC ACTIVITY

I. Introduction

Direct the children to stand in a circle holding hands.

II. Implementation

1. Begin singing the refrain of "Looby Loo" and lead the children in circling to the left.
2. Stop moving and drop hands. Sing the first verse using "hands" as the body part which is put into the circle. (Do not specify "left" hand or "right" hand.) Follow this verse with the refrain as explained in step 1.
3. Repeat step 2 using other body parts, e.g., head, feet, whole body, etc.

III. Techniques and Modifications

1. Sing the song at a tempo which will allow the children enough time to perform the various movements.
2. The refrain can be omitted if the children have difficulty holding hands and moving in a circle.

Resource
"Looby Loo": *Exploring Music—Book 1* (Teacher's Edition), Holt, Rinehart and Winston, Inc., New York, New York, 1971, p. 18

Cross Reference Objectives
Behavior 4
Communication
Socialization 4, 6, 13
Academics 4, 6

A-17.2 Music Therapy Learning Experience

Developmental Therapy Objective A-17/to recognize own body parts

Type of Activity	Area
(Listening)	Academics
Playing	
Singing	*Stage*
(Moving)	(I)
Creating	II
Verbalizing	III
	IV

MUSIC ACTIVITY

I. Introduction

Direct the children to sit on the floor in a semicircle facing the music therapist.

II. Implementation

1. Give the children directions for touching a finger to various body parts, e.g., "Put your finger on your nose."
2. Assist the children in finding the correct body part, e.g., point to a child's body part, take a child's hand and place it on the correct body part.
3. Sing the song "Just Like Me" and lead the children in touching the correct body parts as directed in the song.

III. Techniques and Modifications

1. Before beginning the song it may be helpful to stand with the children in front of a mirror and show them the location of various body parts.
2. If some children have difficulty finding their own body parts, help them to point to the body parts on another child.

Resource
"Just Like Me": Jennie Purvis (Resource 14)

Cross Reference Objectives
Behavior 4
Communication 1, 2, 9
Socialization 1, 2, 4, 7
Academics 4, 6

Developmental Therapy Objective A-18/to recognize uses of objects, toys, etc.

Type of Activity	Area
Listening	Academics
(Playing)	
Singing	Stage
Moving	I
Creating	(II)
(Verbalizing)	III
	IV

MUSIC ACTIVITY

I. Introduction

Direct the children to sit in their chairs in the music area.

II. Implementation

1. Hold the jingle bells in front of the children and ask what they are and how they are used. Direct the children to show how the bells are played.
2. Repeat step 1 using a cow bell.
3. Instruct the children to each ask for the type of bell they prefer to play.
4. When each child has a bell, begin singing the song and lead the children in playing the bells.

III. Techniques and Modifications

1. Encourage the children to use words to describe how each type of bell should be played.
2. For a sequel to this activity, show the children pictures of various musical instruments and have them discuss how each one is played.

Resource
"Ring, Bells, Ring": *Exploring Music—Book K* (Teacher's Edition), Holt, Rinehart and Winston, Inc., New York, New York, 1969, p. 149

cow bells

jingle bells
(at least one instrument per child)

Cross Reference Objectives
Behavior 8, 11
Communication 8, 12
Socialization 13
Academics

A-19.1 Music Therapy Learning Experience

Developmental Therapy Objective A-19/to recognize detail in pictures by gesture or word

Type of Activity	*Area*
Listening	Academics
(Playing)	
(Singing)	*Stage*
(Moving)	I
(Creating)	(II)
(Verbalizing)	III
	IV

MUSIC ACTIVITY

I. Introduction

Direct the children to form a train to the zoo (music area).

II. Implementation

1. Show the children the picture of the zoo animals. Have each child name any one animal and then the characteristic that tells them what it is, e.g., elephant—long trunk. When a characteristic is mentioned, mimic the animal using various body parts, e.g., elephant's long trunk—clasp hands, stretch arms forward, and swing them.
2. Tell the children that they are going to sing a song about the zoo animals, and that when they hear ". . . the little (*animal name*) looks (or sounds) like this, _____," they are to mimic the characteristic of the animal or make the appropriate sound, whichever is designated in the song.
3. Direct one child to select an animal to be sung about and have him demonstrate the appropriate characteristic or sound.
4. Instruct him to strum the guitar strings with the pick. As the child strums the strings, finger the appropriate chords and begin singing the song using the child's suggestion. Encourage the other children to sing and make the appropriate body movement or animal sound.
5. Repeat steps 3 and 4, directing each child to pass the guitar and pick to the next child when his turn is over.

III. Techniques and Modifications

1. If the children suggest zoo animals for the song other than those shown in the picture, use their ideas.
2. If a child is unable to verbally or visually describe an animal's characteristics, make the appropriate movement or sound and verbally and visually associate it with the animal name.

3. A decision about whether to mimic a characteristic of an animal or to use an animal sound in the song will depend upon which is more familiar to the children and easier to do, e.g., use the arm motions mimicking the movement of an elephant trunk rather than the sound of the elephant; use a "roaring" sound to represent a lion.

Resource
"Zoo Sights and Sounds": Shelley Samet (Resource 27)
guitar
pick
a picture of several zoo animals

Cross Reference Objectives
Behavior 9, 12
Communication 8, 11, 12
Socialization 14, 16
Academics

Developmental Therapy Objective A-19/to recognize detail in pictures by gesture or word

Type of Activity	Area
Listening	Academics
Playing	
Singing	Stage
(Moving)	I
Creating	(II)
Verbalizing	III
	IV

MUSIC ACTIVITY

I. Introduction

Direct the children to sit on the floor in a semicircle facing the music therapist.

II. Implementation

1. Show the children the picture of the hand. Tell them the name of each finger. Ask various children to point to specific fingers on the picture.
2. Direct the children to each hold up a hand. Point to each finger on the picture and have the children find the corresponding finger on their own hand.
3. Tell the children to listen to the song and to make each finger "dance" at the appropriate time. Begin playing the record. Perform the finger movements as indicated in the words of the song.

III. Techniques and Modifications

1. Assist the children in holding up the hand which corresponds with the picture, i.e., if the picture is that of a left hand, then the children should each hold up their left hand.
2. To assist the children in finding the correct fingers, point to the fingers in the picture as the directions are given in the song.

Resource
record player
"Dance Thumbkin": *Folk Song Carnival* (AR524), Hap Palmer, Educational Activities, Inc., Freeport, New York
picture of a hand with each finger labeled as follows: thumb, *thumbkin;* index finger, *foreman;* middle finger, *longman;* ring finger, *ringman;* little finger, *littleman*

Cross Reference Objectives
Behavior 11
Communication
Socialization 13
Academics 17, 21

A-20.1 Music Therapy Learning Experience

Developmental Therapy Objective A-20/to rote count to ten

Type of Activity	Area
Listening	Academics
(Playing)	
(Singing)	Stage
Moving	I
Creating	(II)
(Verbalizing)	III
	IV

MUSIC ACTIVITY

I. Introduction

Direct the children to sit in their chairs in the music area.

II. Implementation

1. Tell the children that they will hear a song about ten angels. Direct them to count to ten.
2. Place a rhythm instrument on the floor in front of each child's chair. Tell the children that each time during the band section (chorus) of the song they will be able to play the instruments in a band.
3. Begin singing the verse of the song. Encourage the children to sing the numbers from one to ten at the appropriate time.
4. Immediately before beginning the chorus of the song, instruct the children to pick up their instruments and play them. At the end of the chorus, tell them to put their instruments back on the floor.
5. Sing the song several times, repeating steps 3 and 4.

III. Techniques and Modifications

For a sequel to this activity, show the children a picture of ten angels and ask them to count them. Sing the song and give each child a turn in pointing to the angels.

Resource
"The Angel Band": *Making Music Your Own—Book 1* (Teacher's Edition), Silver Burdett Co., Morristown, New Jersey, 1971, pp. 62–63

variety of rhythm instruments, one instrument for each child

Cross Reference Objectives
Behavior 11, 12
Communication
Socialization
Academics

Developmental Therapy Objective A-21/to count with one-to-one correspondence to five

Type of Activity	Area
(Listening)	Academics
Playing	
(Singing)	***Stage***
Moving	I
Creating	(II)
(Verbalizing)	III
	IV

MUSIC ACTIVITY

I. Introduction

Direct the children to sit in their chairs at the table.

II. Implementation

1. Show the children a picture of a turkey and ask questions, such as, "How do turkeys look?" "Where do you find turkeys?" etc.
2. Give each of five children a picture of a turkey. Instruct them to count the turkeys as they are distributed.
3. Sing the first verse of "Five Fat Turkeys." At the end of the first verse direct the child holding turkey number 1 to make it "fly away" by holding it out of sight under the table. Instruct the children to count the remaining turkeys.
4. Sing the second verse of the song and direct the child with turkey number 2 to make it "fly away" under the table. Have the children count the remaining turkeys.
5. Repeat this procedure for the remaining three turkeys.
6. Redistribute the turkey pictures to those children who have not had the opportunity to participate. Again ask the children to count the turkeys as they are distributed. Repeat steps 3 to 5.

III. Techniques and Modifications

1. The turkey pictures can be made by the children; e.g., have the children trace around their hands with fingers spread apart to produce an outline which resembles a turkey shape.
2. If more than five children are in the group, encourage the children who are not holding turkeys to sing the song and to hold up the correct number of fingers after each verse to indicate how many turkeys are left.

3. This activity can be modified to include something other than turkeys, e.g., dogs, children, etc.; also, more objects than five can be used, e.g., "Ten Fat Turkeys," etc.

Resource
"Five Fat Turkeys": *Exploring Music—Book K* (Teacher's Edition), Holt, Rinehart and Winston, Inc., New York, New York, 1969, p. 144
five pictures of a turkey, with numbers 1 to 5 written on them with one number per turkey

Cross Reference Objectives
Behavior 9, 11
Communication 8, 9
Socialization 14, 19
Academics

A-21.2 Music Therapy Learning Experience

Developmental Therapy Objective A-21/to count with one-to-one correspondence to five

Type of Activity	Area
(Listening)	Academics
(Playing)	
Singing	Stage
Moving	I
Creating	(II)
(Verbalizing)	III
	IV

MUSIC ACTIVITY

I. Introduction

Direct the children to sit in their chairs in a semicircle. Place the snare drum in front of them.

II. Implementation

1. Tell the children to listen as the drum is played and to count the number of drum strokes which they hear.
2. Strike the drum one, two, three, four, or five times. Ask the children how many times the drum is played. Repeat this procedure playing a different number of drum strokes each time.
3. Give each child a turn to play the drum. Whisper to a child how many times to strike the drum (from one to five times). Direct the other children to listen and count the number of times the child strikes the drum.

III. Techniques and Modifications

1. It may be necessary to help the children strike the drum the correct number of times.
2. Encourage the children to count aloud as the drum strokes are heard.
3. After the children have developed skill in this activity, use from five to ten drum strokes.

Resource
snare drum and one drum stick

Cross Reference Objectives
Behavior 9, 11, 12
Communication
Socialization 14
Academics

Developmental Therapy Objective A-22/to name colors(black, purple, orange, green)

Type of Activity	Area
Listening	Academics
Playing	
(Singing)	Stage
Moving	I
Creating	(II)
(Verbalizing)	III
	IV

MUSIC ACTIVITY

I. Introduction

Direct the children to sit on the floor in a circle.

II. Implementation

1. Show the children the bag of plastic fruits and vegetables. Select a child to reach into the bag and pull out one of the food items to show to the group.
2. Ask the children the name and color of the fruit or vegetable which was chosen.
3. Instruct the children to pass the fruit or vegetable around the circle while singing the "Passing Song." Direct the last child to put the item back into the bag.
4. Repeat steps 1 to 3 until each child has had an opportunity to choose a fruit or vegetable.

III. Techniques and Modifications

1. Encourage the children to talk about their favorite foods.
2. A variety of objects can be used in the "Passing Song," e.g., buttons, crayons, rhythm instruments, etc.

Resource
"Passing Song": Jennie Purvis, (Resource 20)
plastic fruits and vegetables (orange, apple, grapes, pepper, corn)
bag

Cross Reference Objectives
Behavior 9, 11
Communication 8, 12
Socialization 14, 16, 18, 19
Academics 18

A-23.1 Music Therapy Learning Experience

Developmental Therapy Objective A-23/to count with one-to-one correspondence to ten

Type of Activity	Area
Listening	Academics
Playing	
(Singing)	Stage
Moving	I
Creating	(II)
(Verbalizing)	III
	IV

MUSIC ACTIVITY

I. Introduction

Direct the children to sit on the floor in a semicircle facing the music therapist.

II. Implementation

1. Show the children the picture of the sky with the ten stars. Choose one child to count the stars. Then, point to the stars and have all of the children count them together.

2. Tell the children to listen to a song about stars. Sing "Twinkle, Twinkle, Little Star." Sing the song again and encourage the children to sing along.

III. Techniques and Modifications

1. This activity can be modified to include different numbers of stars to be counted. Also, the stars can be arranged in groups to determine whether the children can recognize the number of stars by the groupings used instead of counting with one-to-one correspondence.

2. As a sequel to this activity, have the children pretend that they are stars twinkling in the sky, e.g., children stand with arms above head and wiggle their fingers.

Resource
"Twinkle, Twinkle, Little Star":
Teacher's Guide to the Open Court Kindergarten Music Program, Betty N. Smith, T. C. Harter, and Mary W. Walter, Open Court Publishing Co., La Salle, Illinois, 1973, p. 28

picture of sky with ten stars

Cross Reference Objectives
Behavior 11
Communication
Socialization 13
Academics 20, 21

Developmental Therapy Objective A-23/to count with one-to-one correspondence to ten

Type of Activity	Area
Listening	Academics
(Playing)	
Singing	Stage
Moving	I
Creating	(II)
(Verbalizing)	III
	IV

MUSIC ACTIVITY

I. Introduction

Instruct the children to sit on the floor in a semicircle.

II. Implementation

1. Show the bongo drum to the children and ask them the name of the instrument.
2. Hold the drum and begin singing the song. After a child is told how many times to hit the drum, hold the drum in front of him and have him count as he hits the drum. When he has hit the drum the designated number of times, move the drum away from him so that he will not hit the drum more than is necessary.
3. Repeat step 2 until each child has had at least one turn playing the drum.

III. Techniques and Modifications

1. Count with the children if they are not able to coordinate saying each number with hitting the drum.
2. After the children have become familiar with the song, encourage the group to count as a child hits the drum.

Resource

"Drum It": Shelley Samet (Resource 8)
one bongo drum

Cross Reference Objectives
Behavior 9
Communication
Socialization 14
Academics 21

A-23.3 Music Therapy Learning Experience

Developmental Therapy Objective A-23/to count with one-to-one correspondence to ten

Type of Activity	Area
Listening	Academics
(Playing)	
Singing	Stage
Moving	I
Creating	(II)
(Verbalizing)	III
	IV

MUSIC ACTIVITY

I. Introduction

Direct the children to sit on the floor in a semicircle facing the music therapist.

II. Implementation

1. Show the children the clock. Talk with them about telling time. Move the hands to various positions, e.g., 4:00, 5:00, etc., and ask the children what time it is.
2. Place the drum in front of the group. Tell the children that they will each have a turn to play the drum to give the time as shown on the clock.
3. Turn the hands on the clock to 3:00. Ask the children what time it is. Choose one child to strike the drum the number of times as shown by the hour hand on the clock, i.e., three times.
4. Repeat step 3 using different times on the clock until each child has had a turn playing the drum.

III. Techniques and Modifications

1. Tell the children to play the drum with loud, steady strokes so that it will resemble a clock chiming.
2. As each child plays the drum, encourage the other children to count the number of drum strokes.
3. Until the children get more experience in telling time, limit this activity to times which involve keeping the long hand of the clock on twelve, e.g., 1:00, 2:00, etc.

Resource
large drum
mallet
cardboard clock (12 inch diameter)
with moveable hands

Cross Reference Objectives
Behavior 9, 11
Communication 12
Socialization 14
Academics 18, 21

Developmental Therapy Objective A-24/to perform eye-hand coordination activities at the five-year level

Type of Activity	Area
Listening	Academics
Playing	
Singing	Stage
Moving	I
(Creating)	(II)
Verbalizing	III
	IV

MUSIC ACTIVITY

I. Introduction

Direct the children to sit at the table.

II. Implementation

1. Show the triangle to the children and ask them the name of the instrument. Tell them that they will be able to draw a picture of a triangle.
2. Demonstrate how to draw a picture of the instrument by making a simple triangle shape. Give each child a sheet of drawing paper and a pencil. Tell the children to draw a triangle.
3. As each child completes his triangle, give him crayons so that he can color it.
4. Repeat steps 1 to 3 using the drum and the wood block.
5. Collect the pictures and display them on the wall.

III. Techniques and Modifications

1. Put each instrument in the middle of the table as the children are drawing a picture of it.
2. Choose instruments for this activity which can be represented by simple geometric shapes.
3. Encourage the children to talk about the pictures which they draw.
4. As a sequel to this activity, have each child draw an instrument of his choice.

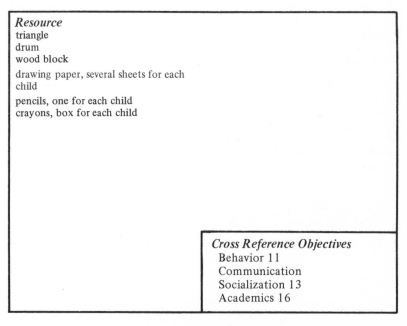

Resource
triangle
drum
wood block
drawing paper, several sheets for each child
pencils, one for each child
crayons, box for each child

Cross Reference Objectives
Behavior 11
Communication
Socialization 13
Academics 16

A-25.1 Music Therapy Learning Experience

Developmental Therapy Objective A-25/to recognize differences among shapes, symbols, numerals, and words

Type of Activity	Area
Listening	Academics
Playing	
Singing	Stage
Moving	I
Creating	(II)
(Verbalizing)	III
	IV

MUSIC ACTIVITY

I. Introduction

Direct the children to sit on the floor in a semicircle facing the music therapist.

II. Implementation

1. Show the children one of the charts with instrument shapes. (Each chart has four shapes; three alike and one different.) Ask the children to decide which instrument is represented by each shape.
2. Direct one child to point to the shape which is different.
3. Repeat steps 1 and 2 for each chart of instrument shapes.

III. Techniques and Modifications

1. Choose instruments which can be represented by simple geometric shapes.
2. Use instruments with which the children are familiar.
3. To modify this activity for use during Work Time, make individual worksheets for each child and show the children how to use a pencil to mark the shapes which are different.

Resource
six 9- by 12-inch charts, each with four instrument shapes; three alike and one different

Example:

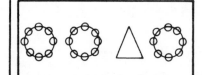

Cross Reference Objectives
Behavior
Communication 8
Socialization
Academics

Developmental Therapy Objective A-26/to categorize items which are different but have generally similar characteristics or associations

Type of Activity	*Area*
(Listening)	Academics
Playing	
Singing	*Stage*
(Moving)	I
Creating	(II)
(Verbalizing)	III
	IV

MUSIC ACTIVITY

I. Introduction

Direct the children to sit on the floor in a semicircle facing the music therapist.

II. Implementation

1. Show the children the six animal pictures. Tell them that some of the animals belong on a farm and the others in the zoo. Hold up the pictures one at a time and have the children decide if each animal is a farm animal or a zoo animal.
2. Tell the children that they will hear a song about the three zoo animals. Each time they hear one of the animals mentioned, they are to stand up and pretend to be that animal. Discuss how each animal looks and moves.
3. Begin playing the record. As each animal is mentioned in the song, lead the children in imitating the movements.

III. Techniques and Modifications

1. Encourage the children to be creative and spontaneous in their animal movements. Emphasize that there are many different ways to do the actions.
2. Direct the children to sit down on the chorus of the song which follows each animal movement.

Resource
record player

"Going to the Zoo": *Folk Song Carnival* (AR524), Hap Palmer, Educational Activities, Inc., Freeport, New York

three pictures of zoo animals: elephant, monkey, seal

three pictures of farm animals: cow, pig, chicken

Cross Reference Objectives
Behavior 11
Communication 8, 12
Socialization 13
Academics

A-27.1 Music Therapy Learning Experience

Developmental Therapy Objective A-27/to write a recognizable approximation of first name, without assistance

Type of Activity	Area
Listening	Academics
(Playing)	
Singing	**Stage**
Moving	I
Creating	(II)
Verbalizing	III
	IV

MUSIC ACTIVITY

I. Introduction

Direct the children to sit at the table.

II. Implementation

1. Give each child a card and magic marker. Direct the children to each write their name on their card.
2. Collect the cards and magic markers.
3. Direct the children to move to the music area and sit on the floor in a circle.
4. Tell the children that they will each be given a pair of rhythm sticks which they are to play when their individual name cards are held up.
5. Give each child a pair of rhythm sticks. Begin playing the record and hold up the name cards one at a time. Encourage the children to watch carefully and to play only when they see their name card.

III. Techniques and Modifications

1. If a child has difficulty writing his name, provide him with a written model to follow.
2. Before using this activity, be certain that each child can recognize his own name.
3. For a sequel to this activity, hold up two or three name cards at the same time as the children play the instruments.

Resource
record player
"It's a Small World": *Mod Marches* (AR 527), Hap Palmer, Educational Activities, Inc., Freeport, New York
rhythm sticks, one pair for each child
5- by 8-inch cards, one for each child
magic markers, one for each child

Cross Reference Objectives
Behavior 11, 12
Communication
Socialization 25
Academics

Developmental Therapy Objective A-28/to discriminate concepts of opposition

Type of Activity	Area
Listening	Academics
Playing	
(Singing)	Stage
(Moving)	I
Creating	(II)
(Verbalizing)	III
	IV

MUSIC ACTIVITY

I. Introduction

Direct the children to sit on the floor in a semicircle facing the music therapist.

II. Implementation

1. Ask the children questions about the differences in tall and small.
2. Sing the song "I'm Tall, I'm Small" and direct the children to stand when they hear the word "tall" and to squat when they hear "small." Sing the song several times and encourage the children to sing along as they perform the movements.
3. Tell the children that they will play a guessing game. Choose a child to be the leader and tell him to pretend to be either tall (standing) or small (squatting). Direct the other children to guess if he is demonstrating tall or small.
4. Repeat step 3 until each child has had a turn being the leader.

III. Techniques and Modifications

1. Sing the song at a tempo which will allow the children enough time to perform the movements successfully.
2. The words of the song may be modified to include other opposite concepts, e.g., fat/thin, happy/sad, etc.

Resource
"I'm Tall, I'm Small": *Exploring Music—Book K* (Teacher's Edition), Holt, Rinehart and Winston, Inc., New York, New York, 1969, p. 2

Cross Reference Objectives
Behavior 11
Communication 8
Socialization 13
Academics

A-28.2 Music Therapy Learning Experience

Developmental Therapy Objective A-28/to discriminate concepts of opposition

Type of Activity	Area
(Listening)	Academics
Playing	
Singing	**Stage**
(Moving)	I
Creating	(II)
Verbalizing	III
	IV

MUSIC ACTIVITY

I. Introduction

Direct the children to sit on the floor in a semicircle facing the music therapist.

II. Implementation

1. Tell the children that they are going to pretend to be Indian hunters. Have them describe how Indian hunters walk, e.g.. quietly, on tiptoe, etc.
2. Play the drum softly to demonstrate the sound of the hunters' feet. Direct the children to walk quietly around the room as the drum is being played very softly.
3. Tell the children to listen for a loud drum stroke which will be the "danger signal" for the Indian hunters. When they hear the loud drum stroke they are to fall on the ground and lie very still until the soft drum strokes are heard again.
4. Alternate loud drum strokes and series of soft drum strokes.

III. Techniques and Modifications

1. After playing a loud drum stroke, pause until all of the children are lying quietly on the floor. Then begin playing a series of soft drum strokes.
2. Encourage the children to move their feet in rhythm with the drum patterns.
3. As a sequel to this activity, allow each child to play the drum to accompany the other children in the movement activity.

Resource
large drum
mallet

Cross Reference Objectives
Behavior 11, 12
Communication
Socialization 13
Academics

Developmental Therapy Objective A-29/to perform body coordination activities at the five-year level

Type of Activity	Area
(Listening)	Academics
Playing	
Singing	*Stage*
(Moving)	I
Creating	(II)
(Verbalizing)	III
	IV

MUSIC ACTIVITY

I. Introduction

Use masking tape to make a circle on the floor. Direct the children to sit on the floor around the circle.

II. Implementation

1. Instruct the children to listen to the song and to try to remember each action mentioned in the words.
2. After the children have listened to the song, ask questions, such as "What do the words of the song tell us to do?" "What action comes first?" etc.
3. Direct the children to stand in circle formation around the masking tape circle on the floor. Begin the music and lead the children around the circle according to the directions given in the song, e.g., running, jumping, etc.
4. At the completion of the song, have the children sit on the floor and guide them in verbally recalling the actions which were performed in the activity.

III. Techniques and Modifications

In the first part of the activity, the children may have difficulty listening and recalling the actions mentioned in the words of the song. It is helpful, therefore, to use brief listening segments interspersed with questions to the children; i.e., stop the record after each new movement and ask the children to name the action.

Resource
record player

"Walk Around the Circle": *Learning Basic Skills Through Music—Vocabulary* (AR521), Hap Palmer, Educational Activities, Inc., Freeport, Long Island, New York

masking tape

Cross Reference Objectives
Behavior
Communication 8, 9
Socialization 13
Academics

A-29.2 Music Therapy Learning Experience

Developmental Therapy Objective A-29/to perform body coordination activities at the five-year level

Type of Activity	Area
Listening	Academics
Playing	
Singing	Stage
(Moving)	I
Creating	(II)
Verbalizing	III
	IV

MUSIC ACTIVITY

I. Introduction

Instruct the children to form a circle with their chairs. The backs of the chairs are to face the center of the circle. Direct them to sit such that they face the center with their legs around the back of the chair.

II. Implementation

1. Instruct the children to imitate the leader's (music therapist's) movements.
2. Begin playing the record and start the first action. Movements should include circular motion of arms, swaying, "running" foot movements, etc., and the incorporation of concepts of fast-slow, high-low, up-down, etc.
3. Allow individual children to suggest actions for the group to imitate.

III. Techniques and Modifications

1. It may be helpful to only use movements that can be done while seated in a chair. This can be expanded to include movements around the chair, beside the chair, etc., after the children have become familiar with the activity.
2. Change movements after all of the children have attempted each action.
3. Verbally associating a familiar situation with a particular movement may help the children to become more involved in the action, e.g., airplane: arms held out to side, upper torso swaying from side to side.

Resource
record player
"Spanish Flea": *Music For Movement Exploration* (L.P. 5090), Karol Lee, Educational Activities and Kimbo Educational Records
chairs, one per child and music therapist

Cross Reference Objectives
Behavior 11
Communication 11
Socialization 13
Academics 17, 28

Developmental Therapy Objective A-30/to recognize groups of objects to five

Type of Activity	*Area*
Listening	Academics
(Playing)	
Singing	*Stage*
Moving	I
Creating	(II)
(Verbalizing)	III
	IV

MUSIC ACTIVITY

I. Introduction

Direct the children to sit in their chairs in a semicircle facing the music therapist.

II. Implementation

1. Show the children pictures of familiar rhythm instruments. Ask questions about each instrument, such as, "What is it called?," "How does it sound?," etc.
2. Show the children the cards of the groups of dots. For each card ask, "How many dots are on this card?"
3. Place the instruments on the floor in front of the children. Hold the two sets of cards, instrument pictures and groups of dots, face down. Have one child choose an instrument picture and a dot card.
4. Instruct him to look at the cards, choose an actual instrument which corresponds to the picture, and strike the instrument the number of times as indicated by the card with the group of dots, e.g., if a child chooses a card with a picture of a drum and a card with a group of four dots, he should strike the drum four times.
5. Direct the other children to listen and count the number of times the child plays the instrument.
6. Repeat steps 3 to 5 for each child.

III. Techniques and Modifications

Be certain that the children are able to recognize the instruments and the number of dots in each group before using the actual instruments.

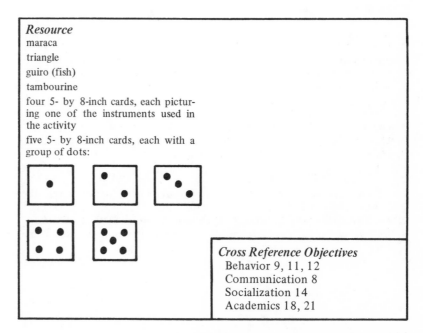

Resource
maraca
triangle
guiro (fish)
tambourine
four 5- by 8-inch cards, each picturing one of the instruments used in the activity
five 5- by 8-inch cards, each with a group of dots:

Cross Reference Objectives
Behavior 9, 11, 12
Communication 8
Socialization 14
Academics 18, 21

A-31.1 Music Therapy Learning Experience

Developmental Therapy Objective A-31/to listen to story telling

Type of Activity	Area
(Listening)	Academics
Playing	
Singing	Stage
(Moving)	I
(Creating)	(II)
(Verbalizing)	III
	IV

MUSIC ACTIVITY

I. Introduction

Direct the children to sit in their chairs at the table.

II. Implementation

1. Tell the story of "Little Cabin in the Wood" and instruct the children to listen so that they can answer the questions about the story when it is over.
2. Ask the children questions concerning the story, such as "Where was the cabin?," "Who lived there?," "What kind of animal came by?," etc.
3. Sing the song while demonstrating actions for the words.
4. Direct the children to imitate the motions as the song is sung again.
5. Ask the children to talk about how the song could be dramatized. Assign parts for a dramatization.
6. Direct the children who are waiting for their turn to participate in the dramatization to sing the song.
7. Repeat the dramatization until all of the children have had an opportunity to have a part in acting out the song.

III. Techniques and Modifications

1. To add to the interest of the activity, use pictures to illustrate the story.
2. Use the ideas of the children for the dramatization of the song.
3. Before beginning the dramatization, discuss the procedures for the activity and be certain that each child understands the steps to be followed.

Resource
"Little Cabin in the Wood": *Exploring Music—Book 1* (Teacher's Edition), Holt, Rinehart and Winston, Inc., New York, New York, 1971, p. 46

Cross Reference Objectives
Behavior 10, 11
Communication 8, 9
Socialization 13, 18, 20
Academics

Developmental Therapy Objective A-32/to recognize groups of objects to ten

Type of Activity	Area
Listening	Academics
Playing	
(Singing)	*Stage*
(Moving)	I
Creating	II
(Verbalizing)	(III)
	IV

MUSIC ACTIVITY

I. Introduction

Direct the children to sit on the floor in a semicircle.

II. Implementation

1. Ask the children if they know the song, "This Old Man." Give the children who know the song an opportunity to sing or speak the words.

2. Sing the song and show the children the actions, which are as follows: "This old man, he plays one" (hold up one finger; on second verse, two fingers, etc.), "He plays knick knack on his thumb" (point to thumb), "Knick knack paddy whack" (slap hands on legs); "Give the dog a bone" (clap hands), "This old man came rolling home" (roll hands over each other).

3. Sing verses one to ten of the song and encourage the children to sing while they engage in the appropriate actions.

4. Show the children the cards, each of which contains a group of dots (groups from one to ten). Hold up each card for brief viewing and ask the children how many dots are in the group.

5. Turn the cards face down and have a child select a card.

6. Ask the child who chose the card to identify the number of dots on the card and then direct the children to sing the verse of "This Old Man" which corresponds with the number of dots, e.g., five dots—sing the fifth verse.

7. Give each child an opportunity to select a card.

III. Techniques and Modifications

1. Sing *a cappella* or with guitar or autoharp accompaniment until the children know the words and actions well enough to sing at the tempo used on the record.

2. Encourage the children to identify the number of dots by the grouping, rather than by counting each dot.

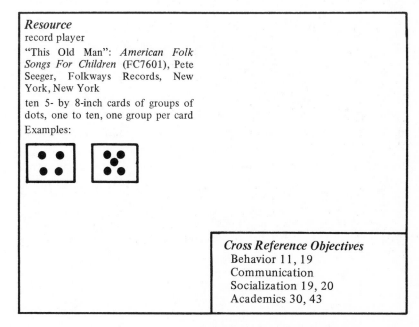

Resource
record player

"This Old Man": *American Folk Songs For Children* (FC7601), Pete Seeger, Folkways Records, New York, New York

ten 5- by 8-inch cards of groups of dots, one to ten, one group per card

Examples:

Cross Reference Objectives
Behavior 11, 19
Communication
Socialization 19, 20
Academics 30, 43

A-33.1 Music Therapy Learning Experience

Developmental Therapy Objective A-33/to demonstrate left to right orientation for visual motor tasks

Type of Activity	Area
Listening	Academics
(Playing)	
Singing	Stage
Moving	I
(Creating)	II
Verbalizing	(III)
	IV

MUSIC ACTIVITY

I. Introduction

Instruct the children to sit in their chairs around the snare drum.

II. Implementation

1. Demonstrate how to hold the drum sticks and how to play a single right hand stroke and a single left hand stroke.
2. Let each child have a turn playing the single strokes, verbally directing the strokes he should play, e.g., right stroke-left stroke, etc.
3. Direct each child to write one line of music on the poster board using a red *L* for a left hand stroke and a blue *R* for a right hand stroke. The number of times each symbol is used and their order within the line should be determined by the child.
4. Direct each child to play his line of music on the snare drum, reading from the left side of the chart to the right.

III. Techniques and Modifications

1. Stand beside the child rather than in front of him when demonstrating left and right hand strokes so as not to provide a mirror image for left and right.
2. To encourage a child to modify his own music, suggest that he play it faster, slower, louder, or softer.
3. After the children play their own lines of music, they can each choose another child's line to play.

Resource
snare drum
drum sticks
two magic markers (one blue, one red)
poster board

Cross Reference Objectives
Behavior 11, 19
Communication 19
Socialization 19, 20
Academics 38

Developmental Therapy Objective A-33/to demonstrate left to right orientation for visual motor tasks

Type of Activity	Area
Listening	Academics
(Playing)	
Singing	Stage
Moving	I
Creating	II
Verbalizing	(III)
	IV

MUSIC ACTIVITY

I. Introduction

Direct the children to sit in a circle on the floor.

II. Implementation

1. Show the group the chart with the instrument symbols and explain what each symbol means, i.e., ♀ = maracas, ✳ = tambourine, ☐ = wood block, ♂♂ = bongo drums.
2. Explain that each child will be given an instrument and that when the leader points to an instrument symbol then the child with that instrument should strike it one time. The child is to try to strike the instrument at the same time the leader points to it.
3. Distribute the instruments to the children.
4. Point to each symbol, moving from left to right across the chart.
5. Allow the children to take turns in pointing to the symbols for the rest of the group.
6. Before each new leader, direct the children to review the procedures for the activity and allow them to exchange instruments.

III. Techniques and Modifications

1. Point to the symbols slowly until the children develop skill in this activity.
2. Use symbols which resemble the shapes of the actual instruments, e.g., ♂♂ = bongo drums. Also, the symbols can be color coded to aid in their recognition.
3. As a sequel to this activity, allow the children to create their own instrument symbols and make their own charts.

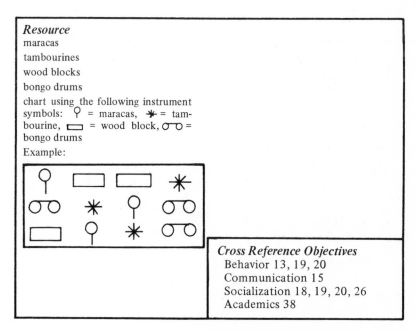

Resource
maracas
tambourines
wood blocks
bongo drums
chart using the following instrument symbols: ♀ = maracas, ✳ = tambourine, ☐ = wood block, ♂♂ = bongo drums
Example:

Cross Reference Objectives
Behavior 13, 19, 20
Communication 15
Socialization 18, 19, 20, 26
Academics 38

A-33.3 Music Therapy Learning Experience

Developmental Therapy Objective A-33/to demonstrate left to right orientation for visual motor tasks

Type of Activity	Area
(Listening)	Academics
Playing	
(Singing)	*Stage*
Moving	I
Creating	II
Verbalizing	(III)
	IV

MUSIC ACTIVITY

I. Introduction

Direct the children to sit on the floor in a semicircle facing the chalk board.

II. Implementation

1. Lead the children in singing the chorus of "Joy to the World" (Three Dog Night). Accompany them using the autoharp.
2. When the song is completed, place the eight word and picture cards (which constitute the chorus of the song) in front of the children. Do not show the cards in the correct sequential order.
3. Sing the chorus of the song again and direct the children to listen carefully to the words. Choose a child to find the card that corresponds to the first part of the song, i.e., *Joy,* and direct him to tape it onto the board.
4. Choose another child to find the next card, i.e., picture of globe. Instruct him to tape it onto the board beside the first card.
5. Repeat step 4 for the remaining cards. Each card should be placed in sequential order on the board, going from left to right, to indicate the order of the words in the song, i.e., *Joy,* picture of globe, *All,* picture of boys and girls, *Joy,* picture of fish in sea, *Joy, You and Me.*
6. When all of the cards have been placed in order on the board, have a child lead the class in singing by pointing to the cards. Accompany the singing with the autoharp.

III. Techniques and Modifications

1. In order for this activity to be successful, the children should be familiar with the words of the song. It may be helpful, therefore, to introduce the song several days before this activity.

2. When a child has difficulty in sequencing a card, it may be necessary to sing the chorus up to the point where that particular card should appear.
3. A modification of this activity would be to give each child a card and as the song is sung the children hold up the appropriate cards.

Resource

"Joy to the World": *Joy to the World and Other Big Hits,* Hoyt Axton, Big 3 Music Corporation, New York, New York, pp. 4–6

autoharp

chalk board and chalk

masking tape

eight 5- by 8-inch cards, one with each of the following words: *Joy* (three cards); *All; You and Me;* picture of globe; picture of boys and girls; picture of fish in sea

---

Cross Reference Objectives
Behavior 19, 20
Communication
Socialization 20, 26
Academics 35, 43

Developmental Therapy Objective A-34/to recognize written names for color words (red, blue, yellow)

Type of Activity	Area
Listening	Academics
(Playing)	
(Singing)	Stage
Moving	I
Creating	II
Verbalizing	(III)
	IV

MUSIC ACTIVITY

I. Introduction

Direct the children to sit on the floor in a circle.

II. Implementation

1. Show the autoharp to the children. Review its name and how to play it.
2. Explain that three of the chord buttons have been covered with colored strips of paper: i.e., C, red; F, blue; G^7, yellow.
3. Tell the group that each child will have a turn to play the autoharp. As the child plays, cards will be held up to indicate chord changes. Each card will have the written name for one of the three colors being used: i.e., *red, blue, yellow.* As the child sees the color word, he is to push the corresponding button on the autoharp which has been marked with that color.
4. Choose a child to play the autoharp. Begin singing the song and hold up the cards to indicate the chord changes. Encourage the other children to sing.
5. Give each child an opportunity to play the autoharp.

III. Techniques and Modifications

1. If the children have difficulty recognizing the written color words, write the words in colors which correspond to the color names, e.g., write *red* using red ink, etc.
2. Have the children suggest other songs which they wish to sing.

Resource
"Shoo, Fly!": *Sigmund Spaeth's Song Session,* Don Wilson, Remick Music Corp., New York, New York, 1958, p. 9

autoharp with three chord buttons (C, F, G^7) covered with slips of colored paper (C, red; F, blue; G^7, yellow)

three 5- by 8-inch cards, each with one of the following color words: *red, blue, yellow*

Cross Reference Objectives
Behavior
Communication 14, 19
Socialization 19
Academics 38

A-34.2 Music Therapy Learning Experience

Developmental Therapy Objective A-34/to recognize written names for color words (red, blue, yellow)

Type of Activity	Area
Listening	Academics
(Playing)	
Singing	Stage
Moving	I
Creating	II
(Verbalizing)	(III)
	IV

2. It may be helpful to frequently alternate the *STOP* card and the "color" cards to maintain the group's attention.
3. Individual children can be leaders by holding up the cards for the group.

MUSIC ACTIVITY

I. Introduction

Direct the group to be seated at the table.

II. Implementation

1. Select two children to work together in putting two 6-foot strips of masking tape on the floor such that they cross midway making four equal-sized squares. (Each square will have two open sides.)
2. Show the cards with the color names to the group asking the children to name them. Select one child at a time to move to one square on the floor and to place one card in the corner. Repeat until one child and one card (green, red, blue, or yellow) are in each square.
3. Instruct the remaining children to select the square in which they would like to sit.
4. Show the group one instrument at a time and ask them to identify the predominant color. Give the instrument to a child sitting in the corresponding color square. Repeat until all children have an instrument.
5. Explain that the second set of cards (hold them up) matches those in the squares. Instruct the children to play their instruments only when the card which corresponds to their instrument color is held up. Ask the group to explain what they are to do when the *STOP* card is held up.
6. Begin playing the record, alternating the color cards singly and in combination.

III. Techniques and Modifications

1. If the children do not know the color words, 1) color code all the words, or, 2) color code the words of the set that will be placed in the squares and write the words on the other set in black.

Resource
record player
"Ob-La-Di, Ob-La-Da": *Mod Marches* (AR527), Hap Palmer, Educational Activities, Inc., Freeport, New York rhythm instruments that have a predominant color of green, red, blue, or yellow, two per child
nine 6- by 9-inch cards (construction paper), two for each word: green, red, yellow, blue; one for *STOP*
masking tape

Cross Reference Objectives
Behavior 11, 12, 19
Communication
Socialization 19, 20, 23
Academics

Developmental Therapy Objective A-35/to recognize written labels

Type of Activity	*Area*
Listening	Academics
(Playing)	
Singing	*Stage*
Moving	I
Creating	II
(Verbalizing)	(III)
	IV

MUSIC ACTIVITY

I. Introduction

Direct the children to move their chairs to the music area and sit in a semicircle facing the music therapist.

II. Implementation

1. Show each of the four cards (*stop, go, loud, soft*) to the children and ask questions such as, "What does this say?" or "What does this mean?"
2. Give each child a rhythm instrument. Instruct the children to begin playing when the *go* card is held up and to play their instruments according to the directions on each card as it is presented.
3. Begin playing the record and hold up the cards one at a time in front of the children, verbally encouraging them to play their instruments.
4. Give each child an opportunity to stand in front of the group and hold up the cards for the other children to follow.

III. Techniques and Modifications

1. For children who are not able to read the words on the cards, it may be helpful to: 1) introduce the written words during other activities before actually using them in the music session, and/or 2) code the words on the cards to aid in their recognition (color code the words *stop* (red) and *go* (green); write *loud* in large print, *soft* in small print).
2. When the children serve as leaders, encourage them to hold up each card long enough for the group to have time to follow the directions on the card.
3. Ask the children to repeat the rules and procedures for the activity before each child has a turn serving as the leader.

Resource
record player
"ABC" (Y-443F), The Jackson Five, Jobete Music Co., Inc.
variety of rhythm instruments, one for each child
four 5- by 8-inch cards, one for each of the following words: *stop, go, loud, soft*.

Cross Reference Objectives
Behavior 11, 13, 19, 20
Communication 15
Socialization 18, 20, 26
Academics

A-35.2 Music Therapy Learning Experience

Developmental Therapy Objective A-35/to recognize written labels

Type of Activity	Area
(Listening)	Academics
Playing	
Singing	Stage
Moving	I
Creating	II
(Verbalizing)	(III)
	IV

MUSIC ACTIVITY

I. Introduction

Instruct the group to sit on the floor, everyone facing the same direction. Place the box of instruments in front of them.

II. Implementation

1. Tell the group that they are going to play a musical guessing game.
2. Show them one instrument, asking them its name.
3. Explain that two cards will be held up, one of which will have the name of that instrument. Ask them what the first letter of the instrument name will be. After they respond hold up the two cards and ask them to select the one that names the instrument.
4. Give one child the card and a piece of masking tape, telling him to tape it to the wall so that everyone can see the word.
5. Repeat steps 2 to 4 for the remaining instruments, no instrument being shown twice.
6. Distribute one of each instrument by presenting them one at a time and asking who would like to play it. If several children want the same instrument, direct the group in a discussion as to how they can share the instrument.
7. Instruct the children to play their instruments and to try to remember the sound each one makes. Place the duplicate set of instruments out of sight behind the children.
8. Explain that behind them are the same type of instruments that they are holding. When they hear one of the instruments being played, the child holding the same instrument is to tell the group that he has it and point to the corresponding instrument word card on the wall.
9. Play the game until each child has had a turn to guess his instrument.
10. Select children to lead the musical guessing game as explained in step

8. After several group members have had a turn, instruct the children to exchange instruments.

III. Techniques and Modifications

1. Before the group selects the corresponding word card for an instrument (step 3), ask them questions about the sounds they hear in the word, e.g., "What is the first letter?" "What is the last letter?" This can be followed by asking which of several sounds come first in the instrument word, e.g., tambourine: *m* or *b*. To avoid dependence on first letters for word recognition, use instruments that begin with the same letter, e.g., triangle and tambourine.
2. After the children have exchanged instruments (step 10), it may be helpful to have each child play his instrument for the group before beginning the activity again.
3. To select leaders for the game, the children can set up an order of turns, or each can select the next leader when his turn has ended.

Resource

two of each of several rhythm instruments, e.g., tambourine, guiro, triangle, bongo drum, wood block, bells (one type of instrument per group member)

5- by 8-inch cards, one for each type of instrument used

box

masking tape

Cross Reference Objectives
Behavior 11
Communication
Socialization 18, 19, 20
Academics

Developmental Therapy Objective A-36/to recognize and write numerals to represent groupings (1 to 10)

Type of Activity	Area
Listening	Academics
(Playing)	
Singing	Stage
Moving	I
Creating	II
(Verbalizing)	(III)
	IV

MUSIC ACTIVITY

I. Introduction

Direct the children to sit on the floor in a semicircle.

II. Implementation

1. Show the cards, one at a time, to the group and direct them to count the number of notes on each card. Encourage them to recognize the number of notes by the grouping used rather than by counting with one-to-one correspondence.
2. Choose one child to hold the cards (the leader) and one child to play the snare drum.
3. Instruct the leader to hold up one of the cards for the drummer, who must strike the drum the number of times as indicated by the group of notes on the card.
4. After the drummer has played the drum the correct number of times, direct him to choose a child to write the corresponding numeral on the chalk board.
5. Repeat steps 2 to 4 until all of the children have had turns writing numerals on the board, being the drummer, and being the leader.

III. Techniques and Modifications

1. Review the cards with the children several times before beginning this activity.
2. The children can be instructed to count aloud as the drummer strikes the drum.

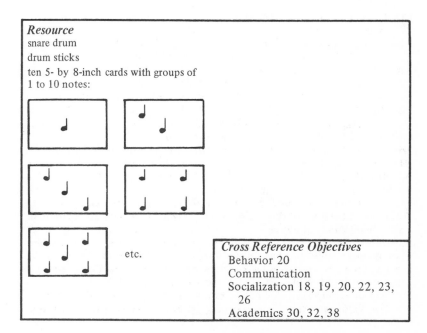

Resource
snare drum
drum sticks
ten 5- by 8-inch cards with groups of
1 to 10 notes:

etc.

Cross Reference Objectives
Behavior 20
Communication
Socialization 18, 19, 20, 22, 23, 26
Academics 30, 32, 38

A-38.1 Music Therapy Learning Experience

Developmental Therapy Objective A-38/to perform eye-hand coordination activities at the six-year level

Type of Activity	Area
Listening	Academics
(Playing)	
Singing	Stage
Moving	I
(Creating)	II
Verbalizing	(III)
	IV

MUSIC ACTIVITY

I. Introduction

Instruct the group to sit on the floor in a semicircle.

II. Implementation

1. Hold up Chart 1 and point to the name of each instrument. Have the group members read them aloud.
2. Point to the first "X" on the chart and ask the children which instrument should be played.
3. Point to two "X's" which appear in a vertical line and ask the children which two instruments should be played.
4. Tell the group that the vertical columns will be pointed to, moving from left to right across the chart. Explain that each child will have an instrument and that they should watch the chart and play their instruments each time an "X" indicates that they should play.
5. Distribute the instruments by asking who would like to play each instrument. If more than one child wants to play the same instrument, have the group devise a method of selection, e.g., take turns, flip a coin, play the instrument together, etc.
6. When everyone has an instrument and is looking at the chart, begin pointing to the "X's," moving from left to right across the chart.
7. Present Chart 2 and tell the children that they are going to create their own composition. Show each child in turn the section he is to write in and have him draw "X's" to indicate the instruments which will be heard.
8. After each child has had an opportunity to complete a section of the composition, ask the group to decide whether they would like to practice their composition before it is tape recorded. Proceed with their decision and lead the group as in step 6. Tape record their performance.
9. Play back the tape and ask the group to comment upon their performance, e.g., whether they liked it, what they would change if they did it again, etc.

III. Techniques and Modifications

1. The instrument names should be written in three different colors, with the "X's" corresponding in color to the instruments they denote.
2. When pointing to the "X's," move from left to right along the bottom of the chart, pointing in turn to each vertical column.
3. Children who play the tone bells should be given one or two individual bells and a mallet.
4. Be certain that the children are familiar with the procedures for the activity before allowing them to create their own composition.

Resource

tape recorder

bongo drums

tambourines

tone bells (sharps and flats which constitute a pentatonic scale)

mallets for tone bells

magic markers, various colors

two charts:

Chart 1

bongo drums	x x		x		x
tambourines		x x		x x	
tone bells		x x	x x		x

Chart 2

bongo drums		
tambourines	(Section	(Section
tone bells	1)	2)

Note: The number of sections on Chart 2 should correspond to the number of children in the group.

Cross Reference Objectives
Behavior 14, 19
Communication 16, 17, 19, 20
Socialization 19, 20, 22
Academics 33, 35

Developmental Therapy Objective A-39/to perform body coordination activities at the six-year level

Type of Activity	Area
Listening	Academics
Playing	
Singing	Stage
(Moving)	I
Creating	II
Verbalizing	(III)
	IV

MUSIC ACTIVITY

I. Introduction

Direct the group to sit on the floor.

II. Implementation

1. Put strips of masking tape on the floor (one for each child and music therapist). The strips should be parallel and long enough so that the children can stand on them an arm's length away from each other.
2. Tell the children to pretend they are at a circus. Explain that they are going to be high wire walkers and that the masking tape strips are wires.
3. Designate one of the teachers to pretend she is taking pictures of the high wire acts. Direct the children to stand at the end of their individual strips of tape.
4. Begin the record and slowly move onto the tape. Perform a short movement sequence (which can include slow sideward walking, turns, bends, etc.) and direct the children to imitate the actions on their individual "wires."
5. Encourage various children to lead the group in movement sequences.

III. Techniques and Modifications

1. To create the atmosphere of a circus, talk to the children as a "master of ceremony," announcing various circus acts and the "dangerous" tightrope walking.
2. Movements should be slow. Emphasize the need to be careful so as not to fall off the wire.
3. If the children are not following the instructions, remind them that the cameraman is taking pictures.

Resource
record player
"Midnight Cowboy": *Midnight Cowboy* (UAS 6725), Ferrante & Teicher, United Artists Records, Inc., New York, New York
masking tape

Cross Reference Objectives
Behavior 11, 20
Communication
Socialization 20, 26
Academics

A-39.2 Music Therapy Learning Experience

Developmental Therapy Objective A-39/to perform body coordination activities at the six-year level

Type of Activity	Area
(Listening)	Academics
Playing	
Singing	Stage
(Moving)	I
Creating	II
Verbalizing	(III)
	IV

MUSIC ACTIVITY

I. Introduction

Direct the children to stand in the music area. Tell them to each choose a child for a partner. The partners should stand facing each other approximately 5 feet apart.

II. Implementation

1. Explain that each pair of children will throw a yarn ball back and forth in rhythm with the music. Each time the speed of the music is changed, they are to change the speed at which they are throwing the yarn ball in order to match the tempo of the music.
2. Give a yarn ball to each pair of children. Begin singing the song, using the guitar for accompaniment. Frequently change the tempo at which the song is being sung and praise those children who are able to change the speed with which they are throwing the ball.

III. Techniques and Modifications

1. If the children are having difficulty catching the ball, tell them to stand closer together.
2. Until the children develop skill in this activity, use tempo changes which are quite obvious, e.g.. extremely slow to very fast.

Resource
"Michael Finnigan": *Songs For Fun And Fellowship—#1*, William Reynolds and Cecil McGee, Broadman Press, Nashville, Tennessee, 1959, p. 23

guitar

yarn balls, one for every two children

Cross Reference Objectives
Behavior
Communication 14
Socialization 17, 18, 20, 23
Academics

Developmental Therapy Objective A-39/to perform body coordination activities at the six-year level

Type of Activity	Area
(Listening)	Academics
(Playing)	
Singing	Stage
Moving	I
Creating	II
Verbalizing	(III)
	IV

MUSIC ACTIVITY

I. Introduction

Direct the children to sit on the floor in a semicircle facing the music therapist.

II. Implementation

1. Show the children the hand drum and ask them questions, such as "How is this played?" "What is it called?" etc.
2. Play a simple rhythm pattern and ask, "Who can play it so it will sound just the same?"
3. Give each child an opportunity to imitate a rhythm pattern. If a child has difficulty duplicating the pattern, play it for him again.
4. Ask various children to play rhythm patterns for the other children to imitate.

III. Techniques and Modifications

1. In order to make this a successful experience for every child it is important to begin with very simple rhythms. Children who do not imitate a rhythm pattern correctly should be given support and help in playing it. (It may be necessary to shorten the pattern or take a child's hand and help him to play it correctly.)
2. Children who serve as leaders will probably need help in playing a rhythm which is simple enough for the other children to imitate.

Resource
two hand drums

Cross Reference Objectives
Behavior 11, 19, 20
Communication
Socialization 18, 20, 22, 26
Academics

A-40.1 Music Therapy Learning Experience

Developmental Therapy Objective A-40/to recognize and write numerals to represent groupings (11 to 20)

Type of Activity	Area
Listening	Academics
(Playing)	
Singing	*Stage*
Moving	I
Creating	II
Verbalizing	(III)
	IV

MUSIC ACTIVITY

I. Introduction

Direct the children to sit on the floor in a semicircle in front of the chalk board.

II. Implementation

1. Show the children the cards with the group of dots. Direct them to say the numeral which corresponds to each group of dots.
2. Distribute the rhythm instruments. Hold the cards with the groups of dots face down in front of a child. Direct him to take the top card, look at it, and then go to the chalk board and write the numeral which corresponds to the number of dots.
3. When the child has written the numeral on the board, tell him to lead the other children in playing their instruments the number of times as indicated by the numeral.
4. Repeat steps 2 and 3 until each child has had a turn in writing a numeral.

III. Techniques and Modifications

1. Encourage the children to try to recognize the number of dots by the groupings used rather than by counting with one-to-one correspondence.
2. Some of the children may need assistance in writing the numerals on the board.
3. Encourage the children to think of ways in which the leader can help the group to play together, e.g., verbal cues, visual cues, etc.

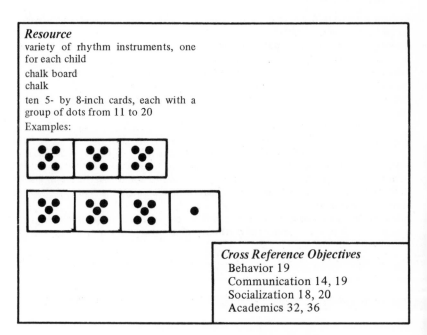

Resource
variety of rhythm instruments, one for each child

chalk board

chalk

ten 5- by 8-inch cards, each with a group of dots from 11 to 20

Examples:

Cross Reference Objectives
Behavior 19
Communication 14, 19
Socialization 18, 20
Academics 32, 36

Developmental Therapy Objective A-41/to write alphabet or simple words

Type of Activity	Area
(Listening)	Academics
(Playing)	
Singing	**Stage**
Moving	I
Creating	II
Verbalizing	(III)
	IV

2. To aid the children in playing the melodies, remove all of the bells which will not be used.

MUSIC ACTIVITY

I. Introduction

Direct the children to sit on the floor in a semicircle facing the chalk board.

II. Implementation

1. Direct the children one at a time to go to the chalk board and write a specific letter of the alphabet which is dictated to them. Instruct the children to write the letters in a horizontal line from left to right across the board. Use the letters A through G and assign the letters to the children in such a way that they will form the beginning melody line of a familiar song. (For example, the following letters indicate the beginning melodic line of "Row, Row, Row": C C C D E E D E F G. In this activity, therefore, the first child would be directed to write a C on the board, the second child a C, the third child a C, the fourth child, a D, etc., until the complete melodic line appears on the board.)

2. Place the set of tone bells in front of the chalk board. Direct one child to play the bells which correspond to the letters on the board (each bell is marked with a letter). Tell the child to play each bell as the corresponding letter is pointed to on the board. Point to the letters in such a manner as to indicate the correct rhythm of the melody.

3. Tell the other group members to try to determine the name of the melody. When they identify the melody, have the child play it again and encourage the children to sing.

4. Repeat steps 1 to 3 giving each child an opportunity to play a melody.

III. Techniques and Modifications

1. Use simple melodies which will be easy for the children to recognize.

Resource
set of tone bells
one mallet
chalk board and chalk

Cross Reference Objectives
Behavior
Communication 14, 19
Socialization
Academics 33, 38

A-43.1 Music Therapy Learning Experience

Developmental Therapy Objective A-43/to use ordinal concepts verbally

Type of Activity	Area
Listening	Academics
(Playing)	
Singing	Stage
Moving	I
Creating	II
Verbalizing	(III)
	IV

MUSIC ACTIVITY

I. Introduction

Direct the children to sit in a semicircle on the floor. Place the six soda pop bottles in front of them so that the bottle on the extreme left has the greatest amount of water progressing to the bottle on the far right which has the least amount of liquid.

II. Implementation

1. Blow across the top of each bottle to demonstrate the sound they make. Explain how different amounts of water produce variations in the pitch of the sound.
2. Point to each bottle from left to right and tell the children to count them in the following way: first bottle, second bottle, etc.
3. One at a time, hold up the ordinal number cards and direct the children to read them aloud.
4. Select a child to take the six cards and arrange them in any order from left to right on the floor in front of the bottles.
5. Instruct the other children to read the cards from left to right while the child who arranged them plays the corresponding bottle as each word is read: e.g., *third*, child plays the third bottle.
6. Repeat steps 3 to 5 for each child.

III. Techniques and Modifications

1. Encourage the children to describe the sound of the melodies which they create.
2. If the children cannot read the written labels (*first, second*, etc.), then include numerals on the cards, e.g., *first(1), second(2)*, etc.
3. If the children have difficulty producing a sound by blowing across the bottles, give them a metal object such as a spoon with which they can strike the bottles to make a sound.

Resource

six soda pop bottles, each filled with a different amount of water (ranging from very little water to a bottle which is almost full)

six cards, each with one of the following written labels: *first, second, third, fourth, fifth, sixth*

Cross Reference Objectives
Behavior
Communication 19, 20
Socialization 19, 20
Academics 33, 35

Developmental Therapy Objective A-44/to listen to a story and respond with appropriate answers to questions: by comments or gestures

Type of Activity	Area
(Listening)	Academics
Playing	
Singing	Stage
Moving	I
Creating	II
(Verbalizing)	(III)
	IV

MUSIC ACTIVITY

I. Introduction

Direct the children to sit on the floor in a semicircle.

II. Implementation

1. Show the children the title of the book, "The Sorcerer's Apprentice," and ask them to discuss the meaning of sorcerer and apprentice.
2. Begin to tell the story, showing the pictures. Start playing the music when the sorcerer tells the apprentice that he is going away and dictates what he is to do while he is gone.
3. Upon completion of the story, ask questions, such as, "How did the apprentice learn to do magic?" "What would you do if you were the sorcerer?" etc.

III. Techniques and Modifications

1. The music should be tape recorded so that it can be edited to correspond to the length of the story (approximately 7 minutes long). The middle section of the music can be eliminated.
2. If the children are not familiar with the terms of "sorcerer" and "apprentice," change them to "magician" and "helper" when telling the story.
3. Upon completion of the book, the group can discuss acting out the story. Encourage them to give suggestions for costumes, props, parts to be played, etc.

Resource
tape recorder

The Sorcerer's Apprentice (MS-7165), Paul Dukas, Columbia Records, New York, New York

"The Sorcerer's Appretice" [story], adapted by Makoto Oishi, translated by Ann Brannen, Fantasia Pictorial Series, Gakken Co., Tokyo, Japan, 1971

Cross Reference Objectives
Behavior
Communication 16, 20
Socailization
Academics 31

A-44.2 Music Therapy Learning Experience

Developmental Therapy Objective A-44/to listen to a story and respond with appropriate answers to questions: by comments or gestures

Type of Activity	*Area*
(Listening)	Academics
Playing	
Singing	*Stage*
Moving	I
(Creating)	II
(Verbalizing)	(III)
	IV

MUSIC ACTIVITY

I. Introduction

Direct the group to sit in their chairs at the table.

II. Implementation

1. Tell the story to the children using pictures for illustration.
2. Stop when the story is almost completed and ask the children to draw their own ending. Tell them that music will be played to help them think of an end to the story.
3. Distribute a sheet of drawing paper and a box of crayons to each child. Play the tape recording of "Pantomime."
4. When the children have finished their drawings, ask each child to hold up his picture and to tell the group his ending to the story.

III. Techniques and Modifications

1. Accept each child's interpretation of the story ending.
2. After each child explains his picture, encourage the other group members to talk about the characteristics of the music (tempo, volume, instrumentation, etc.) which may have influenced what was drawn.

Resource
tape recorder
"Pantomime" From *The Comedians* (Kabalevsky): *Making Music Your Own—Book K, Record III,* Silver Burdett Company, Morristown, New Jersey
"Pretend Time": *Making Music Your Own—Book K* (Teacher's Edition), Silver Burdett Company, Morristown, New Jersey, 1971, p. 69
drawing paper, one sheet per child; crayons; enough for each child; pictures: cowboy, submarine, rocket, fire station, police station, postman, hill with tree at top and birds and airplanes in the air

Cross Reference Objectives
Behavior 19
Communication 16, 19, 20
Socialization 20
Academics 31

Developmental Therapy Objective A-44/to listen to a story and respond with appropriate answers to questions: by comments or gestures

Type of Activity	Area
(Listening)	Academics
Playing	
(Singing)	Stage
Moving	I
Creating	II
Verbalizing	(III)
	IV

MUSIC ACTIVITY

I. Introduction

Direct the children to sit in their chairs at the table.

II. Implementation

1. Sing "Over the River and Through the Woods." Show the picture cards at the appropriate times to correspond with the words.
2. Pass out the cards to the children. (Each child can hold two cards.) Tell the children to hold up the picture cards as the corresponding words are sung in the song.
3. Begin singing the song. Encourage the children to sing along and hold up the cards at the correct time.
4. Collect the cards. Redistribute them and sing the song again.

III. Techniques and Modifications

1. Sing the song at a tempo which will allow the children enough time to hold up the cards.
2. This activity can be used with a wide variety of children's songs.

Resource
"Over the River and Through the Woods": *Making Music Your Own—Book K* (Teacher's Edition), 1971, p. 80

eleven 5- by 8-inch cards, each with a picture of one of the following: 1) river, 2) woods, 3) house, 4) horse, 5) sleigh, 6) snow, 7) river, 8) woods, 9) wind, 10) toes, 11) snow

Cross Reference Objectives
Behavior 11
Communication
Socialization 19, 20
Academics

A-44.4 Music Therapy Learning Experience

Developmental Therapy Objective A-44/to listen to a story and respond with appropriate answers to questions: by comments or gestures

Type of Activity	*Area*
(Listening)	Academics
(Playing)	
Singing	*Stage*
Moving	I
Creating	II
Verbalizing	(III)
	IV

MUSIC ACTIVITY

I. Introduction

Direct the group to sit on the floor in a semicircle.

II. Implementation

1. Explain to the children that they are going to tape record a story about a circus.
2. Hold up one instrument at a time and ask who would like to play it. As each child selects his instrument, tell him the word which is his cue to play his instrument. Place the appropriate word card on the floor in front of him.
3. Emphasize that the children are to play only when they hear their word in the story.
4. Before beginning the story, have a practice session so that the children will know what to do.
5. Turn on the tape recorder and begin reading the story.
6. Replay the tape.

III. Techniques and Modifications

1. The number of words to be represented by instruments will depend upon the number of children in the group.
2. Rather than assigning specific instruments to represent different words in the story, the children can select instruments which they feel are appropriate. This can be done in several ways: 1) The music therapist presents a word, the children present alternative instrumentations, and the group votes on these choices. 2) Each child is assigned a word. He then selects an instrument to represent that word with the selection being based on his own decision or on suggestions made by other group members.

3. Enhance the story telling through changes in voice and facial expressions.
4. If the children are not following the verbal cues in the story, have them review the procedure as to when each child is supposed to play his instrument.
5. At the end of the story it may be necessary to collect the instruments before replaying the tape.
6. Encourage the children to create other sound stories.

Resource
tape recorder
"The Circus Surprise" [story]: Shelley Samet (Resource 5)
tambourine
cymbals
tone bells (three)
bongo drum
guiro
five 6- by 9-inch cards (construction paper), one for each word to be represented by instruments: *animal tamer* (tambourine); *circus* (cymbals); *clowns* (tone bells); *lion* (bongo drum); *people* (guiro)

Cross Reference Objectives
Behavior 11, 12, 13, 19
Communication 15, 19
Socialization 19
Academics 31, 35

Developmental Therapy Objective A-44/to listen to a story and respond with appropriate answers to questions: by comments or gestures

Type of Activity	Area
(Listening)	Academics
Playing	
(Singing)	Stage
Moving	I
Creating	II
Verbalizing	(III)
	IV

MUSIC ACTIVITY

I. Introduction

Direct the children to sit on the floor near the record player.

II. Implementation

1. Tell the children to listen carefully to the song. Play a short segment on the record player and ask questions pertaining to who is singing (man, woman, children, etc.), what instrument is being played, and what the title of the song might be.
2. Play the first version of the song and instruct the children to echo each musical phrase immediately after it is heard (the record allows sufficient time for the children to echo each phrase).
3. As the children listen to the second version of the song (in which the last rhyming word of each phrase is missing), direct them to sing or say the missing word.
4. Play the third version of the song in which the entire phrases are missing. Direct the children to sing the missing phrases at the appropriate time.

III. Techniques and Modifications

1. Encourage those children who are reluctant to sing by directing them to "speak" the missing words.
2. If the children have difficulty remembering missing words and phrases, the words or clues for the words can be written on cards and presented at the appropriate time.
3. Since the three versions of the song become progressively more difficult, allow a sufficient amount of practice on versions one and two before introducing the third version.

Resource
record player
"No More Pie": *Play Your Instruments and Make a Pretty Sound* (FC7665), Ella Jenkins, Folkways Records, New York, New York

Cross Reference Objectives
Behavior 11, 19
Communication
Socialization 20
Academics

A-45.1 Music Therapy Learning Experience

Developmental Therapy Objective A-45/to read basic primary vocabulary words spontaneously in sentences

Type of Activity	*Area*
Listening	Academics
Playing	
Singing	*Stage*
(Moving)	I
Creating	II
(Verbalizing)	(III)
	IV

MUSIC ACTIVITY

I. Introduction

Direct the children to stand in a circle in the music area.

II. Implementation

1. Tell the children that they will each be given in turn a slip of paper on which is written instructions for a specific movement, e.g., *touch the floor five times.*
2. Tell the group that when a child receives a slip of paper, he is to silently read the written instructions and perform the designated movement with the music. The other children are to imitate the child's actions, being careful to do the movement the same number of times as he does it.
3. Give a slip of paper to one child and instruct him to read it silently. Begin playing the record and direct the child to start the movement.
4. Stop the music after the movement and encourage the group members to talk about the instructions which were written on the paper.
5. Repeat steps 3 and 4 until all the children have had a turn.

III. Techniques and Modifications

1. Write clear, concise directions for movement, using a simple vocabulary.
2. When necessary assist the children in reading the instructions on the slips of paper.
3. As a sequel to this activity, allow the children to write their own directions for movement.

Resource
record player
"Jungle Boogie" (PST 1261), Kool and the Gang, Delightful Music/Gang Music
slips of paper, each with instructions for movement

Cross Reference Objectives
Behavior 19, 20
Communication
Socialization 20, 22, 26
Academics 39

Developmental Therapy Objective A-47/to write basic words from memory or dictation

Type of Activity	*Area*
Listening	Academics
Playing	
Singing	*Stage*
Moving	I
Creating	II
(Verbalizing)	(III)
	IV

MUSIC ACTIVITY

I. Introduction

Direct the children to sit in their chairs at the table.

II. Implementation

1. Give each child a card and a magic marker. Dictate a different animal name to each child and instruct the children to write the word which is assigned to them on their card.
2. Collect the magic markers and completed cards. Hold up each card and direct the children to say the word and imitate the sound which the animal makes.
3. Show the children a chart on which is written patterns with the animal names. Tell the children that they all are to make the appropriate animal sound one time each time an animal name appears. An "X" indicates that no sound should be made.
4. Point to the words on the chart one at a time, moving from left to right. Remind the group to make an animal sound only one time for each word and to remain silent when an "X" appears.

III. Techniques and Modifications

1. The children may need assistance in writing the animal names on the cards.
2. Be certain that most of the children can recognize the names of the animals before using this activity. The words on the chart can be color coded or picture coded to aid in their recognition.
3. As a sequel to this activity, assign an animal name to each child and direct the group to respond individually as their words are pointed to on the chart.

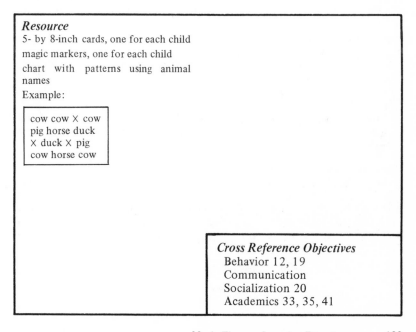

Resource

5- by 8-inch cards, one for each child

magic markers, one for each child

chart with patterns using animal names

Example:

cow cow X cow
pig horse duck
X duck X pig
cow horse cow

Cross Reference Objectives
Behavior 12, 19
Communication
Socialization 20
Academics 33, 35, 41

A-48.1 Music Therapy Learning Experience

Developmental Therapy Objective A-48/to participate in group activity for writing an experience story, dictating to teacher, or working on murals

Type of Activity	Area
Listening	Academics
(Playing)	
(Singing)	*Stage*
Moving	I
(Creating)	II
(Verbalizing)	(III)
	IV

2. It is not necessary for the song to be elaborate or complex in rhythm or melody. Most of the children will probably say the words rather than sing them when giving suggestions, so it will be necessary for the music therapist to create the melody.

3. This activity can be used with a variety of children's stories.

MUSIC ACTIVITY

I. Introduction

Direct the children to sit on the floor in a semicircle facing the music therapist.

II. Implementation

1. Read "Captain Blooper's Pirates" to the children and ask them questions about the story. Then, tell them that they will be able to make up a song about the story.

2. While playing one chord on the autoharp, create the first line of the song and sing it to the children. Leave out the last word and encourage the children to think of an appropriate word, e.g., "We are the pirates big and _____." The children suggest a word for the end of the line, such as "strong."

3. Ask the children to think of more words for the song. As suggestions are made, fit them into a simple melody using only two or three chord changes.

4. As the children compose the song, ask someone to write the words on a sheet of poster paper.

5. When the song is complete, instruct the children to look at the words and sing the song. At the time the children may express a desire to change some of the words in order to make the song "sound better."

6. When the children are satisfied with the song, give each child an opportunity to strum the autoharp (music therapist presses the buttons) while the class sings the song.

III. Techniques and Modifications

1. Adapt the song so as to incorporate as many of the children's ideas as possible, thereby making it "their" song.

> **Resource**
> "Captain Blooper's Pirates" [story]:
> *Dusokit, D-1,* American Guidance Service, Inc., Circle Pines, Minnesota
> autoharp
> sheet of poster paper
>
> **Cross Reference Objectives**
> Behavior 11, 19
> Communication 16, 19, 20
> Socialization 18, 19, 20, 22
> Academics 31, 33, 41, 44, 47

Developmental Therapy Objective A-50/to read and write basic use vocabulary spontaneously in complete sentences

Type of Activity	Area
(Listening)	Academics
Playing	
Singing	Stage
Moving	I
Creating	II
(Verbalizing)	III
	(IV)

MUSIC ACTIVITY

I. Introduction

Instruct the group to sit at the table.

II. Implementation

1. Direct the children to think of questions which might be asked about musical selections, e.g., "What is the tempo?" "Is the selection vocal or instrumental?" "What instruments are used?" "How does the music make you feel?"
2. Ask a child to write the questons on the borad as the group dictates them.
3. Direct the children to choose several musical selections which they wish to hear.
4. Distribute pencils and paper.
5. Play the selections and instruct the children to answer the questions for each selection.
6. Have the children read and discuss each group member's answers.

III. Techniques and Modifications

1. After the children present basic ideas, they may need aid in phrasing questions or answers. Present alternative ways of writing the same idea and encourage the group to select the one they want to use.
2. A modification of this activity would be to use the questions and answers for a "musical quiz program" in which one child asks the questions and the other group members form a panel to answer the questions.

Resource
record player
variety of records (classical, folk, rock, etc.)
chalk board and chalk
paper and pencils, one of each per group member

Cross Reference Objectives
Behavior
Communication 20, 23, 26
Socialization
Academics 47

Developmental Therapy Objective A-52/to contribute to group projects requiring expressive skills

Type of Activity	Area
Listening	Academics
Playing	
Singing	*Stage*
(Moving)	I
(Creating)	II
(Verbalizing)	III
	(IV)

MUSIC ACTIVITY

I. Introduction

Direct the group to sit at the table.

II. Implementation

1. Tell the children that they will be able to dramatize "The Sorcerer's Apprentice." (The children are already familiar with the story and music.)
2. Briefly review the characters in the story:
   1) the sorcerer: powerful, tells the apprentice what to do;
   2) the apprentice: wants to learn magic, has the brooms doing his work, but cannot stop them;
   3) the brooms: mechanical, constantly bringing water from the river to the castle.
3. Tell the group to make a decision as to who will play each part. Discuss the role of each character.
4. Distribute the costumes and place the props around the room as shown in the following diagram.

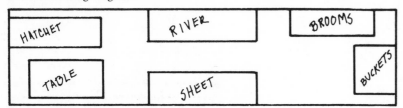

Have the children discuss each area of the room in terms of what they will be doing. Direct the sorcerer and apprentice to stand near the table; tell the brooms to stand in the opposite corner.
5. Begin playing the music and start the narration.

6. Upon completion, encourage the children to discuss their feelings about the drama.

III. Techniques and Modifications

1. The children should be familiar with the story and music before attempting a dramatic portrayal.
2. The music should be tape recorded so that it can be edited to correspond with the desired length of the drama.
3. Be spontaneous and flexible with the narration. Include affective terms to provide cues for various characters, e.g., "The apprentice was very happy when the brooms began to do his work." Also, verbally reflect the spontaneous actions of the children in order to incorporate their ideas into the drama as well as to redirect behaviors. Example: If a broom pretends to throw water on the other brooms, the narrator might state that the brooms were pouring water everywhere, and not where the apprentice wanted them to pour it.
4. Use of video tape can make this activity even more motivating and can provide feedback to the children as to how well they are able to work together.

Resource
tape recorder
tape recording of *The Sorcerer's Apprentice* (MS-7165), Paul Dukas, Columbia Records, New York, New York
narration for the drama
costumes and props:
sorcerer cape, cone-shaped hat
apprentice cape, cone-shaped hat
brooms (strands of yarn to hang from knees to ankles, brown material to wrap around middle of body)
buckets, one for each "broom"
one sheet to represent the overflowing water
one cardboard hatchet
one table
one sign with the following word: *River*

Cross Reference Objectives
Behavior 19, 20
Communication 20, 22, 23, 24, 25, 26, 27
Socialization 24, 26, 28, 30
Academics

Developmental Therapy Objective A-53/to write individual experience stories

Type of Activity	Area
(Listening)	Academics
Playing	
Singing	Stage
Moving	I
(Creating)	II
(Verbalizing)	III
	(IV)

MUSIC ACTIVITY

I. Introduction

Direct the children to sit at the table. Place the record player close to the table.

II. Implementation

1. Instruct the children to listen to the musical selection and to recall recent experiences which are brought to mind by the sound of the music. Begin playing the record.
2. Distribute pencils and paper and direct the children to write stories about the experiences they thought of while listening to the music.
3. When the children have completed their stories, encourage them to share their experiences with the group, either by reading or telling the story they wrote.
4. Discuss the characteristics of the music (rhythm patterns, tempo, instruments, etc.) which may have influenced each child's story.

III. Techniques and Modifications

1. A wide variety of musical selections may be used with this activity.
2. Present ideas and suggestions to the children if they are having difficulty developing their own ideas.
3. Assist the children in spelling difficult words.
4. Instead of one musical selection, two contrasting selections may be used in order to give the children a choice as to what they write.
5. A sequel to this activity could be the writing of a group experience story, dictated to the music therapist by the group members.

Resource
record player
"Ballet of the Unhatched Chicks":
Pictures At An Exhibition (ML5401), Modeste Moussorgsky (transcribed for orchestra by Maurice Ravel), Columbia Masterworks, New York, New York
pencils and paper, enough for each child

Cross Reference Objectives
Behavior
Communication 20, 23, 26, 28
Socialization 27
Academics 47, 50

chapter 4

ORIGINAL RESOURCE MATERIALS

Animal Song/Shelley Samet

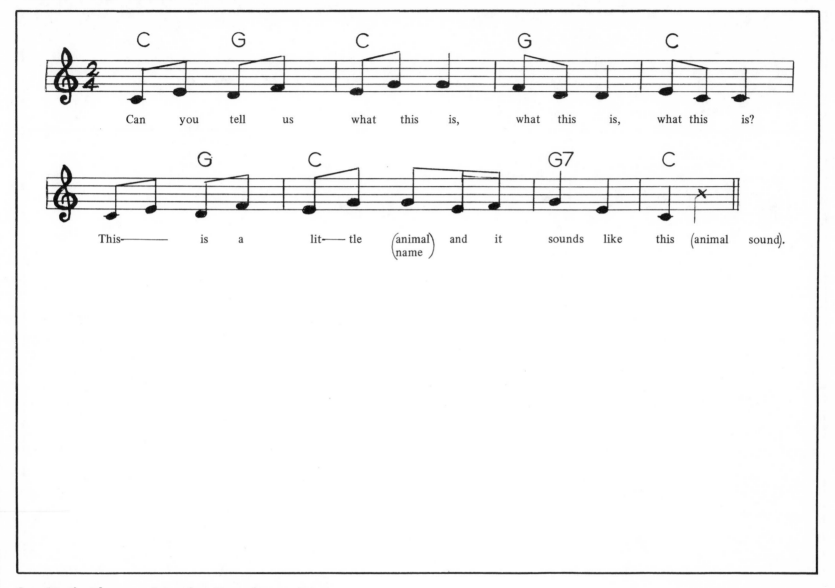

See Music Therapy Learning Experience C-3.2

Body Part Song/Beleta Griffith

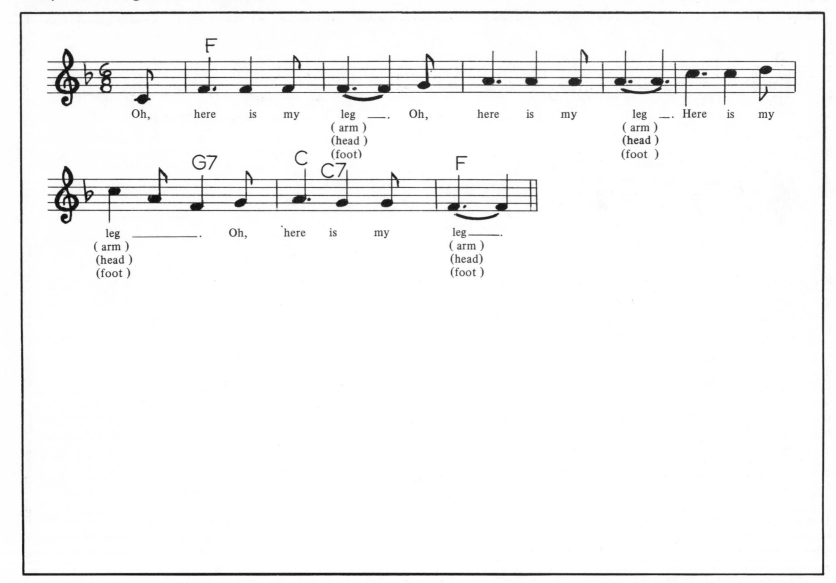

See Music Therapy Learning Experience C-2.1

Button-up Song/Jennie Purvis

See Music Therapy Learning Experience A-16.2

Circle Song/Clementine Gigliotti

See Music Therapy Learning Experience A-13.2

The Circus Surprise/Shelley Samet

The circus had come to town; all the lions, tigers, bears, and clowns. It was opening night. Thousands of people came to see the greatest show on earth. Such excitement! Everyone was watching the center ring where the animal tamer was going to direct the lions, tigers and bears to do their tricks. The spotlight was turned on; all the people became quiet. Even the clowns were watching with excitement.

Out came the animal tamer and the animals behind him—the biggest attraction of the circus. It began—the tigers were jumping through hoops and the bears were walking on big rubber balls. Suddenly, one of the lions refused to do anything the animal tamer wanted him to do. The lion began walking around the ring growling at the people. They were scared!

The animal tamer and the clowns tried to bring the lion back to the ring. All of a sudden, the lion began turning his head around and around until it came right off! And what do you think happened?—A clown came out laughing. It was all part of the big circus.

See Music Therapy Learning Experience A-44.4

6 Resource

Drawing Song/Jennie Purvis

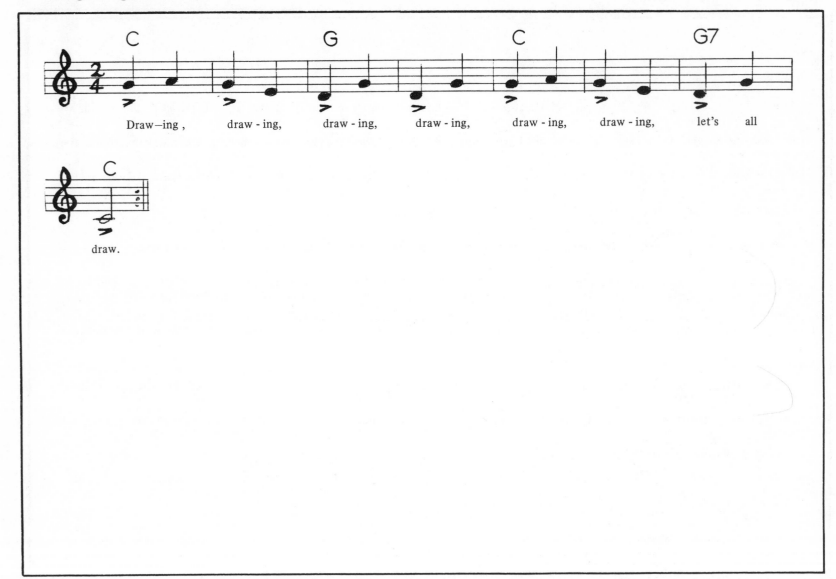

See Music Therapy Learning Experience A-5.1

The Dream/Shelley Samet

> *pounding begins;*
> *bird sounds begin*

I was awakened by an unearthly pounding. At first I thought it was thunder, but when I opened my eyes I could see the morning sun streaming in my window and there wasn't a cloud in the sky. How could it be thunder? I lay there quietly as I heard the sound over and over again.

> *pounding continues;*
> *bird sounds stop;*

The sudden *yelping of the dogs* overshadowed the twittering of the birds. I was drawn to the window by the sound of my neighbor's front *door slamming.* I heard her yell, *"What is it? Where is it coming from?"* As if in a trance, she walked out into the field toward the nearby forest. Fear held me back for only a moment before I felt compelled to follow her. I ran frantically to the door and out of the house to catch up with her. As I reached the woods all I could follow were her footprints. I followed and followed until suddenly I heard a piercing *scream* and I ran even faster to get to her.

> *pounding stops*

The pounding stopped as I reached the last footprint—I was alone.

See Music Therapy Learning Experience S-20.5

Drum It/Shelley Samet

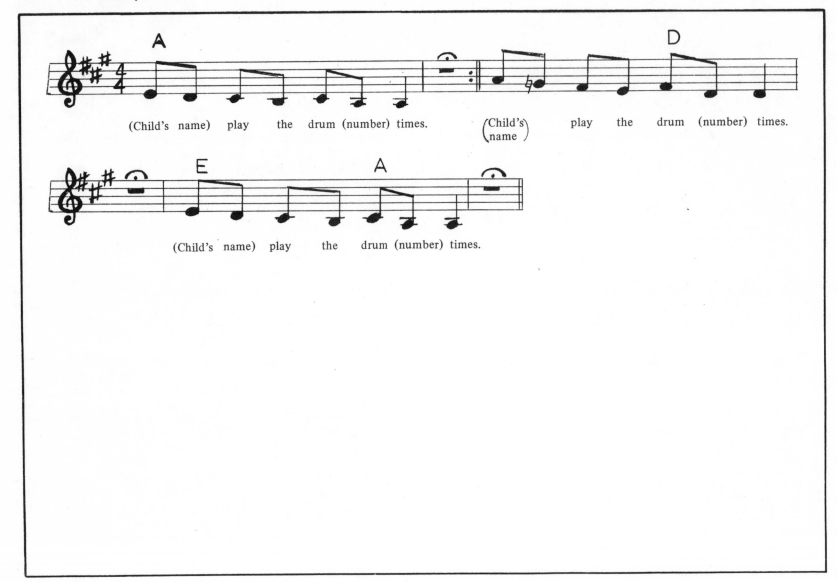

See Music Therapy Learning Experience A-23.2

Drum Song/Jennie Purvis

See Music Therapy Learning Experience B-1.1

Go Find It/Jennie Purvis

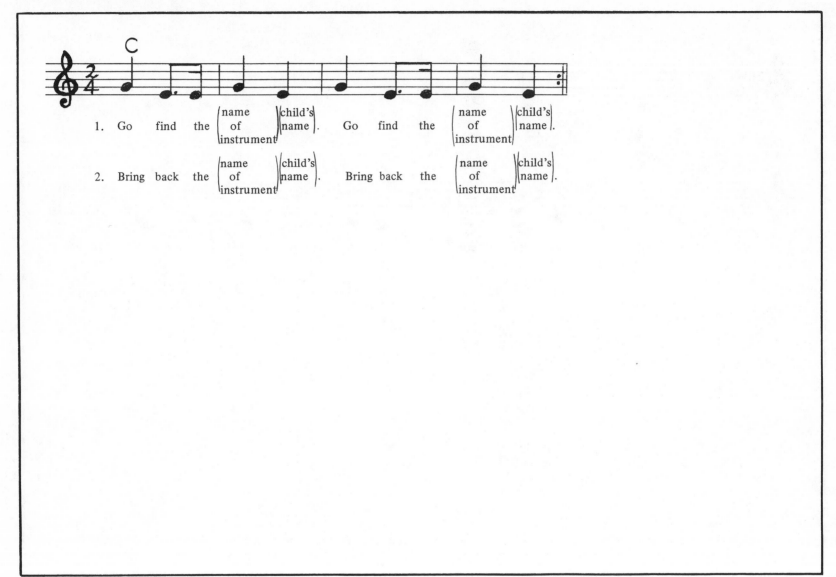

See Music Therapy Learning Experience S-7.1

Hello/Shelley Samet

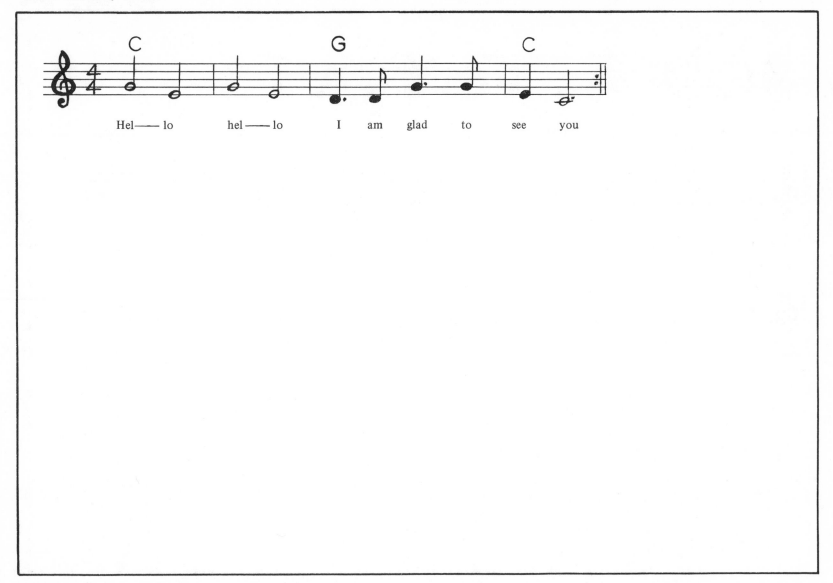

See Music Therapy Learning Experience S-1.1

I Can Touch/Beleta Griffith

See Music Therapy Learning Experience S-11.1

Jumping/Shelley Samet

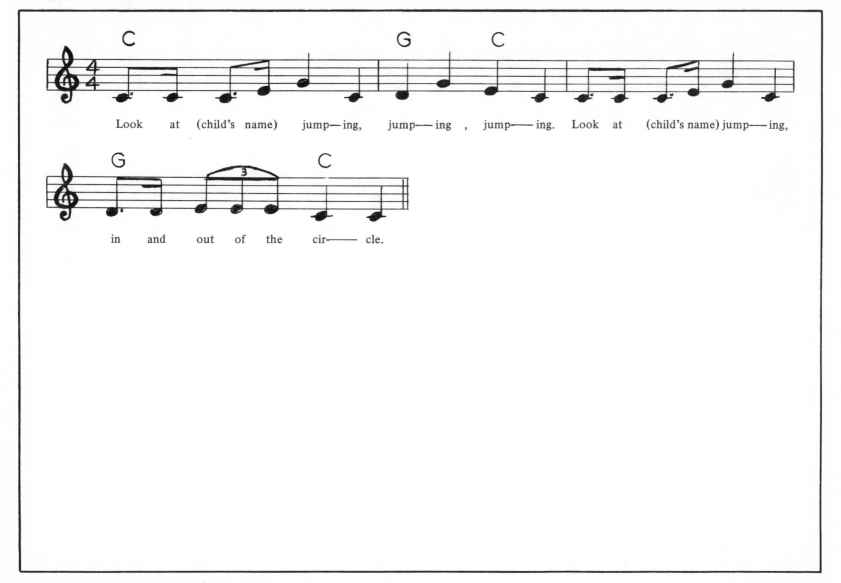

See Music Therapy Learning Experience S-6.1

Just Like Me/Jennie Purvis

See Music Therapy Learning Experience A-17.2

Let Everybody Walk/Shelley Samet

See Music Therapy Learning Experience S-4.2

Let's Go/Jennie Purvis

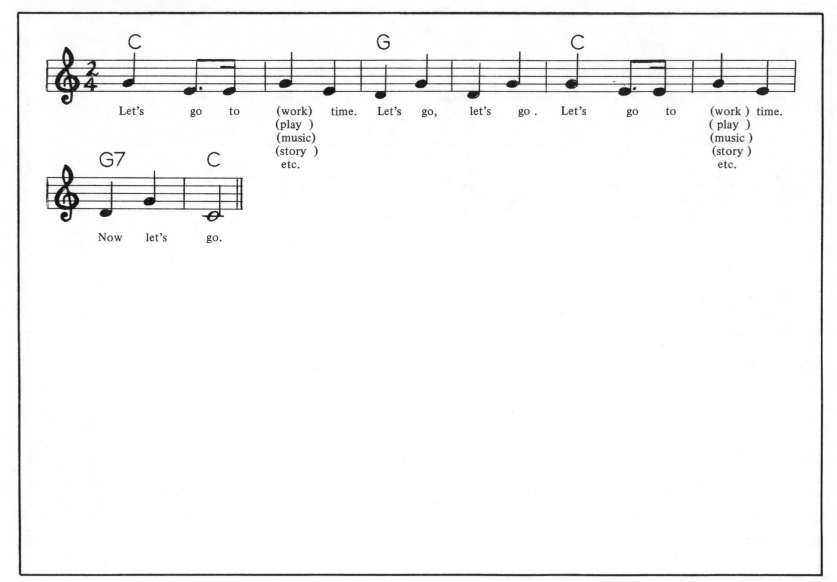

See Music Therapy Learning Experience B-7.1

Let's Walk the Circle All Around/Shelley Samet

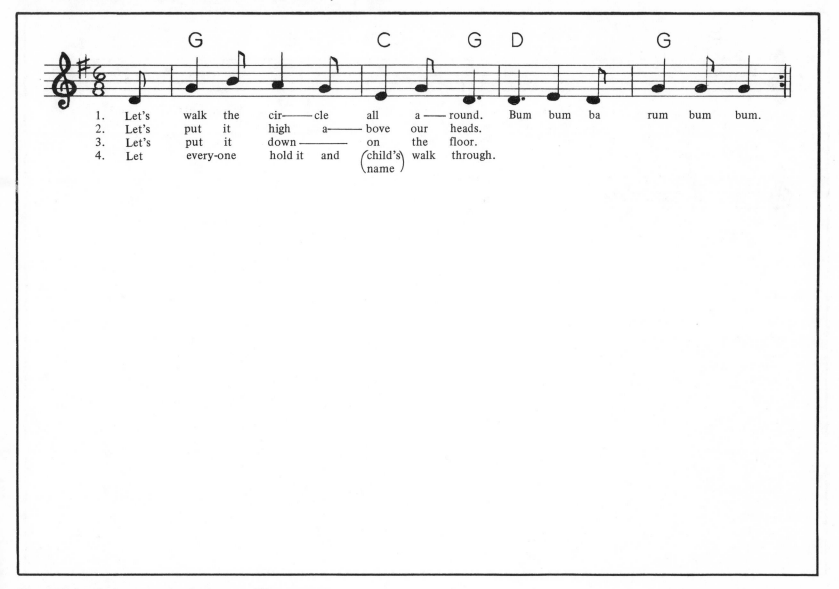

See Music Therapy Learning Experience S-3.2

Match the Face/Shelley Samet

See Music Therapy Learning Experience C-10.2

Move On/Jennie Purvis

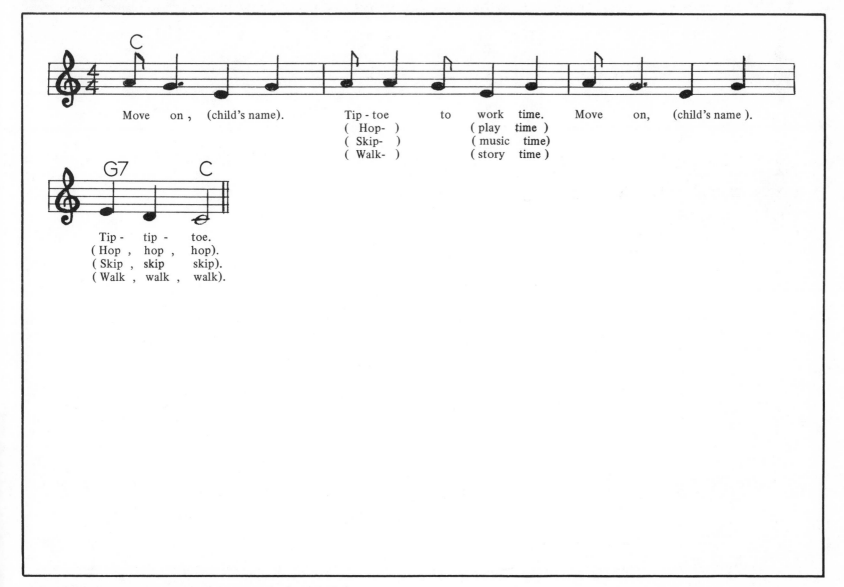

See Music Therapy Learning Experience B-12.1

Passing Song/Jennie Purvis

See Music Therapy Learning Experience A-22.1

Play the Band/Clementine Gigliotti

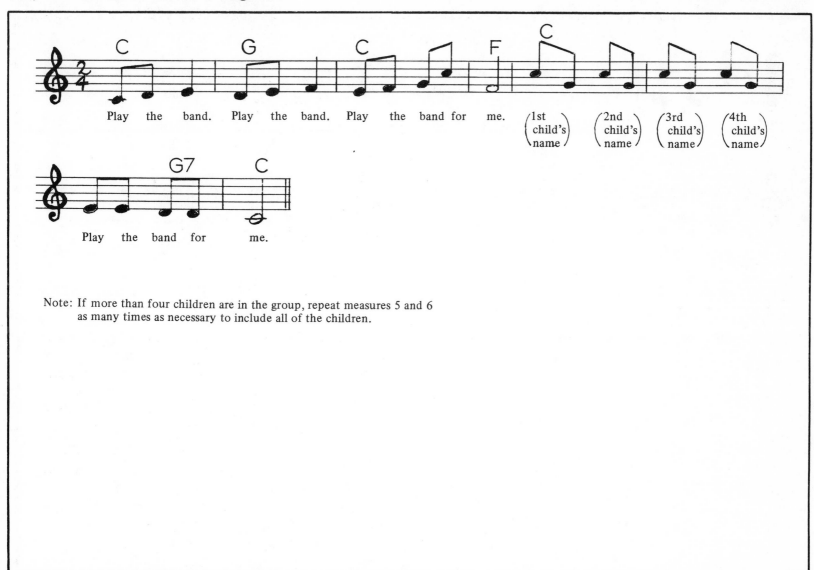

Note: If more than four children are in the group, repeat measures 5 and 6
as many times as necessary to include all of the children.

See Music Therapy Learning Experience C-5.1; A-11.1; A-15.1

Play the Bells/Jennie Purvis

See Music Therapy Learning Experience C-3.1

Tambourine Song/Jennie Purvis

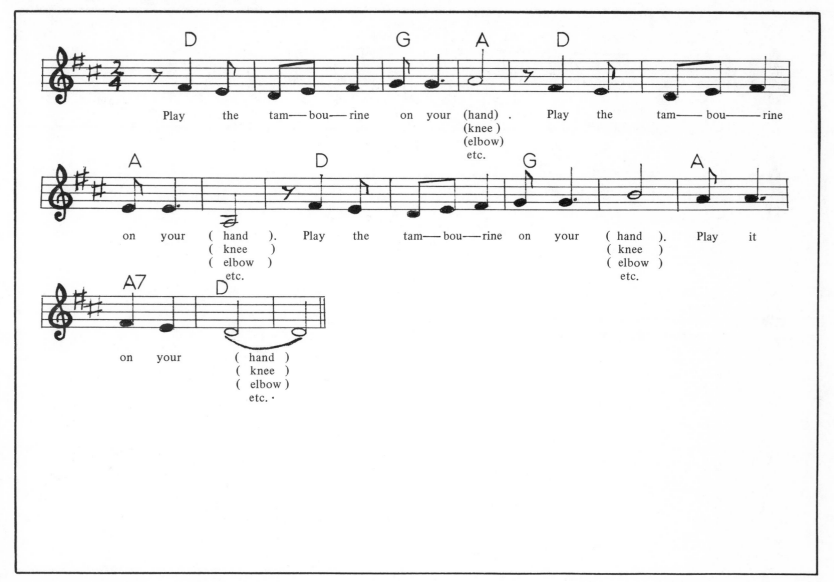

See Music Therapy Learning Experience A-6.1

Up in the Air/Shelley Samet

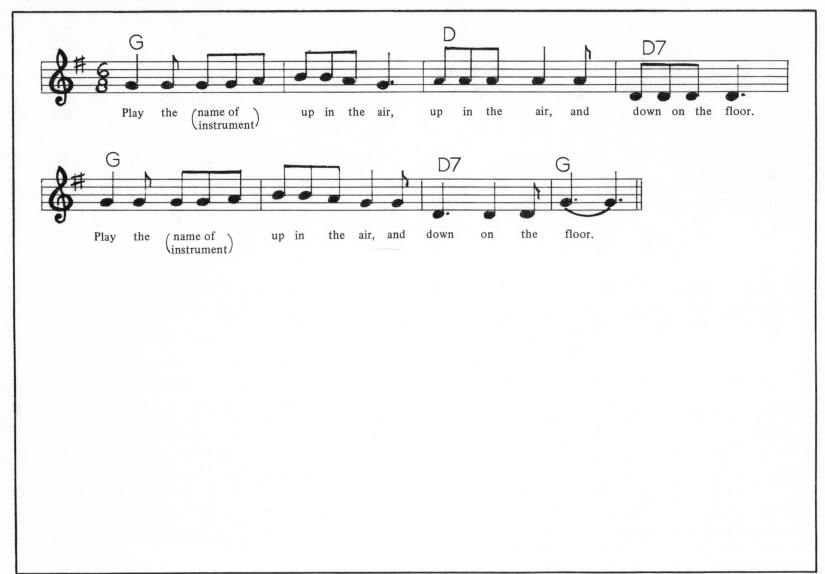

See Music Therapy Learning Experience A-7.2

Washing Song/Jennie Purvis

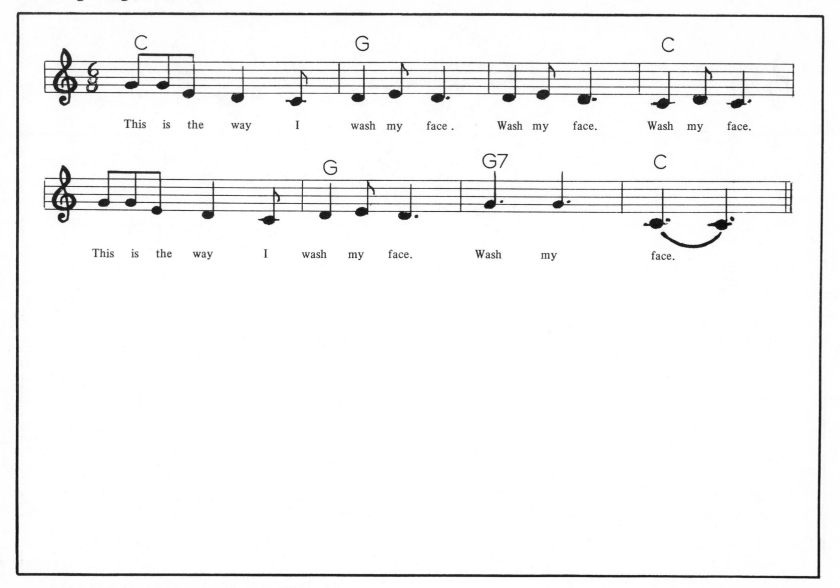

See Music Therapy Learning Experience B-5.1

Work Song/Jennie Purvis

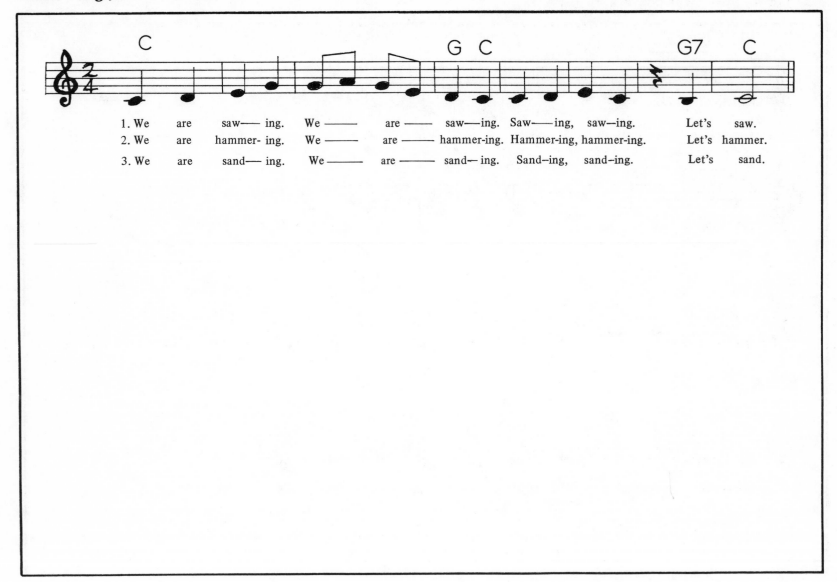

See Music Therapy Learning Experience B-2.1

Zoo Sights and Sounds/Shelley Samet

See Music Therapy Learning Experience A-19.1

SELECTED BIBLIOGRAPHY

Developmental Therapy Reference Materials

Developmental Music Therapy [Monograph]. Lawrence, Kansas: National Association for Music Therapy, 1974.

Wood, M. M. (Ed.) *Developmental Therapy*. Baltimore, Maryland: University Park Press, 1975.

Wood, M. M. (Ed.) *The Rutland Center Model for Treating Emotionally Disturbed Children*. Second Edition. Athens, Georgia: Technical Assistance Office, Rutland Center, 1972.

Music Series

Exploring Music, Books K and 1. New York, New York: Holt, Rinehart and Winston, Inc., 1969, 1971.

Making Music Your Own, Books K, 1, 2, and 3. Morristown, New Jersey: Silver Burdett Co., 1971.

Silver Burdett Music, Books 1 and 2. Morristown, New Jersey: General Learning Corporation, 1974.

This Is Music, Book K. Boston, Massachusetts: Allyn and Bacon, Inc., 1971.

Records

Bacharach, Burt. *Butch Cassidy and the Sundance Kid* (SP4227). Hollywood, California: A & M Records.

Beethoven, L. van. *Symphony No. 6 in F Major,* Op. 68 ("Pastoral") (Everest 3074). Hollywood, California: Everest Records.

Checker, Chubby, "The Twist" (811). Parkway Records, Inc.

Como, Perry. "Catch A Falling Star" (47-7128). Camden, New Jersey: RCA Victor.

Copland, Aaron. *Billy the Kid* (LM-2195). New York, New York: RCA Victor Records.

Donegan, Lonnie. "Does Your Chewing Gum Lose Its Flavor?" (45-15911). Hollywood, California: Dot Records, Inc.

Dukas, Paul. *The Sorcerer's Apprentice* (MS-7165). New York, New York: Columbia Records.

Ferrante and Teicher. *Midnight Cowboy* (UAS 6725). New York, New York: United Artists, Inc.

The Fifth Dimension. "Save the Country" (895). New York, New York: Bell Records.

Four Tops. *Four Tops Greatest Hits–Volume I* (M5-662). Detroit, Michigan: Motown Record Co.

Gershwin, George. *American in Paris* (LM-2367). New York, New York: RCA Victor Records.

Ginglend, David, and Stiles, Winifred. *More Learning As We Play* (FC 7658). New York, New York: Folkways Records.

Grofé, Ferde. *Grand Canyon Suite* (SDBR 3044). Hollywood, California: Everest Records.

Guthrie, Arlo. *Alice's Restaurant* (6267). New York, New York: Reprise Records.

Happy Folk Dances (EPA-4129). Camden, New Jersey: RCA Victor.

Holst, Gustav. *The Planets* (M31125). New York, New York: Columbia Masterworks.

Jackson Five. "ABC" (Y-443F). Jobete Music Co., Inc.

Jenkins, Ella. *Play Your Instruments and Make a Pretty Sound* (FC7665). New York, New York: Folkways Records.

Lee, Karol. *Music For Movement Exploration* (LP 5090). Educational Activities and Kimbo Educational Records.

Lennon, John, and McCartney, Paul. *Sgt. Pepper's Lonely Hearts Club Band* (2653). Hollywood, California: Capitol Records.

The Marketts. *The Batman Theme* (WS 1642). Hollywood, California: Warner Brothers Records.

Moussorgsky, Modeste. *Pictures at an Exhibition* (ML 5401). New York, New York: Columbia Records.

Nelson, Esther, and Haack, Bruce. *Dance, Sing and Listen Again and Again–Volume III* (D121). Bronx, New York: Dimension 5.

Palmer, Hap. *Folk Song Carnival* (AR 524). Freeport, New York: Educational Activities, Inc.

Palmer, Hap. *Getting to Know Myself* (AR543). Freeport, New York: Educational Activities, Inc.

Palmer, Hap. *Learning Basic Skills Through Music–Vocabulary* (AR521). Freeport, New York: Educational Activities, Inc.

Palmer, Hap. *Learning Basic Skills Through Music–Volume I.* (AR 514). Freeport, New York: Educational Activities, Inc.

Palmer, Hap. *Mod Marches* (AR527). Freeport, New York: Educational Activities, Inc.

Polk, Elizabeth. *Popular and Folk Tunes For Dancing and Rhythmic Movements* (HLP-4074). Waldwick, New Jersey: Hoctor Dance Records.

Schuller, Gunther. *Scott Joplin: The Red Back Book* (S-2-36060). New York, New York: Angel Records.

Sea Train. *Sea Train* (SP4171). Hollywood, California: A & M Records.

Seeger, Pete. *American Folk Songs For Children* (FC 7601). New York, New York: Folkways Records.

Sharp, Dee Dee. "Mashed Potato Time" (C-212). Cameo Records.

War. *Deliver the Word.* Los Angeles, California: United Artists, Inc.

Song Books

Axton, Hoyt. *Joy to the World and Other Big Hits.* New York, New York: Big 3 Music Corporation.

Dollin, Leon, and Dollin, Lynn. *Heritage Songster.* Dubuque, Iowa: William C. Brown, Co., 1972.

Ginglend, David, and Stiles, Winifred. *Music Activities For Retarded Children.* Nashville, Tennessee: Abingdon Press, 1965.

Reynolds, William, and McGee, Cecil. *Songs For Fun And Fellowship—#1.* Nashville, Tennessee: Broadman Press, 1959.

Reynolds, William, and McGee, Cecil. *Songs For Fun And Fellowship—#2.* Nashville, Tennessee: Broadman Press, 1961.

Simon, William L. *Reader's Digest Treasury of Best Loved Songs.* Pleasantville, New York: Reader's Digest Association, 1972.

Smith, Betty N., Harter, T. C., and Walter, Mary W. *Teacher's Guide to the Open Court Kindergarten Music Program.* La Salle, Illinois: Open Court Publishing Co., 1973.

Wilson, Don. *Sigmund Spaeth's Song Session.* New York, New York: Remick Music Corp., 1958.

Stories

Dusokit, D-1. Circle Pines, Minnesota: American Guidance Service.

Oishi, Makota, and Brannen, Ann. "The Sorcerer's Apprentice" [story]. Tokyo, Japan: Fantasia Pictorial Series, Gakken Co., 1971

INDEX OF
RESOURCE MATERIALS

Resource	Music Therapy Learning Experience

"Wiggle Song": *This Is Music—Book K,* Allyn and Bacon, Inc., Boston, Massachusetts,
  1971, p. 77. . . . . C-8.1
"Work Song": Jennie Purvis (Resource 26). B-2.1
"Yellow Rose of Texas": *Popular and Folk Tunes For Dancing and Rhythmic Movements*
  (HLP-4074), Elizabeth Polk, Hoctor Dance Records, Waldwick, New Jersey. S-18.5; S-19.1
"Yellow Submarine": *Mod Marches* (AR527), Hap Palmer, Educational Activities, Inc.,
  Freeport, New York. B-11.3; B-11.4; S-18.2
"Zoo Sights and Sounds": Shelley Samet (Resource 27). A-19.1

INDEX OF
MUSIC THERAPY
LEARNING
EXPERIENCES

CLASSIFIED BY
TYPE OF
MUSIC ACTIVITY

Listening

	Behavior	Communication	Socialization	Academics
STAGE I	B-4.3; B-7.1	C-2.1	S-3.2; S-7.1; S-11.1	A-7.1; A-7.2; A-13.1; A-15.1; A-17.1; A-17.2
STAGE II	B-9.2; B-9.4; B-10.1; B-11.3; B-11.4; B-12.1; B-12.2	C-8.2; C-9.1; C-10.2; C-13.1	S-13.1; S-13.2; S-16.1; S-18.4	A-21.1; A-21.2; A-26.1; A-28.2; A-29.1; A-31.1
STAGE III	B-14.1;	C-14.1; C-19.1; C-20.1; C-20.2	S-19.4; S-20.3; S-20.5; S-22.2; S-24.1	A-33.3; A-35.2; A-39.2; A-39.3; A-41.1; A-44.1; A-44.2; A-44.3; A-44.4; A-44.5
STAGE IV	B-20.1	C-26.1; C-28.1		A-50.1; A-53.1

Playing

	Behavior	Communication	Socialization	Academics
STAGE I	B-1.1; B-3.1; B-4.1; B-6.1	C-3.1; C-4.1; C-5.1; C-6.1; C-7.1	S-5.1	A-6.1; A-7.2; A-10.1; A-11.1; A-12.1; A-15.1; A-15.2; A-16.1
STAGE II	B-9.1; B-9.2; B-11.3; B-11.4	C-10.3; C-11.1	S-16.1; S-18.2; S-18.5; S-18.6; S-18.7	A-18.1; A-19.1; A-20.1; A-21.2; A-23.2; A-23.3; A-27.1; A-30.1
STAGE III	B-14.2; B-15.1; B-16.1; B-19.5; B-19.6	C-14.1; C-19.1; C-20.1; C-20.2	S-19.1; S-19.3; S-19.4; S-20.2; S-20.4; S-21.1; S-22.2	A-33.1; A-33.2; A-34.1; A-34.2; A-35.1; A-36.1; A-38.1; A-39.3; A-40.1; A-41.1; A-43.1; A-44.4; A-48.1
STAGE IV	B-20.4	C-25.1; C-25.2		

Singing

	Behavior	Communication	Socialization	Academics
STAGE I				
STAGE II	B-9.1; B-9.3	C-8.2; C-10.1; C-10.2; C-12.1	S-15.1; S-16.1	A-20.1; A-21.1; A-22;1; A-23.1; A-28.1
STAGE III	B-19.1; B-19.6	C-19.1	S-20.6; S-24.1	A-32.1; A-33.3; A-34.1; A-44.3; A-44.5; A-48.1
STAGE IV				

Moving

	Behavior	Communication	Socialization	Academics
STAGE I	B-2.1; B-4.2; B-4.3; B-5.1; B-7.1	C-1.1; C-2.1	S-1.1; S-2.1; S-3.1; S-3.2; S-4.1; S-4.2; S-4.3; S-5.1; S-6.1; S-7.1; S-11.1	A-12.1; A-13.1; A-13.2; A-13.3; A-14.1; A-16.2; A-17.1; A-17.2
STAGE II	B-8.1; B-10.1; B-11.1; B-11.2; B-12.1; B-12.2	C-8.1; C-9.1; C-11.2	S-13.1; S-13.2; S-17.1; S-18.1; S-18.3; S-18.4	A-19.1; A-19.2; A-26.1; A-28.1; A-28.2; A-29.1; A-29.2; A-31.1
STAGE III	B-13.1; B-14.2; B-19.1; B-19.2; B-19.3; B-19.4		S-19.2; S-20.1; S-20.3; S-22.1; S-22.2	A-32.1; A-39.1; A-39.2; A-45.1
STAGE IV	B-20.2; B-20.3		S-30.1	A-52.1

Creating

	Behavior	Communication	Socialization	Academics
STAGE I				A-5.1
STAGE II		C-9.1; C-10.3; C-11.2	S-18.3; S-18.6; S-18.7	A-19.1; A-24.1; A-31.1
STAGE III	B-19.4; B-19.5	C-14.1; C-16.1; C-20.2	S-19.3; S-20.1; S-20.3; S-20.5; S-22.2; S-22.3	A-33.1; A-38.1; A-43.1; A-44.2; A-48.1
STAGE IV	B-20.3; B-20.4	C-25.1; C-25.2; C-28.1	S-25.1; S-30.1	A-52.1; A-53.1

Verbalizing

	Behavior	Communication	Socialization	Academics
STAGE I	B-4.1; B-5.1	C-3.1; C-3.2; C-4.1; C-5.1; C-6.1; C-7.1	S-4.1	A-6.1; A-10.1; A-12.1; A-16.1; A-16.2
STAGE II	B-9.4; B-11.2; B-11.4	C-8.1; C-8.2; C-10.1; C-10.3; C-11.1; C-11.2; C-12.1; C-13.1	S-15.1; S-18.6; S-18.7	A-18.1; A-19.1; A-20.1; A-21.1; A-21.2; A-22.1; A-23.1; A-23.2; A-23.3; A-25.1; A-26.1; A-28.1; A-29.1; A-30.1; A-31.1
STAGE III	B-13.1; B-14.1; B-14.2; B-15.1; B-16.1; B-19.1; B-19.2; B-19.5	C-16.1; C-20.1; C-20.2	S-20.1; S-20.2; S-20.4; S-21.1; S-22.3; S-23.1; S-24.1	A-32.1; A-34.2; A-35.1; A-35.2; A-36.1; A-43.1; A-44.1; A-44.2; A-45.1; A-47.1; A-48.1
STAGE IV	B-20.1; B-20.4; B-25.1	C-25.1; C-25.2; C-26.1; C-28.1	S-25.1; S-30.1	A-50.1; A-52.1; A-53.1